World Facts

The Earth

AREA: 196,938,000 sq mi (510,066,000 sq km)

LAND: 57,393,000 sq mi (148,647,000 sq km)— 29.1%

WATER: 139,545,000 sq mi (361,419,000 sq km)— 70.9%

POPULATION: 7,176,024,000 people

The Continents

	AREA (sq mi)	(sq km)	Percent of Earth's Land
Asia	17,208,000	44,570,000	30.0
Africa	11,608,000	30,065,000	20.2
North America	9,449,000	24,474,000	16.5
South America	6,880,000	17,819,000	12.0
Antarctica	5,100,000	13,209,000	8.9
Europe	3,841,000	9,947,000	6.7
Australia	2,970,000	7,692,000	5.2

Highest Point On Each Continent

	feet	meters
Mount Everest, Asia	29,035	8,850
Cerro Aconcagua, South America	22,831	6,959
Mount McKinley (Denali), N. America	20,320	6,194
Kilimanjaro, Africa	19,340	5,895
El'brus, Europe	18,510	5,642
Vinson Massif, Antarctica	16,066	4,897
Mount Kosciuszko, Australia	7,310	2,228

Lowest Point On Each Continent

	feet	meters
Dead Sea, Asia	-1,385	-422
Lake Assal, Africa	-512	-156
Laguna del Carbón, South America	-344	-105
Death Valley, North America	-282	-86
Caspian Sea, Europe	-92	-28
Lake Eyre, Australia	-52	-16
Bentley Subglacial Trench, Antarctica (ice covered)	-8,383	-2,555

Ten Longest Rivers

	LENGTH miles	kilometers
Nile, Africa	4,160	6,695
Amazon, South America	4,150	6,679
Yangtze (Chang), Asia	3,880	6,244
Mississippi-Missouri, North America	3,710	5,970
Yenisey-Angara, Asia	3,610	5,810
Yellow (Huang), Asia	3,590	5,778
Ob-Irtysh, Asia	3,362	5,410
Congo, Africa	2,900	4,700
Paraná-Rio de la Plata, South America	2,917	4,695
Amur, Asia	2,744	4,416

Ten Largest Lakes

	AREA (sq mi)	(sq km)	GREATEST DEPTH (feet)	(meters)
Caspian Sea, Europe-Asia	143,200	371,000	3,363	1,025
Superior, N. America	31,700	82,100	1,332	406
Victoria, Africa	26,800	69,500	269	82
Huron, N. America	23,000	59,600	751	229
Michigan, N. America	22,300	57,800	922	281
Tanganyika, Africa	12,600	32,600	4,823	1,470
Baikal, Asia	12,200	31,500	5,371	1,637
Great Bear, N. America	12,100	31,300	1,463	446
Malawi, Africa	11,200	28,900	2,280	695
Great Slave, N. America	11,000	28,600	2,014	614

Ten Largest Islands

	AREA (sq mi)	(sq km)
Greenland, North America	836,000	2,166,000
New Guinea, Asia-Oceania	306,000	792,500
Borneo, Asia	280,100	725,500
Madagascar, Africa	226,600	587,000
Baffin, North America	196,000	507,500
Sumatra, Asia	165,000	427,300
Honshu, Asia	87,800	227,400
Great Britain, Europe	84,200	218,100
Victoria, North America	83,900	217,300
Ellesmere, North America	75,800	196,200

The Oceans

	AREA (sq mi)	(sq km)	Percent of Earth's Water Area
Pacific	65,436,200	169,479,000	46.8
Atlantic	35,338,500	91,526,400	25.3
Indian	28,839,800	74,694,800	20.6
Arctic	5,390,000	13,960,100	3.9

Deepest Point In Each Ocean

	feet	meters
Challenger Deep, Mariana Trench, Pacific	-36,070	-10,994
Puerto Rico Trench, Atlantic	-28,232	-8,605
Java Trench, Indian	-23,376	-7,125
Molloy Deep, Arctic	-18,599	-5,669

Ten Largest Seas

	AREA (sq mi)	(sq km)	AVERAGE DEPTH (feet)	(meters)
Coral Sea	1,615,260	4,183,510	8,107	2,471
South China Sea	1,388,570	3,596,390	3,871	1,180
Caribbean Sea	1,094,330	2,834,290	8,517	2,596
Bering Sea	972,810	2,519,580	6,010	1,832
Mediterranean Sea	953,320	2,469,100	5,157	1,572
Sea of Okhotsk	627,490	1,625,190	2,671	814
Gulf of Mexico	591,430	1,531,810	5,066	1,544
Norwegian Sea	550,300	1,425,280	5,801	1,768
Greenland Sea	447,050	1,157,850	4,734	1,443
Sea of Japan (East Sea)	389,290	1,008,260	5,404	1,647

Earth's Extremes

HOTTEST PLACE: Dalol, Danakil Desert, Ethiopia; annual average temperature— 93°F (34°C)

COLDEST PLACE: Ridge A, Antarctica; annual average temperature— -94°F (-74°C)

WETTEST PLACE: Mawsynram, Assam, India; annual average rainfall— 467 in (1,187 cm)

DRIEST PLACE: Atacama Desert, Chile; rainfall barely measurable

HIGHEST WATERFALL: Angel Falls, Venezuela— 3,212 ft (979 m)

LARGEST HOT DESERT: Sahara, Africa— 3,475,000 sq mi (9,000,000 sq km)

LARGEST ICE DESERT: Antarctica— 5,100,000 sq mi (13,209,000 sq km)

LARGEST CANYON: Grand Canyon, Colorado River, Arizona; 277 mi (446 km) long along river, 600 ft (180 m) to 18 mi (29 km) wide, about 1 mi (1.6 km) deep

LONGEST REEF: Great Barrier Reef, Australia— 1,429 mi (2,300 km)

GREATEST TIDAL RANGE: Bay of Fundy, Nova Scotia, Canada— 52 ft (16 m)

MOST PREDICTABLE GEYSER: Old Faithful, Wyoming, U.S.; annual average interval— 66 to 80 minutes

LARGEST CAVE SYSTEM: Mammoth Cave, Kentucky, U.S.; over 330 mi (530 km) of passageways mapped

Abbreviations

COUNTRY NAMES

ARM.	Armenia
AZERB.	Azerbaijan
B. & H.; BOSN. & HERZG.	Bosnia and Herzegovina
BELG.	Belgium
CRO.	Croatia
EST.	Estonia
HUNG.	Hungary
KOS.	Kosovo
LATV.	Latvia
LIECH.	Liechtenstein
LITH.	Lithuania
LUX.	Luxembourg
MACED.	Macedonia
MOLD.	Moldova
MONT.	Montenegro
N.Z.	New Zealand
NETH.	Netherlands
SLOV.	Slovenia
SWITZ.	Switzerland

U.A.E.	United Arab Emirates
U.K.	United Kingdom
U.S.	United States

PHYSICAL FEATURES

I.-s.	Island-s
L.	Lake
Mt.-s.	Mont, Mount-ain-s
R.	River

OTHER

ALA.	Alabama
ARK.	Arkansas
CONN.	Connecticut
D.C.	District of Columbia
Eq.	Equatorial
FLA.	Florida
ILL.	Illinois
IND.	Indiana
KY.	Kentucky

LA.	Louisiana
MASS.	Massachusetts
MD.	Maryland
MINN.	Minnesota
MISS.	Mississippi
N.H.	New Hampshire
N.Y.	New York
PA.	Pennsylvania
P.E.I.	Prince Edward Island
Pop.	Population
Rep.	Republic
R.I.	Rhode Island
St.-e.	Saint-e
TENN.	Tennessee
VA.	Virginia
VT.	Vermont
WASH.	Washington
WIS.	Wisconsin
W.VA.	West Virginia
&	and

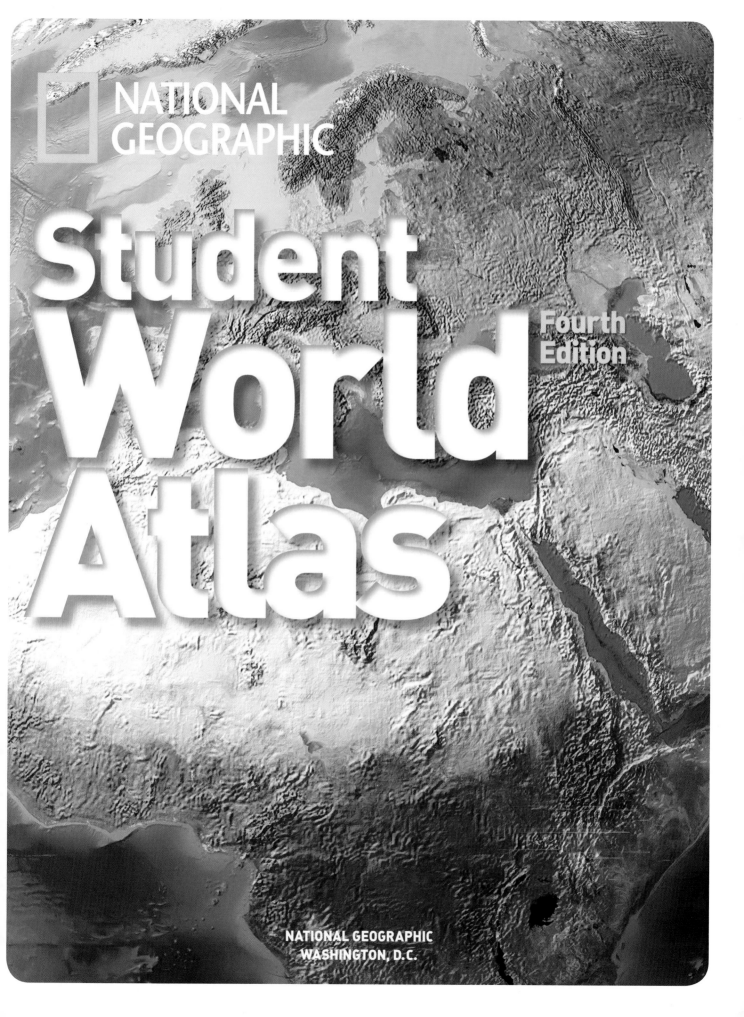

NATIONAL GEOGRAPHIC

Student World Atlas

Fourth Edition

NATIONAL GEOGRAPHIC
WASHINGTON, D.C.

Table of Contents

FRONT OF THE BOOK

ABOUT EARTH
Earth in Space   4

LEARNING ABOUT MAPS
Map Projections   6
Reading Maps   8
Types of Maps   10
Time Zones   12

PHYSICAL SYSTEMS
The Physical World   14
Earth's Geologic History   16
Earth's Land &
    Water Features   18
Earth's Climates   20
Climate Controls   22
Earth's Natural Vegetation   24
Earth's Water   26
Environmental Hot Spots   28

HUMAN SYSTEMS
The Political World   30
World Population   32
World Refugees   34
Quality of Life   36
World Cities   38
World Languages   40
World Religions   42
Predominant
    World Economies   44
World Food   46
World Energy &
    Mineral Resources   48
Globalization   50
Cultural Diffusion   52

NORTH AMERICA   54

Physical & Political Maps   56
Climate & Precipitation   58
Population &
    Predominant Economies   60
Canada:
    Elevation & Political   62
United States:
    Elevation & Political   64
Mexico:
    Elevation & Political   66
Focus On: Natural Hazards   68

SOUTH AMERICA   70

Physical & Political Maps   72
Climate & Precipitation   74
Population &
    Predominant Economies   76
Focus On:
    Amazon Rain Forest   78

EUROPE   80

Physical & Political Maps   82
Climate & Precipitation   84
Population &
    Predominant Economies   86
Focus On:
    European Waterways   88

North America:
Floods, page 68

South America:
Three-toed sloth,
page 78

ASIA 90

Physical & Political Maps	92
Climate & Precipitation	94
Population & Predominant Economies	96
Focus On: East Asia Ports	98

AUSTRALIA & OCEANIA 110

Physical & Political Maps	112
Climate & Precipitation	114
Population & Predominant Economies	116
Focus On: Great Barrier Reef	118

AFRICA 100

Physical & Political Maps	102
Climate & Precipitation	104
Population & Predominant Economies	106
Focus On: Protected Areas	108

ANTARCTICA 120

Physical Maps	122
Political Map	124
Focus On: Antarctica's Extreme Environment	125

Asia:
Taj Mahal,
pages 90–91

Antarctica:
Emperor penguins, page 125

Africa: Giraffe, page 108

BACK OF THE BOOK

RESOURCES

Flags & Stats	126
Glossary	134
Web Sites	136
Thematic Index	137
Place-Name Index	138
Illustration Credits	143

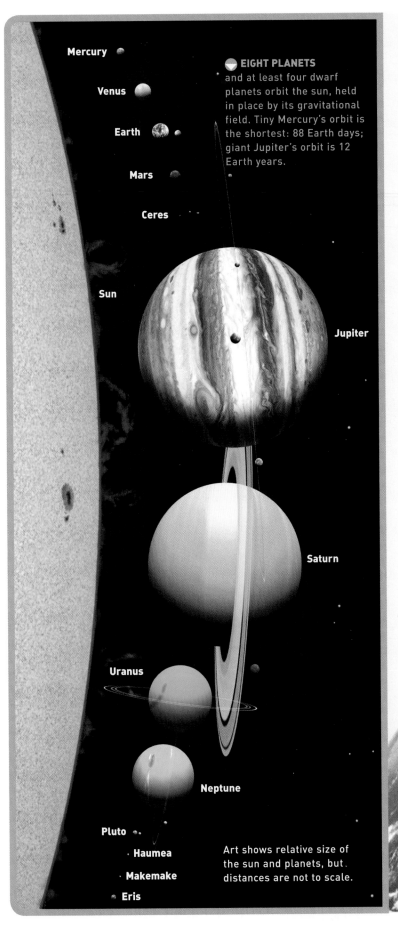

Mercury

Venus

Earth

Mars

Ceres

Sun

Jupiter

Saturn

Uranus

Neptune

Pluto

Haumea

Makemake

Eris

EIGHT PLANETS and at least four dwarf planets orbit the sun, held in place by its gravitational field. Tiny Mercury's orbit is the shortest: 88 Earth days; giant Jupiter's orbit is 12 Earth years.

Art shows relative size of the sun and planets, but distances are not to scale.

Earth in Space

At the center of our solar system is the sun, a huge mass of hot gas that is the source of both light and warmth for Earth. Third in a group of eight planets that revolve around the sun, Earth is a terrestrial, or mostly rocky, planet. So are Mercury, Venus, and Mars. Earth is about 93 million miles (150 million km) from the sun, and its journey, or revolution, around the sun takes 365¼ days. Farther away from the sun, four more planets—Jupiter, Saturn, Uranus, and Neptune (all made up primarily of gases)—plus at least five dwarf planets (Ceres, Pluto, Haumea, Makemake, and Eris) complete the main bodies of our solar system. The solar system, in turn, is part of the Milky Way galaxy.

SPRING
Northern Hemisphere

WINTER
Northern Hemisphere

EARTH'S SEASONS change throughout the year because the planet tilts 23.5° on its axis as it revolves around the sun. For example, when the Northern Hemisphere is tilted toward the sun, summer occurs there; when it's tilted away from the sun, it experiences winter.

SUMMER
Northern Hemisphere

FALL
Northern Hemisphere

North Pole

Tropic of Cancer

Equator

Tropic of Capricorn

South Pole

AN ENVELOPE OF AIR SURROUNDS EARTH. Called the atmosphere, it is made up of a mix of nitrogen, oxygen, and other gases. It is 300 miles (483 km) thick. The troposphere, which extends upward as much as 10 miles (16 km) from Earth's surface, is called the zone of life. The combination of gases, moderate temperatures, and water in this layer supports plants, animals, and other forms of life on Earth.

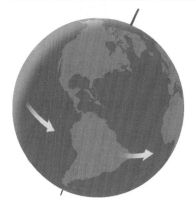

EARTH ROTATES WEST TO EAST on its axis, an imaginary line that runs through Earth's center from Pole to Pole. Each rotation takes 24 hours, or one full cycle of day and night. One complete rotation equals one Earth day. One complete revolution around the sun equals one Earth year.

Map Projections

Maps tell a story about physical and human systems, places and regions, patterns and relationships. This atlas is a collection of maps that tell a story about Earth.

Understanding that story requires a knowledge of how maps are made and a familiarity with the special language used by cartographers, the people who create maps.

Globes present a model of Earth as it is—a sphere—but they are bulky and can be difficult to use and store. Flat maps are much more convenient, but certain problems result from transferring Earth's curved surface to a flat piece of paper, a process called projection. There are many different types of projections, all of which involve some form of distortion: area, distance, direction, or shape.

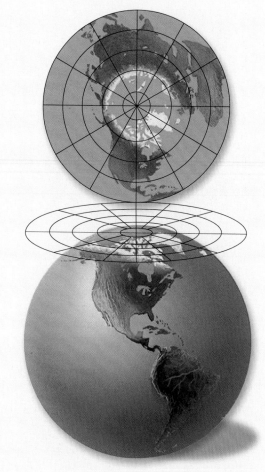

◉ **AZIMUTHAL MAP PROJECTION.** This kind of map is made by projecting a globe onto a flat surface that touches the globe at a single point, such as the North Pole. These maps accurately represent direction along any straight line extending from the point of contact. Away from the point of contact, shape is increasingly distorted.

◐ **MAKING A PROJECTION.** Imagine a globe that has been cut in half as this one has. If a light is shined into it, the lines of latitude and longitude and the shapes of the continents will cast shadows that can be "projected" onto a piece of paper, as shown here. Depending on how the paper is positioned, the shadows will be distorted in different ways.

CONIC MAP PROJECTION. This kind of map is made by projecting a globe onto a cone. The part of Earth being mapped touches the sides of the cone. Lines of longitude appear as straight lines; lines of latitude appear as parallel arcs. Conic projections are often used to map mid-latitude areas with great east-west extent, such as North America.

CYLINDRICAL MAP PROJECTION. A cylindrical projection map is made by projecting a globe onto a cylinder that touches Earth's surface along the Equator. Latitude and longitude lines on this kind of map show true compass directions, which makes it useful for navigation. But there is great distortion in the size of high-latitude landmasses.

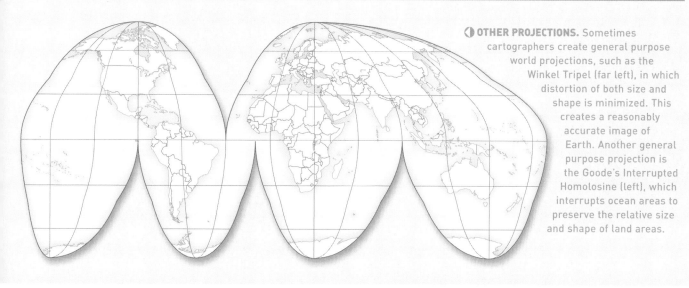

OTHER PROJECTIONS. Sometimes cartographers create general purpose world projections, such as the Winkel Tripel (far left), in which distortion of both size and shape is minimized. This creates a reasonably accurate image of Earth. Another general purpose projection is the Goode's Interrupted Homolosine (left), which interrupts ocean areas to preserve the relative size and shape of land areas.

Reading Maps

People can use maps to find locations, to determine direction or distance, and to understand information about places. Cartographers rely on a special graphic language to communicate through maps.

An imaginary system of lines, called the global grid, helps us locate particular points on Earth's surface. The global grid is made up of lines of latitude and longitude that are measured in degrees, minutes, and seconds. The point where these lines intersect identifies the absolute location of a place. No other place has the exact same address.

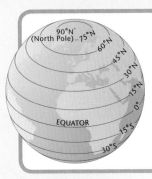

LATITUDE. Lines of latitude—also called parallels because they are parallel to the Equator—run east to west around the globe and measure location north or south of the Equator. The Equator is 0° latitude.

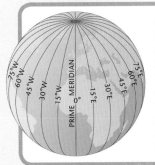

LONGITUDE. Lines of longitude—also called meridians—run from Pole to Pole and measure location east or west of the prime meridian. The prime meridian is 0° longitude, and it runs through Greenwich, near London, England.

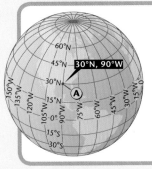

GLOBAL GRID. When used together, latitude and longitude form a grid that provides a system for determining the exact, or absolute, location of every place on Earth. For example, the absolute location of point A is 30°N, 90°W.

DIRECTION. Cartographers put a north arrow or a compass rose, which shows the four cardinal directions—north, south, east, and west—on a map. On this map, point Ⓑ is northwest (NW) of point Ⓐ. Northwest is an example of an intermediate direction, which means it is between two cardinal directions. Grid lines can also be used to indicate north.

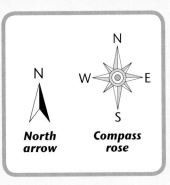

North arrow   **Compass rose**

SCALE. A map represents a part of Earth's surface, but that part is greatly reduced. Cartographers include a map scale to show what distance on Earth is represented by a given length on the map. Scale can be graphic (a bar), verbal, or a ratio. To determine how many miles point Ⓐ is from point Ⓑ, place a piece of paper on the map above and mark the distance between Ⓐ and Ⓑ. Then compare the marks on the paper with the bar scale on the map.

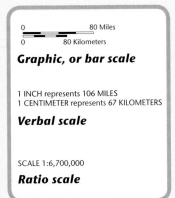

Graphic, or bar scale

1 INCH represents 106 MILES
1 CENTIMETER represents 67 KILOMETERS

Verbal scale

SCALE 1:6,700,000

Ratio scale

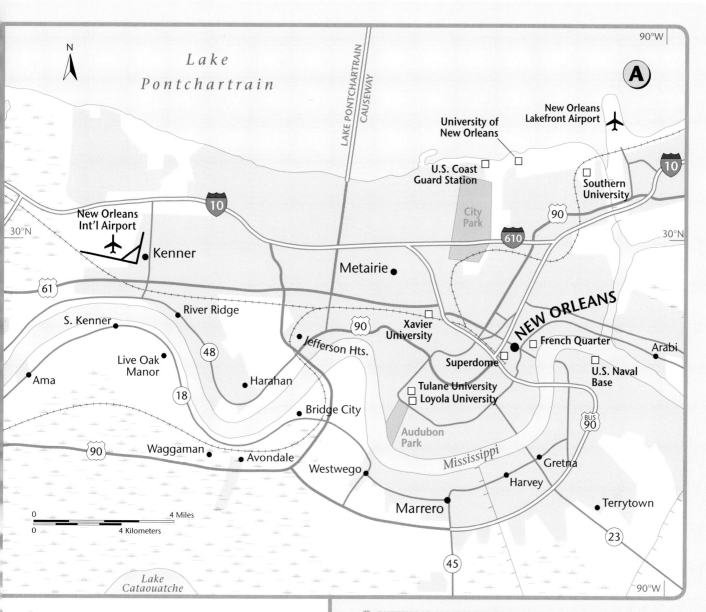

A

Finally, cartographers use a variety of symbols, which are identified in a map key or legend, to tell us more about the places represented on the map. There are three general types of symbols:

●● **POINT SYMBOLS** show exact location of places (such as cities) or quantity (a large dot can mean a more populous city).

⊢⊢⊢ **LINE SYMBOLS** show boundaries or connections (such as roads, canals, and other trade links).

▭ **AREA SYMBOLS** show the form and extent of a feature (such as a lake, park, or swamp).

Additional information may be coded in color, size, and shape.

PUTTING IT ALL TOGETHER. We already know from the map on page 8 which states A and B are located in. But to find out more about city A, we need a larger scale map—one that shows a smaller area in more detail (see above).

MAP LEGEND

▭	Metropolitan area	═══	Road
▭	Lake or river	⊢⊢⊢	Railroad
▭	Park	◁	Runway
▭	Swamp	✈	Airport
⊣⊣⊣	Canal	□	Point of interest
═══	Highway	●●●	Town

Types of Maps

This atlas includes many different types of maps so that a wide variety of information about Earth can be presented. Three of the most commonly used types of maps are physical, political, and thematic.

A **physical map** identifies natural features, such as mountains, deserts, oceans, and lakes. Area symbols of various colors and shadings may indicate height above sea level or, as in the example here, ecosystems. Similar symbols could also show water depth.

A **political map** shows how people have divided the world into countries. Political maps can also show states, counties, or cities within a country. Line symbols indicate boundaries, and point symbols show the locations and sometimes sizes of cities.

Thematic maps use a variety of symbols to show distributions and patterns on Earth. For example, a choropleth map uses shades of color to represent different values. The example here shows the amount of energy consumed each year by various countries. Thematic maps can show many different things, such as patterns of vegetation, land use, and religions.

A **cartogram** is a special kind of thematic map in which the size of a country is based on some statistic other than land area. In the cartogram at far right, population size determines the size of each country. This is why Nigeria—the most populous country in Africa— appears much larger than Algeria, which has more than double the land area of Nigeria (see the political map). Cartograms allow for a quick visual comparison of countries in terms of a selected statistic.

◗ **THIS GLOBE** is useful for showing Africa's position and size relative to other landmasses, but very little detail is possible at this scale. By using different kinds of maps, mapmakers can show a variety of information in more detail.

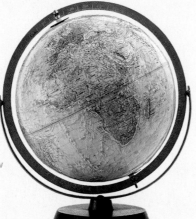

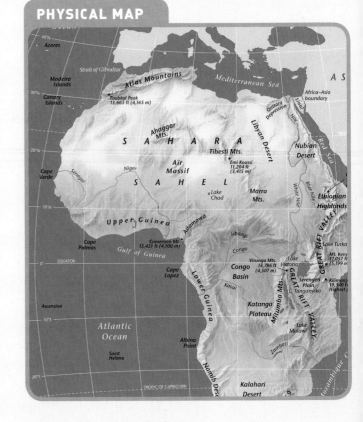

PHYSICAL MAP

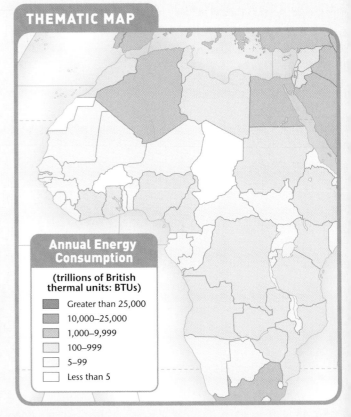

THEMATIC MAP

Annual Energy Consumption

(trillions of British thermal units: BTUs)

- Greater than 25,000
- 10,000–25,000
- 1,000–9,999
- 100–999
- 5–99
- Less than 5

POLITICAL MAP

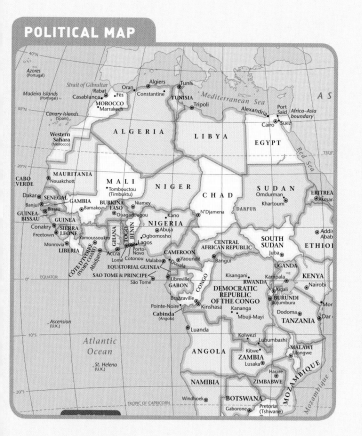

CARTOGRAM

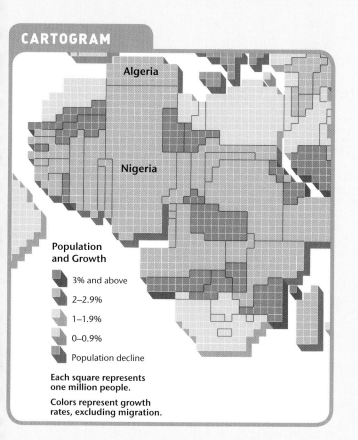

Population and Growth

- 3% and above
- 2–2.9%
- 1–1.9%
- 0–0.9%
- Population decline

Each square represents one million people.

Colors represent growth rates, excluding migration.

SATELLITE IMAGE MAPS

Satellites orbiting Earth transmit images of the surface to computers on the ground. These computers translate the information into special maps (below) that use colors to show various characteristics. Such maps are valuable tools for identifying patterns or comparing changes over time.

CLOUD COVERAGE

TOPOGRAPHY/BATHYMETRY

SEA LEVEL VARIABILITY

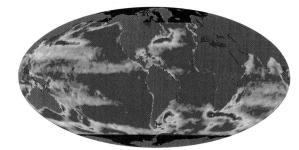

SEA SURFACE TEMPERATURE

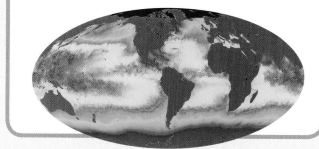

Time Zones

The *Fiji Times*, a newspaper published in Suva, capital of the Fiji Islands, carries the message "The First Newspaper Published in the World Every Day" on the front page of each edition. How can this newspaper from a small island country make such a claim? Fiji lies west of the date line, an invisible boundary designated to mark the beginning of each new day. The date line is just part of the system we have adopted to keep track of the passage of days.

For most of human history, people determined time by observing the position of the sun in the sky. Slight differences in time did not matter until, in the mid-19th century, the spread of railroads and telegraph lines changed forever the importance of time. High-speed transportation and communications required schedules, and schedules required that everyone agree on the time.

In 1884, an international conference, convened in Washington, D.C., established an international system of 24 time zones based on the fact that Earth turns from west to east 15 degrees of longitude every hour. Each time zone has a central meridian and is 15 degrees wide, 7½ degrees to either side of the named central meridian.

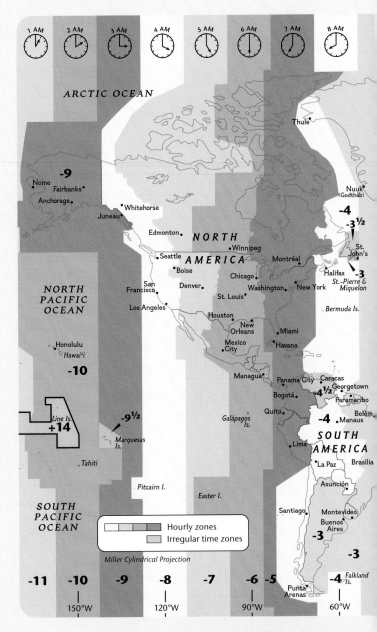

◖ **WORLD TIME CLOCK,** in Alexanderplatz in Berlin, Germany, features a large cylinder that is marked with the world's 24 time zones and major cities found in each zone. The cylinder rises almost 33 feet (10 m) above the square and weighs 16 tons (14.5 MT).

◐ **A SYSTEM OF STANDARD TIME** put trains on schedule, which helped reduce the chance of collisions and the loss of lives and property caused by them.

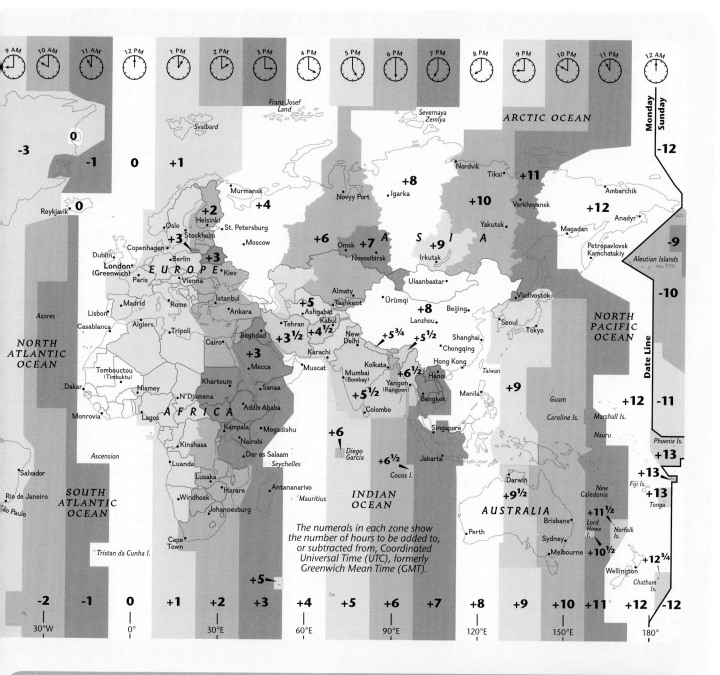

9 AM | 10 AM | 11 AM | 12 PM | 1 PM | 2 PM | 3 PM | 4 PM | 5 PM | 6 PM | 7 PM | 8 PM | 9 PM | 10 PM | 11 PM | 12 AM

Monday / Sunday

ARCTIC OCEAN

-3   **0**   **-1**   **0**   **+1**

Franz Josef Land

Svalbard

Severnaya Zemlya

-12

Nordvik

Tiksi

+11

Ambarchik

Reykjavik **0**

Murmansk

+8

Novyy Port

Igarka

Verkhoyansk

+12

Anadyr

Oslo   Helsinki   St. Petersburg

+2

+4

Magadan

-9

Stockholm

+3

Moscow

+6

Omsk **+7**

A   S   I   A

Yakutsk

+9

Petropavlovsk-
Kamchatskiy

Aleutian Islands

Copenhagen   Berlin

+3

Novosibirsk

Irkutsk

Vladivostok

-10

Dublin

London
(Greenwich)

E U R O P E

Kiev

Ulaanbaatar

NORTH
PACIFIC
OCEAN

Paris   Vienna

Almaty

Ürümqi

Date Line

Madrid   Rome   Istanbul

Tashkent

+5

+8

Seoul

Tokyo

Azores

Lisbon   Ankara

Ashgabat

Kabul

Beijing

Casablanca   Algiers

Tehran

+4½

Lanzhou

Algiers   Tripoli

+3½

New
Delhi

+5¾

+5½

Shanghai

NORTH
ATLANTIC
OCEAN

Cairo

Baghdad

Karachi

Chongqing

Hong Kong

Tombouctou
(Timbuktu)

+3

Mecca

Muscat

Kolkata

Mumbai
(Bombay)

+6½

Hanoi

Taiwan

Dakar   Niamey   Khartoum

Sanaa

Yangon
(Rangoon)

Bangkok

Manila

+9

Guam

Marshall Is.

+12

-11

N'Djamena   Addis Ababa

+5½

Caroline Is.

Monrovia   Lagos

A F R I C A

Colombo

Nauru

Phoenix Is.

Ascension   Kampala   Mogadishu

+6

Singapore

+13

Kinshasa   Nairobi

Diego
Garcia

Jakarta

+13

Salvador

Luanda   Dar es Salaam

Seychelles

Cocos I.

+6½

+13

Fiji Is.

Rio de Janeiro

SOUTH
ATLANTIC
OCEAN

Lusaka   Antananarivo

INDIAN
OCEAN

Darwin

+9½

New
Caledonia

Tonga

São Paulo

Windhoek   Harare

Mauritius

AUSTRALIA

+11½

+12¾

Johannesburg

Perth

Brisbane

Lord
Howe
Is.

Norfolk
Is.

Tristan da Cunha I.

Cape
Town

+5½

Sydney

Melbourne

+10½

Wellington

Chatham
Is.

The numerals in each zone show
the number of hours to be added to,
or subtracted from, Coordinated
Universal Time (UTC), formerly
Greenwich Mean Time (GMT).

-2   **-1**   **0**   **+1**   **+2**   **+3**   **+4**   **+5**   **+6**   **+7**   **+8**   **+9**   **+10**   **+11**   **+12**   **-12**

30°W   0°   30°E   60°E   90°E   120°E   150°E   180°

THE DATE LINE (180°) is directly opposite the prime meridian (0°). As Earth rotates, each new day officially begins as the 180° line passes midnight. If you travel west across the date line, you advance one day; if you travel east across the date line, you fall back one day. Notice on the map how the line zigs to the east as it passes through the South Pacific so that the islands of Fiji will not be split between two different days. Also notice that India is 5½ hours ahead of Coordinated Universal Time (formerly Greenwich Mean Time), and China has only one time zone, even though the country spans more than 60 degrees of longitude. These differences are the result of decisions made at the country level.

The Physical World

Realms of land and water make up the physical world. More than two-thirds of Earth's surface is covered by water: oceans, lakes, and rivers. The rest is land: continents and islands. People inhabit every continent except Antarctica, which lies frozen beneath a vast ice cap at Earth's South Pole. Each continent is unique, but all show evidence of dynamic forces at work. Some forces build up mountains such as the Rockies, the Andes, and the Himalaya; other forces wear down Earth's surface, creating vast sedimentary plains and lowlands. Powerful rivers such as the Mississippi, the Congo, and the Yangtze (Chang) cut through the land and empty billions of gallons of freshwater into the oceans and seas each day.

THE OCEAN FLOOR. Beneath Earth's oceans lies a landscape as varied as any on land. The Mid-Atlantic Ridge is part of a global mountain range that winds 40,000 miles (64,000 km) across the ocean floor. Volcanic islands rise up from the seabed, while the Mariana Trench plunges more than 36,070 feet (10,994 m)—deep enough to submerge Mount Everest.

ARCTIC OCEAN

GREENLAND

Greenland Sea

Severnaya Zemlya

New Siberian Islands

Laptev Sea

East Siberian Sea

ARCTIC CIRCLE

Iceland

Svalbard

Barents Sea

Novaya Zemlya

Kara Sea

Central Siberian Plateau

60°N

Bering Sea

Kamchatka Peninsula

Aleutian Is.

Norwegian Sea

Scandinavia

Ural Mountains

Ob

West Siberian Plain

Yenisey

Lena

Lena

Sea of Okhotsk

British Isles

North Sea

Northern European Plain

Oh

Irtysh

Angara

Lake Baikal

Amur

Hokkaido

JAPAN

Nampo Shoto

Ireland

Great Britain

Baltic

EUROPE

Alps

Volga

The Steppes

Altay Mountains

Tian Shan

ASIA

GOBI

Sea of Japan (East Sea)

Honshu

30°N

Azores

Danube

El'brus 18,510 ft (5,642 m)

Black Sea

Caspian Sea

Caucasus Mts.

Zagros Mountains

Taklimakan Desert

Kunlun Mountains

Plateau of Tibet

Yellow (Huang)

North China Plain

Yangtze (Chang)

Korea

Yellow Sea

East China Sea

Ryukyu Islands

Mediterranean Sea

Atlas Mountains

Dead Sea -1,385 ft (-422 m)

ARABIAN PENINSULA

Indus

HIMALAYA

Mt. Everest 29,035 ft (8,850 m)

Brahmaputra

Ganges

Salween

Mekong

Taiwan

Hainan

PACIFIC

Canary Islands

SAHARA

Libyan Desert

Nile

Red Sea

Arabian Sea

INDIA

Deccan Plateau

Bay of Bengal

Indochina Peninsula

South China Sea

Luzon

Philippine Sea

Mariana Islands

OCEAN

Cape Verde Islands

SAHEL

Niger

Lake Chad

White Nile

Blue Nile

Gulf of Aden

Somali Peninsula

Andaman Islands

Andaman Sea

Philippine Islands

MICRONESIA

Marshall Islands

Upper Guinea

AFRICA

Ethiopian Highlands

Sri Lanka

Nicobar Is.

Malay Peninsula

Gilbert Islands

Gulf of Guinea

Congo

Lake Victoria

Kilimanjaro 19,340 ft (5,895 m)

Maldive Islands

Seychelles

Borneo

INDONESIA

Greater Sunda Islands

Celebes

Moluccas

New Guinea

Bismarck Archipelago

MELANESIA

OCEAN

Lower Guinea

Congo Basin

Lake Tanganyika

Great Rift Valley

INDIAN

Sumatra

Java

Timor

Solomon Islands

Namib Desert

Zambezi

Comoros Islands

Madagascar

Mascarene Islands

OCEAN

Arafura Sea

New Caledonia

Coral Sea

Vanuatu

Fiji Islands

Kalahari Desert

Drakensberg

Great Sandy Desert

AUSTRALIA

Lake Eyre -52 ft (-16 m)

Great Victoria Desert

Central Lowlands

Great Dividing Range

Darling

Murray

Tasman Sea

North Island

NEW ZEALAND

0 miles 2000

0 kilometers 3000

Winkel Tripel Projection

Kerguelen Islands

Mt. Kosciuszko 7,310 ft (2,228 m)

Tasmania

South Island

Auckland Islands

South Sandwich Islands

ANTARCTIC CIRCLE

60°S

Weddell Sea

Queen Maud Land

Transantarctic Mountains

Victoria Land

MOUNTAINS

ANTARCTICA

⬤ **THE PHYSICAL WORLD.** Great landmasses called continents break Earth's global ocean into four smaller ones. Each continent is unique in terms of the landforms and rivers that etch its surface and the ecosystems that lend colors ranging from the deep greens of the tropical forests of northern South America and southeastern Asia to the browns and yellows of the arid lands of Africa and Australia. Most of Antarctica's features are hidden beneath its ice cap.

Earth's Geologic History

Earth is a dynamic planet. Its outer shell, or crust, is broken into huge pieces called plates. These plates ride on the slowly moving molten rock, or magma, that lies beneath the crust. Their movement constantly changes Earth's surface. Along one convergent boundary—a place where two plates meet—the Indian Plate moves northward, colliding with the Eurasian Plate and heaving up the still growing Himalaya. Along another convergent boundary, the Nasca Plate dives beneath the South American Plate—a process called subduction that can trigger volcanoes, under-water earthquakes, and giant ocean waves called tsunamis. Along transform faults, such as California's San Andreas Fault, plates grind past each other, resulting in destructive earthquakes. Along divergent boundaries, plates are pushed apart, as in the Mid-Atlantic Ridge where the ocean floor is spread-ing apart allowing molten rock to rise, and Africa's Great Rift Valley where the continental plate is separating.

⊙ **OUR CHANGING PLANET.** The Latin phrase *terra firma* implies planet Earth is solid and unchanging. However, Earth's surface has been anything but unchanging. Geologic evidence suggests that moving plates have collided and moved apart more than once over the course of the planet's long history. As the main map shows, the forces of change show no signs of stopping.

PANGAEA. About 240 million years ago, all of Earth's continents collided to form a vast landmass (now called Pangaea) that stretched from Pole to Pole.

DRIFTING APART. By 94 million years ago, Pangaea had been pulled apart into smaller landmasses. In the warm global climate, dinosaurs evolved into Earth's dominant animal group.

PHYSICAL SYSTEMS

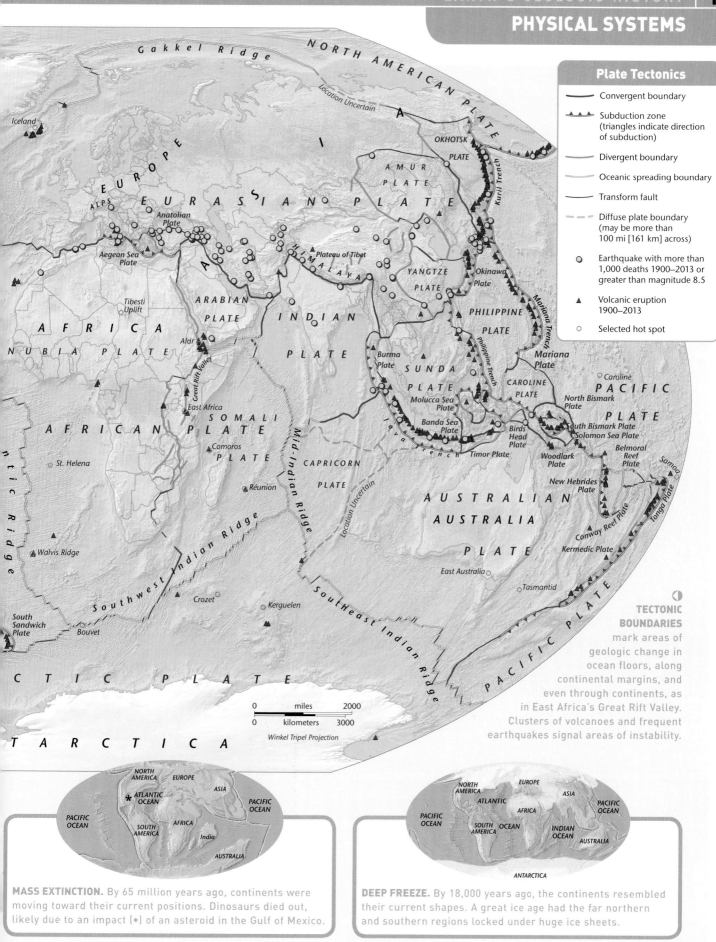

Plate Tectonics

Convergent boundary

Subduction zone
(triangles indicate direction
of subduction)

Divergent boundary

Oceanic spreading boundary

Transform fault

Diffuse plate boundary
(may be more than
100 mi [161 km] across)

⊙ Earthquake with more than
1,000 deaths 1900–2013 or
greater than magnitude 8.5

▲ Volcanic eruption
1900–2013

○ Selected hot spot

**TECTONIC
BOUNDARIES**
mark areas of
geologic change in
ocean floors, along
continental margins, and
even through continents, as
in East Africa's Great Rift Valley.
Clusters of volcanoes and frequent
earthquakes signal areas of instability.

0   miles   2000
0   kilometers   3000
Winkel Tripel Projection

MASS EXTINCTION. By 65 million years ago, continents were
moving toward their current positions. Dinosaurs died out,
likely due to an impact (∗) of an asteroid in the Gulf of Mexico.

DEEP FREEZE. By 18,000 years ago, the continents resembled
their current shapes. A great ice age had the far northern
and southern regions locked under huge ice sheets.

Earth's Land & Water Features

The largest land and water features on Earth are the continents and the oceans, but many other features—large and small—make each place unique. Mountains, plateaus, and plains give texture to the land. The Rockies and the Andes rise high above the lowlands of North and South America. In Asia, the Himalaya and the Plateau of Tibet form the rugged core of Earth's largest continent. These features are the result of powerful forces within Earth pushing up the land. Other landforms, such as canyons and valleys, are created when weathering and erosion wear down parts of Earth's surface.

Dramatic features are not limited to the land. Submarine mountains, appearing like pale blue threads against the deep blue on the satellite map, rise from the seafloor and trace zones of underwater geologic activity. Deep trenches form where plates collide, causing one to dive beneath the other.

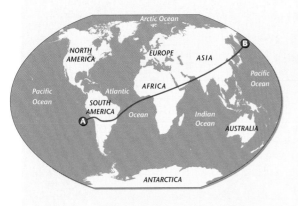

A SLICE OF EARTH. This cross section of Earth's surface extends from Lake Titicaca near South America's Pacific coast to the Kuril Islands in the northwestern Pacific Ocean. It shows towering mountains, eroded highlands, broad coastal plains, and deep ocean basins.

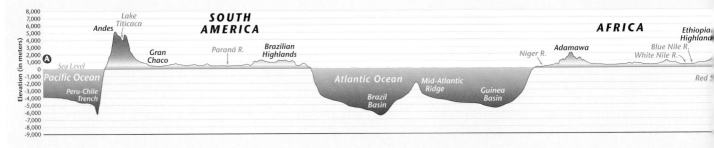

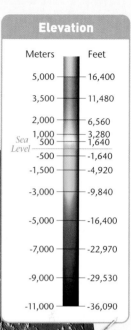

Elevation

Meters		Feet
5,000		16,400
3,500		11,480
2,000		6,560
1,000		3,280
500		1,640
Sea Level	—	
-500		-1,640
-1,500		-4,920
-3,000		-9,840
-5,000		-16,400
-7,000		-22,970
-9,000		-29,530
-11,000		-36,090

◖ **EARTH'S HIGHS AND LOWS** above and below sea level are clearly evident in this color-enhanced satellite map. Mountain ranges and ice caps, which rise above the land, stand out in shades of red; broad expanses of lowlands are shown in green. Pale aqua marks shallow seas along continental margins and over peaks and ridges rising from the ocean floor.

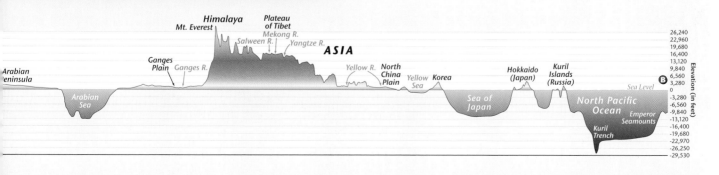

Earth's Climates

Climate is not the same as weather. Climate is the long-term average of conditions in the atmosphere at a particular location on Earth's surface. Weather refers to the momentary conditions of the atmosphere. Climate is important because it influences vegetation and soil development. It also influences people's choices about how and where to live.

There are many different systems for classifying climates. One commonly used system was developed by Russian-born climatologist Wladimir Köppen and later modified by American climatologist Glenn Trewartha. Köppen's system identifies five major climate zones based on average precipitation and temperature, and a sixth zone for highland, or high elevation, areas. Except for continental climate, all climate zones occur in mirror image north and south of the Equator.

CLIMATE GRAPHS. A climate graph is a combination bar and line graph that shows monthly averages of precipitation and temperature for a particular place. The bar graph shows precipitation in inches and centimeters; the line graph shows temperature in degrees Fahrenheit and Celsius. The graphs below are typical for places in the climate zone represented by their background color. The seeming inversion of the temperature lines for Alice Springs, in Australia, and McMurdo, in Antarctica, reflects the reversal of seasons south of the Equator, where January is midsummer. The abbreviations for months are across the bottom of each graph.

Resolute
Fairbanks
60°N

NORTH AMERICA

Subarctic Current

North Pacific Drift

Des Moines

30°N

Gulf Stream

North Atlantic Drift

Labrador Current

TROPIC OF CANCER

Monterrey

PACIFIC

OCEAN

ATLANTIC

Equatorial Countercurrent

150°W   120°W   EQUATOR   90°W

0°

Belém

South Equatorial Current

SOUTH AMERICA

Peru Current

TROPIC OF CAPRICORN

30°S

| 0 | miles | 2000 |

| 0 | kilometers | 3000 |

Winkel Tripel Projection

Falkland Current

West Wind Drift

60°S

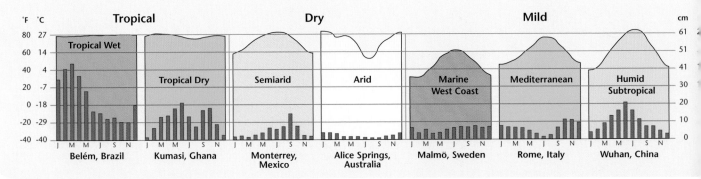

		Tropical	**Dry**	**Mild**	
°F	°C				cm
80	27	Tropical Wet			61
60	14			Marine	51
40	4	Tropical Dry	Semiarid	Arid	West Coast	Mediterranean	Humid Subtropical	41
20	-7				30
0	-18				20
-20	-29				10
-40	-40				0

J M M J S N   J M M J S N   J M M J S N   J M M J S N   J M M J S N   J M M J S N   J M M J S N

Belém, Brazil   Kumasi, Ghana   Monterrey, Mexico   Alice Springs, Australia   Malmö, Sweden   Rome, Italy   Wuhan, China

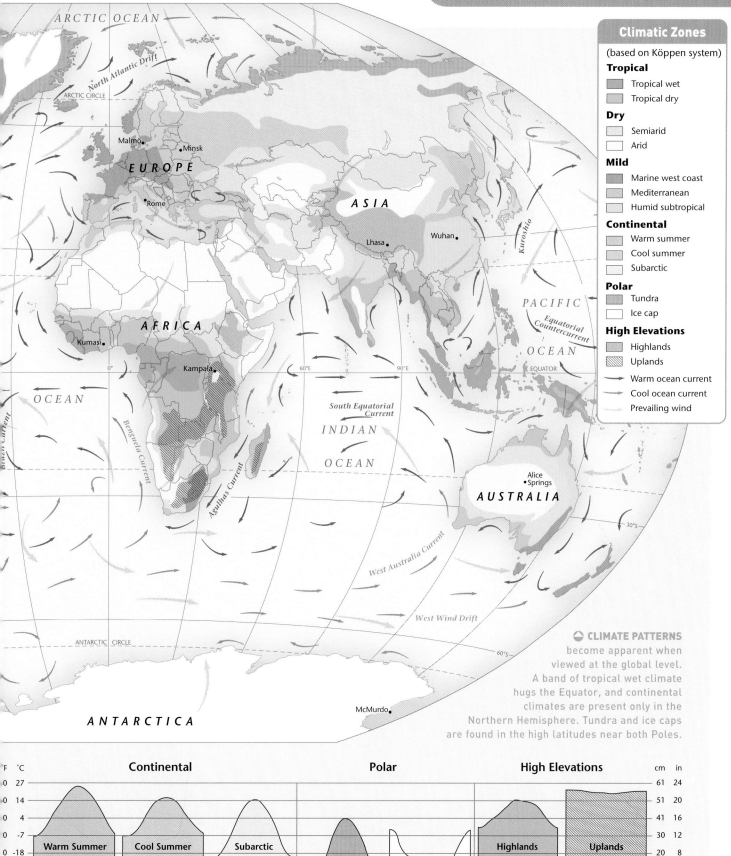

ARCTIC OCEAN

North Atlantic Drift

ARCTIC CIRCLE

60°N

Malmö

Minsk

EUROPE

Rome

ASIA

Lhasa   Wuhan

Kuroshio

PACIFIC

Equatorial
Countercurrent

OCEAN

AFRICA

Kumasi

Kampala

0°   60°E   90°E   EQUATOR   30°S

OCEAN

Benguela Current

Agulhas Current

South Equatorial
Current

INDIAN

OCEAN

Brazil Current

Alice
Springs

AUSTRALIA

30°S

West Australia Current

West Wind Drift

60°S

ANTARCTIC CIRCLE

McMurdo

ANTARCTICA

Climatic Zones

(based on Köppen system)

Tropical
- Tropical wet
- Tropical dry

Dry
- Semiarid
- Arid

Mild
- Marine west coast
- Mediterranean
- Humid subtropical

Continental
- Warm summer
- Cool summer
- Subarctic

Polar
- Tundra
- Ice cap

High Elevations
- Highlands
- Uplands
- → Warm ocean current
- → Cool ocean current
- → Prevailing wind

◯ **CLIMATE PATTERNS**
become apparent when
viewed at the global level.
A band of tropical wet climate
hugs the Equator, and continental
climates are present only in the
Northern Hemisphere. Tundra and ice caps
are found in the high latitudes near both Poles.

°F	°C				cm	in
	27	**Continental**	**Polar**	**High Elevations**	61	24
	14				51	20
	4				41	16
	-7				30	12
	-18	Warm Summer	Cool Summer	Subarctic	Tundra	Ice Cap	Highlands	Uplands	20	8
	-29				10	4
	-40				0	0

Des Moines, Iowa, U.S.A. | Minsk, Belarus | Fairbanks, Alaska, U.S.A. | Resolute, Nunavut, Canada | McMurdo, Antarctica | Lhasa, China | Kampala, Uganda

Climate Controls

The patterns of climate vary widely. Some climates, such as those near the Equator and the Poles, are nearly constant year-round. Others experience great seasonal variations, such as the wet and dry patterns of the tropical dry zone and the monthly average temperature extremes of the subarctic.

Climate patterns are not random. They are the result of complex interactions of basic climate controls: latitude, elevation, prevailing winds, ocean currents, landforms, and location.

These controls combine in various ways to create the bands of climate that can be seen on the world climate map on pages 20–21 and on the climate maps in the individual continent sections of this atlas. At the local level, however, special conditions may create microclimates that differ from those that are more typical of the region.

LATITUDE

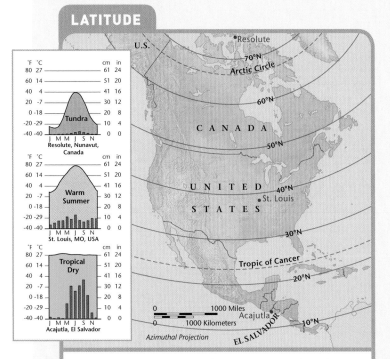

Latitude affects the amount of solar energy received. As latitude (distance north or south of the Equator) increases, the angle of the sun's energy becomes increasingly oblique, or slanted. Less energy is received from the sun, and annual average temperatures fall. Therefore, the annual average temperature decreases as latitude increases from Acajutla, El Salvador, to St. Louis, Missouri, to Resolute, Canada.

ELEVATION

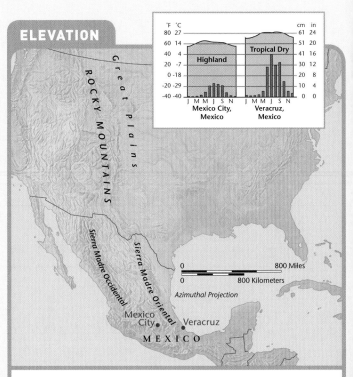

Not all locations at the same latitude experience similar climates. Air at higher elevations is cooler and holds less moisture than air at lower elevations. This explains why the climate at Veracruz, Mexico, which is near sea level, is warm and wet, and the climate at Mexico City, which is more than 7,000 feet (2,100 m) above sea level, is cooler and drier.

LANDFORMS

When air carried by prevailing winds blows across a large body of water, such as the ocean, it picks up moisture. If that air encounters a mountain when it reaches land, it is forced to rise and the air becomes cooler, causing precipitation on the windward side of the mountain (see Portland graph). When air descends on the side away from the wind— the leeward side—the air warms and absorbs available moisture. This creates a dry condition known as rain shadow (see Wallowa graph).

PREVAILING WINDS AND OCEAN CURRENTS

Earth's rotation combined with heat energy from the sun creates patterns of movement in Earth's atmosphere called prevailing winds. In the oceans, similar movements of water are called currents. Prevailing winds and ocean currents bring warm and cold temperatures to land areas. They also bring moisture or take it away. The Gulf Stream and the North Atlantic Drift, for example, are warm-water currents that influence average temperatures in eastern North America and northern Europe. Prevailing winds—trade winds, polar easterlies, and westerlies—also affect temperature and precipitation averages.

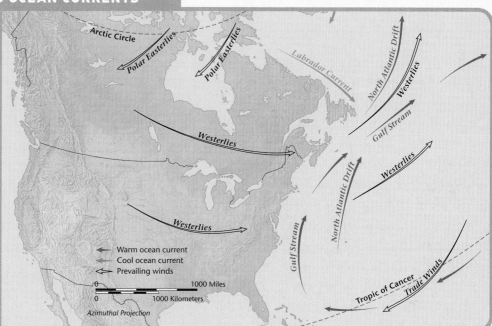

LOCATION

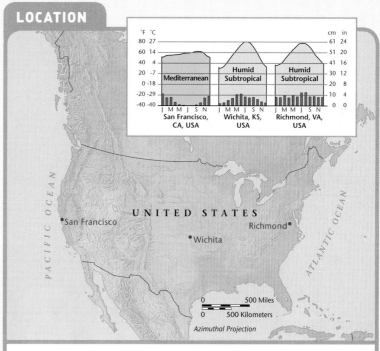

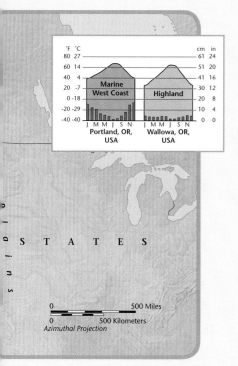

Marine locations—places near large bodies of water—have mild climates with little temperature variation because water gains and loses heat slowly (see San Francisco graph). Interior locations—places far from large water bodies—have much more extreme climates. There are great temperature variations because land gains and loses heat rapidly (see Wichita graph). Richmond, which is relatively near the Atlantic Ocean but which is also influenced by prevailing westerly winds blowing across the land, has moderate characteristics of both conditions.

Earth's Natural Vegetation

Natural vegetation is plant life that would be found in an area if it were undisturbed by human activity. Natural vegetation varies widely depending on climate and soil conditions. In rain forests, trees tower as much as 200 feet (60 m) above the forest floor. In the humid mid-latitudes, deciduous trees shed their leaves during the cold season, while coniferous trees remain green throughout the year. Areas receiving too little rainfall to support trees have grasses. Dry areas have plants such as cacti that tolerate long periods without water. In the tundra, dwarf species of shrubs and flowers are adaptations to harsh conditions at high latitudes and high elevations.

Vegetation is important to human life. It provides oxygen, food, fuel, products with economic value, even lifesaving medicines. Human activities, however, have greatly affected natural vegetation (see pages 28–29). Huge forests have been cut to provide fuel and lumber. Grasslands have yielded to the plow as people extend agricultural lands. As many as one in eight plants may become extinct due to human interference.

🌐 **TYPES OF VEGETATION.** Vegetation creates a mosaic of colors and textures across Earth's surface. Grasslands dominate in places where there is too little precipitation to support trees. In the wet conditions of the tropics, rain forests and mangroves flourish. Desert shrubs are adapted to dry climates, and tundra plants survive a short growing season. These photographs show some of the plants found in various vegetation regions. Each is keyed to the map by color and number.

NORTH AMERICA

SOUTH AMERICA

PACIFIC OCEAN

ATLANTIC

TROPIC OF CANCER

EQUATOR

TROPIC OF CAPRICORN

```
0      miles      2000
0    kilometers   3000
```
Winkel Tripel Projection

1

TUNDRA

2

NORTHERN CONIFEROUS FOREST

4

TEMPERATE BROADLEAF FOREST

5

TEMPERATE GRASSLAND

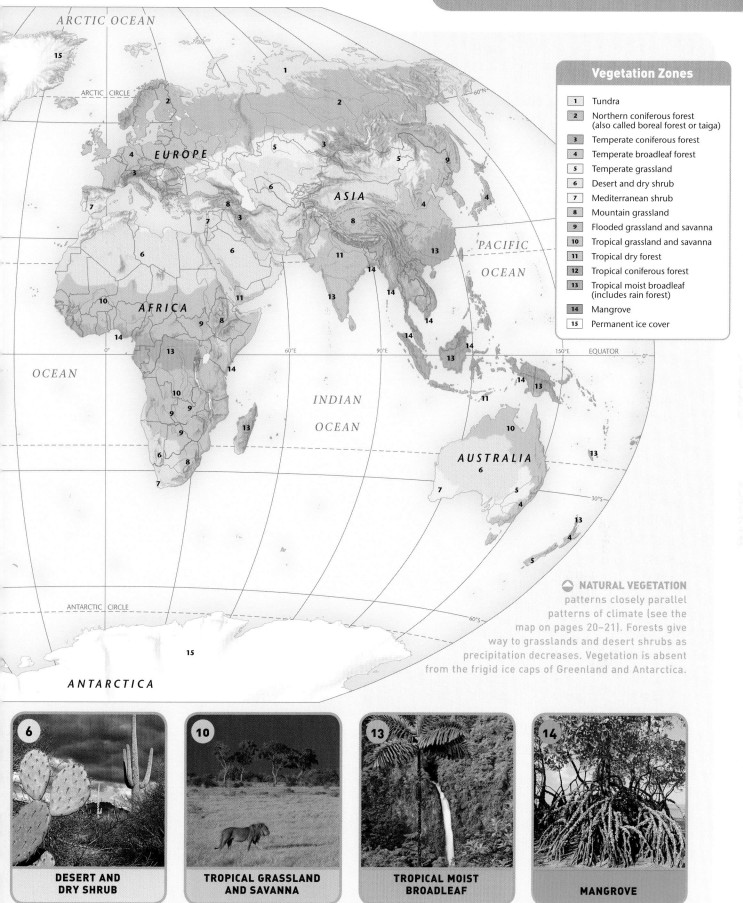

ARCTIC OCEAN

15

ARCTIC CIRCLE

EUROPE

ASIA

AFRICA

PACIFIC OCEAN

OCEAN

INDIAN OCEAN

AUSTRALIA

ANTARCTIC CIRCLE

15

ANTARCTICA

Vegetation Zones

1	Tundra
2	Northern coniferous forest (also called boreal forest or taiga)
3	Temperate coniferous forest
4	Temperate broadleaf forest
5	Temperate grassland
6	Desert and dry shrub
7	Mediterranean shrub
8	Mountain grassland
9	Flooded grassland and savanna
10	Tropical grassland and savanna
11	Tropical dry forest
12	Tropical coniferous forest
13	Tropical moist broadleaf (includes rain forest)
14	Mangrove
15	Permanent ice cover

NATURAL VEGETATION patterns closely parallel patterns of climate (see the map on pages 20–21). Forests give way to grasslands and desert shrubs as precipitation decreases. Vegetation is absent from the frigid ice caps of Greenland and Antarctica.

6 DESERT AND DRY SHRUB

10 TROPICAL GRASSLAND AND SAVANNA

13 TROPICAL MOIST BROADLEAF

14 MANGROVE

Earth's Water

Water is essential for life and is one of Earth's most valuable natural resources. It is even more important than food. More than 70 percent of Earth's surface is covered with water in the form of oceans, lakes, rivers, and streams, but most of this water—about 97 percent—is salty and without treatment is unusable for drinking or growing crops. The remaining 3 percent is fresh, but most of this is either trapped in glaciers or ice caps or lies too deep underground to be tapped economically.

Water is a renewable resource that can be used over and over because the hydrologic, or water, cycle purifies water as it moves through the processes of evaporation, condensation, precipitation, runoff, and infiltration. However, careless use can diminish the supply of usable fresh water when pollution results from industrial dumping, runoff of fertilizers or pesticides from cultivated fields, or discharge of urban sewage. Like other natural resources, water is unevenly distributed on Earth. Some regions, such as the eastern United States, have sufficient water to meet the needs of the people living there. But in other regions, such as large areas of Asia, the demand for water places great stress on available supply (see the map).

NORTH AMERICA

PACIFIC OCEAN

ATLANTI

SOUTH AMERICA

60°N

30°N

TROPIC OF CANCER

0°

150°W · 120°W · EQUATOR · 90°W · 60°W

30°S

66°S

Water Stress

Withdrawls as a Percentage of Available Supply

- Less than 10%
- 10–19.9%
- 20–39.9%
- 40–80%
- Greater than 80%
- Arid with low demand
- No data

WATER USES   Note: Percentages shown are for annual use; 2011 data.

Domestic 12%

DOMESTIC. In many less developed regions, women, such as these in Central America, haul water for daily use.

Agricultural 70%

AGRICULTURAL. Irrigation has made agriculture possible in dry areas such as the San Pedro Valley in Arizona, shown here.

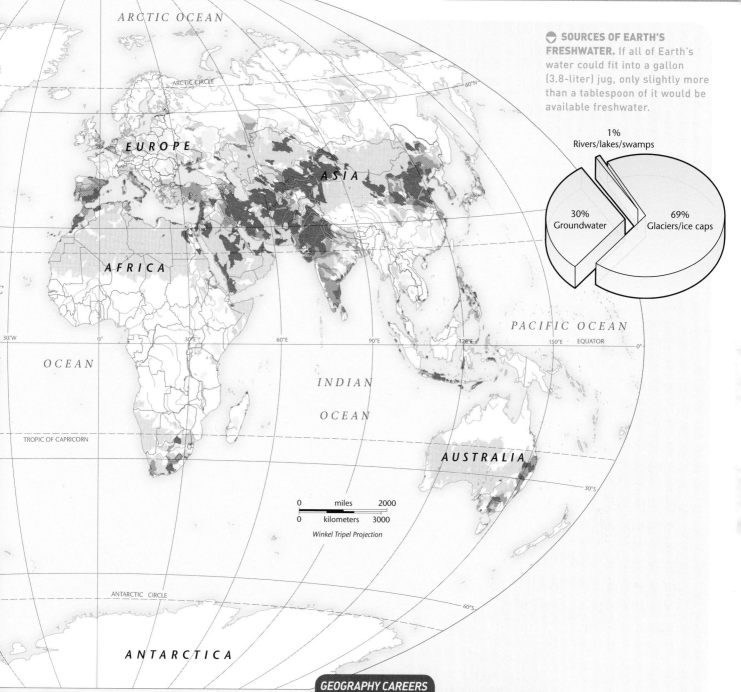

ARCTIC OCEAN

ARCTIC CIRCLE

EUROPE

ASIA

AFRICA

OCEAN

INDIAN

OCEAN

PACIFIC OCEAN

TROPIC OF CAPRICORN

AUSTRALIA

0 miles 2000
0 kilometers 3000

Winkel Tripel Projection

ANTARCTIC CIRCLE

ANTARCTICA

⬤ **SOURCES OF EARTH'S FRESHWATER.** If all of Earth's water could fit into a gallon (3.8-liter) jug, only slightly more than a tablespoon of it would be available freshwater.

1%
Rivers/lakes/swamps

30%
Groundwater

69%
Glaciers/ice caps

Industrial 18%

INDUSTRIAL. Hydroelectric dams, such as this one in Tucuruí, Brazil, generate electricity to power industry.

GEOGRAPHY CAREERS

NG EXPLORER: SANDRA POSTEL

Sandra Postel, a freshwater conservationist, has spent over 25 years promoting water conservation and better water management. She founded the Global Water Policy Project in order to promote the preservation and sustainable uses of Earth's freshwater sources and works to accomplish this goal through research, writing, outreach, public speaking, and teaching. *national geographic.com/explorers/bios/sandra-postel*

Environmental Hot Spots

As Earth's human population increases, pressures on the natural environment also increase. In industrialized countries, landfills overflow with the volume of trash produced. Industries generate waste and pollution that foul the air and water. Farmers use chemical fertilizers and pesticides that run off into streams and groundwater. Cars release exhaust fumes that pollute the air and perhaps also contribute to global climate change.

In less developed countries, forests are cut and not replanted, making the land vulnerable to erosion. Fragile grasslands turn to deserts when farmers and herders move onto marginal land as they try to make a living. And cities struggle with issues such as water safety, sanitation, and basic services that accompany the explosive urban growth that characterizes many less developed countries.

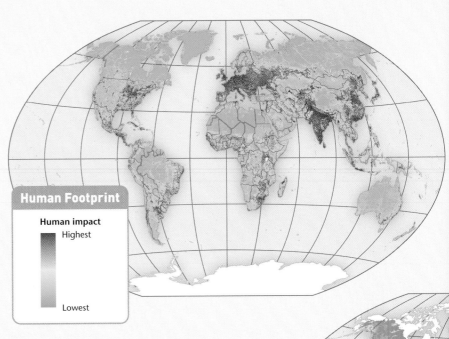

Human Footprint

Human impact
Highest

Lowest

🌐 **HUMAN ACTIVITY** has altered nearly 75 percent of Earth's habitable surface. Referred to as the "human footprint," this disturbance is greatest in areas of high population.

◑ Forests play a critical role in Earth's natural systems. They regulate water flow, release oxygen and retain carbon, cycle nutrients, and build soils. But humans have cut, burned, altered, and replaced half of all forests that stood 8,000 years ago.

Fragile Forests

Current frontier forest (large, relatively undisturbed forest)

Current non-frontier forest (degraded, regrown, replanted, plantation, or other forest areas)

Estimated extent of frontier forest 8,000 years ago

DESERT SANDS, moved by high winds, cover large areas of Mauritania. The shifting sands threaten to cover an important transportation route (upper right), which must be cleared daily. A grid of branches has been laid over the sand to try to slow the advancing desert, which has been expanding since the mid-1960s.

DEFORESTATION in Haiti (left side of photograph above) clearly defines its border with the Dominican Republic. Haiti was once 30 percent forested, but loss of trees for timber and subsistence agriculture has reduced forest cover to less than 2 percent.

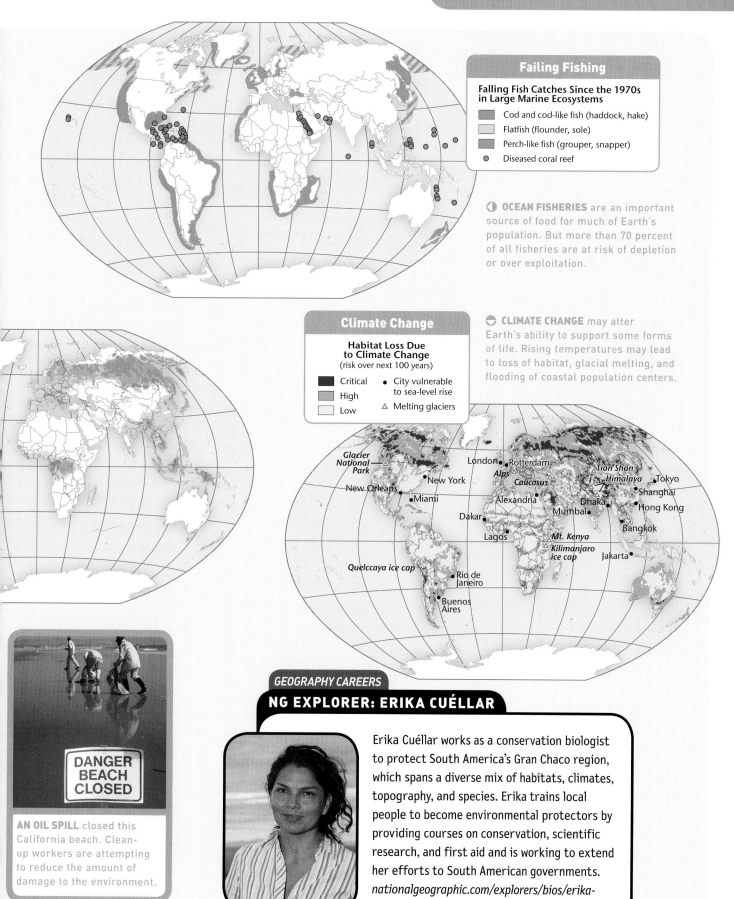

Failing Fishing

Falling Fish Catches Since the 1970s in Large Marine Ecosystems

- Cod and cod-like fish (haddock, hake)
- Flatfish (flounder, sole)
- Perch-like fish (grouper, snapper)
- ○ Diseased coral reef

OCEAN FISHERIES are an important source of food for much of Earth's population. But more than 70 percent of all fisheries are at risk of depletion or over exploitation.

Climate Change

Habitat Loss Due to Climate Change
(risk over next 100 years)

- Critical
- High
- Low
- • City vulnerable to sea-level rise
- △ Melting glaciers

CLIMATE CHANGE may alter Earth's ability to support some forms of life. Rising temperatures may lead to loss of habitat, glacial melting, and flooding of coastal population centers.

Glacier National Park • London • Rotterdam Tian' Shan Tokyo
Alps Himalaya
New York Caucasus Shanghai
New Orleans Alexandria Dhaka Hong Kong
Miami Mumbai
Dakar Bangkok
Lagos Mt. Kenya
Kilimanjaro ice cap Jakarta
Quelccaya ice cap
Rio de Janeiro
Buenos Aires

AN OIL SPILL closed this California beach. Clean-up workers are attempting to reduce the amount of damage to the environment.

DANGER BEACH CLOSED

GEOGRAPHY CAREERS

NG EXPLORER: ERIKA CUÉLLAR

Erika Cuéllar works as a conservation biologist to protect South America's Gran Chaco region, which spans a diverse mix of habitats, climates, topography, and species. Erika trains local people to become environmental protectors by providing courses on conservation, scientific research, and first aid and is working to extend her efforts to South American governments. *nationalgeographic.com/explorers/bios/erika-cuellar*

The Political World

A map with the names and boundaries of countries shows the political world. Boundaries—some arrived at peacefully, others after years of conflict and war—carve up the land into 195 independent units, or countries, early in the 21st century. Boundaries are dynamic, meaning they change over time as political power shifts. For example, in 1990, West and East Germany became one country, removing a boundary that had separated them since 1949. In 2011, a new boundary was established to separate the new country of South Sudan from Sudan.

Countries vary in size. Russia, the largest, stretches across northern Asia into Europe. Other countries are small enough to fit inside another country. For instance, the country of Lesotho lies entirely within the country of South Africa.

◖ THE SCALE OF THIS MAP makes it impossible to name all 195 independent countries and their capital cities. For a complete listing, refer to pages 126–133 or use the place-name index and the political maps in each continent section.

◖ VIEW FROM THE NORTH POLE. Ocean, not land, surrounds the area of the North Pole, so there are no political boundaries there. The Arctic Ocean, icebound much of the year, is part of the coastal waters of Earth's northernmost countries.

ARCTIC OCEAN

Greenland (Denmark)

Greenland Sea

Franz Josef Land

Barents Sea

Severnaya Zemlya

New Siberian Islands

East Siberian Sea

Laptev Sea

Kara Sea

Svalbard (Norway)

Novaya Zemlya

Norwegian Sea

ARCTIC CIRCLE

ICELAND
• Reykjavik

60°N

Bering Sea

Sea of Okhotsk

Kamchatka Peninsula

NORWAY

SWEDEN

FINLAND

• Helsinki

Oslo

Stockholm

R U S S I A

Sakhalin

Hokkaido

UNITED KINGDOM

North Sea

DENMARK

EST.

LATV.

LITH.

• Minsk

• Moscow

Astana

Honshu

JAPAN

Dublin

IRELAND

London

Copenhagen

NETH.

Berlin

BELG.

GERMANY

POLAND

Warsaw

BELARUS

UKRAINE

Kiev

KAZAKHSTAN

Ulaanbaatar ⊛

MONGOLIA

NORTH KOREA

Beijing ⊛

Pyongyang

Seoul

SOUTH KOREA

Tokyo

Osaka

Kyushu

See Europe, pp. 82-83

FRANCE

Paris

CZECH REP.

SLOV.

AUSTRIA

SWITZ.

SLO.

HUNG.

CRO.

MOLD.

ROMANIA

SERBIA

Astana

Tashkent

UZBEKISTAN

Bishkek

KYRGYZSTAN

Dushanbe

TAJIKISTAN

C H I N A

30°N

PORTUGAL

Madrid

ITALY

Rome

BOS.

MONTENEGRO

ALBANIA

MACED.

KOSOVO

Black Sea

GEORGIA

ARM.

AZER.

TURKMENISTAN

Ashgabat

Kabul

Chongqing •

Shanghai •

TAIWAN

Azores (Portugal)

Lisbon

SPAIN

Tunis

BULGARIA

GREECE

Athens

TURKEY

Ankara

Istanbul

Caspian Sea

PACIFIC

Madeira Is. (Portugal)

Rabat

Algiers

TUNISIA

CYPRUS

LEBANON

SYRIA

Damascus

IRAQ

Baghdad

IRAN

Tehran

AFGHANISTAN

Islamabad ⊛

Thimphu

BHUTAN

Guangzhou

Shenzhen

Taipei

Taiwan

The People's Republic of China claims Taiwan as its 23rd province. Taiwan's government (Republic of China) maintains that there are two political entities.

Canary Is. (Spain)

MOROCCO

Western Sahara (Morocco)

ALGERIA

LIBYA

Tripoli

Cairo

ISRAEL

JORDAN

KUWAIT

BAHRAIN

QATAR

Riyadh

U.A.E.

Muscat

PAKISTAN

Karachi

NEPAL

New Delhi

Kathmandu

BANGLADESH

Dhaka

MYANMAR (BURMA)

Hanoi

Hainan

South China Sea

Luzon

Philippine Sea

Northern Mariana Islands (U.S.)

OCEAN

MAURITANIA

CABO VERDE

GAMBIA

SENEGAL

Dakar

GUINEA-BISSAU

MALI

Nouakchott ⊛

Bamako

NIGER

Niamey

CHAD

N'Djamena

SUDAN

Khartoum

ERITREA

Asmara

YEMEN

Sanaa

Red Sea

EGYPT

SAUDI ARABIA

OMAN

Arabian Sea

Mumbai (Bombay)

INDIA

Bay of Bengal

Yangon

Vientiane

LAOS

THAILAND

Bangkok

CAMBODIA

Phnom Penh

VIETNAM

Manila

Guam (U.S.)

MARSHALL ISLANDS

BURKINA FASO

Ouagadougou

NIGERIA

Abuja ⊛

DJIBOUTI

SOMALILAND

Socotra (Yemen)

Bangalore

Colombo

SRI LANKA

BRUNEI

Bandar Seri Begawan

PHILIPPINES

Mindanao

PALAU

FEDERATED STATES OF MICRONESIA

KIRIBATI

Conakry

GUINEA

SIERRA LEONE

Freetown

LIBERIA

Monrovia

GHANA

Accra

Lomé

TOGO

BENIN

Lagos

CENTRAL AFRICAN REPUBLIC

Bangui

SOUTH SUDAN

Juba

ETHIOPIA

Addis Ababa

SOMALIA

Male

MALDIVES

Mogadishu

Kuala Lumpur

MALAYSIA

SINGAPORE

Borneo

INDONESIA

Jakarta

Java

Celebes

New Guinea

PAPUA NEW GUINEA

EQUATOR

NAURU

YAMOUSSOUKRO

CÔTE D'IVOIRE (IVORY COAST)

Abidjan

CAMEROON

Yaoundé

EQ. GUINEA

GABON

Libreville

SAO TOME AND PRINCIPE

CONGO

Brazzaville

DEMOCRATIC REPUBLIC OF THE CONGO

Kinshasa

UGANDA

Kampala

KENYA

Nairobi

RWANDA

Kigali

BURUNDI

Bujumbura

TANZANIA

Dodoma

Dar es Salaam

SEYCHELLES

INDIAN

Port Moresby

SOLOMON ISLANDS

Honiara

TUVALU

60°E

90°E

150°E

0°

CABINDA (Angola)

Luanda

ANGOLA

ZAMBIA

Lusaka

COMOROS

Moroni

OCEAN

VANUATU

Port-Vila

FIJI

Suva

New Caledonia (France)

OCEAN

NAMIBIA

Windhoek

BOTSWANA

Gaborone

ZIMBABWE

Harare

MOZAMBIQUE

MALAWI

Lilongwe

MADAGASCAR

Antananarivo

MAURITIUS

Port Louis

Réunion (France)

Coral Sea

AUSTRALIA

Pretoria (Tshwane)

Maputo

SWAZILAND

Bloemfontein

LESOTHO

SOUTH AFRICA

Cape Town

Great Australian Bight

Canberra ⊛

Tasman Sea

North Island

30°S

Tasmania

NEW ZEALAND

Wellington ⊛

South Island

Kerguelen Islands (France)

Meridian of Greenwich (London)

ANTARCTIC CIRCLE

60°S

Weddell Sea

A N T A R C T I C A

▷ **VIEW FROM THE SOUTH POLE.** Covered by ice, the continent of Antarctica has been set aside by treaty for scientific research. It has no permanent population and no political boundaries, although 7 countries claim territory there and 20 operate year-round research stations (see map page 124).

Ross Sea

0°

ATLANTIC OCEAN

30°W

30°E

ANTARCTIC CIRCLE

60°W

Weddell Sea

60°E

Antarctic Peninsula

Ronne Ice Shelf

90°W

West Antarctica

South Pole

East Antarctica

90°E

INDIAN OCEAN

A N T A R C T I C A

Ross Ice Shelf

120°W

PACIFIC OCEAN

Ross Sea

120°E

0 mi 600

0 km 900

150°W

180°

150°E

Azimuthal Equidistant Projection

World Population

In mid-2013, the United Nations estimated Earth's population to be 7.2 billion. Although more than 86 million people are added each year, the rate, or annual percent, at which the population is growing is gradually decreasing. Earth's population has very uneven distribution, with huge clusters in Asia and in Europe. Population density, the number of people living in each square mile (or square kilometer) on average, is high in these regions. For example, on average there are more than 2,815 people per square mile (1,087 per sq km) in Bangladesh. Other areas, such as deserts and Arctic tundra, have fewer than 2 people per square mile (1 person per sq km).

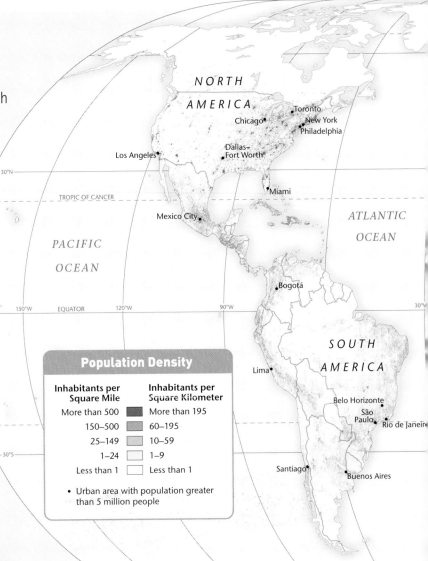

Population Density

Inhabitants per Square Mile		Inhabitants per Square Kilometer
More than 500		More than 195
150–500		60–195
25–149		10–59
1–24		1–9
Less than 1		Less than 1

• Urban area with population greater than 5 million people

🔘 **CROWDED STREETS,** like this one in Shanghai, China, may become commonplace as Earth's population continues to increase and as more people move to urban areas.

POPULATION GROWTH OVER TIME

The population's rate of increase—the percentage by which it changes each year—was slow until industrial and scientific discoveries in the 1800s brought improved health, a more reliable food supply, and other changes that improved the quality of life. Although the rate of increase is slowing, the United Nations projects that Earth's population will reach 9.6 billion by 2050.

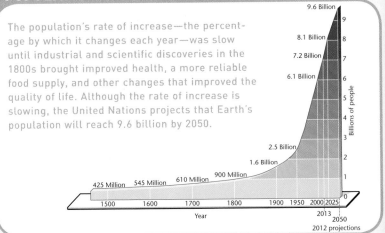

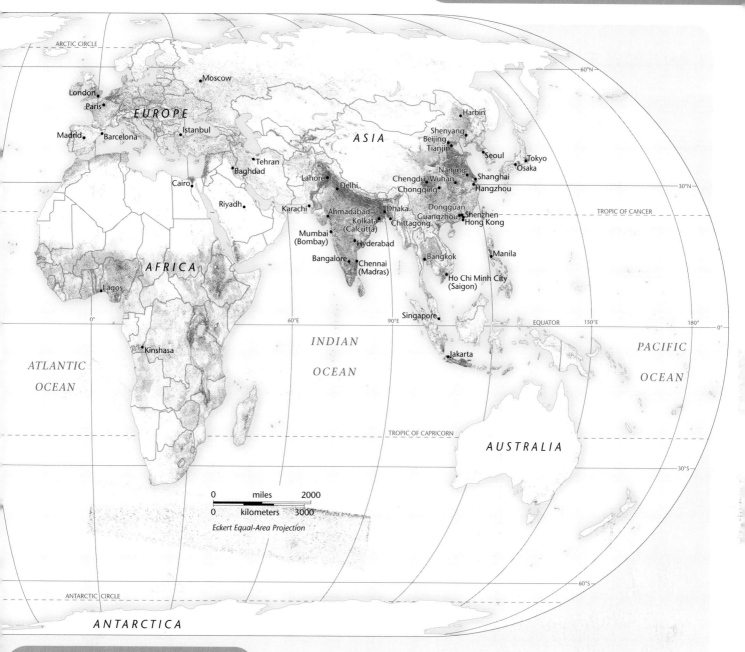

THREE POPULATION PYRAMIDS

A population pyramid is a special type of bar graph that shows the distribution of a country's population by sex and age. Italy has a very narrow pyramid, which shows that most people are in middle age. Its population is said to be aging, meaning the median age is increasing. The United States also has a narrow pyramid, but one that shows some growth due to a median age of about 37 years and a young immigrant population. By contrast, Nigeria's pyramid has a broad base, showing it has a young population. Almost half of its people are younger than 15 years.

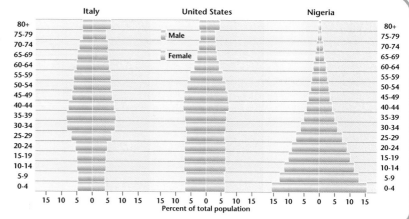

World Refugees

Every day, people relocate to new cities, new states, even new countries. Most move by choice, but some people, called refugees, move to escape war and persecution that make it impossible to remain where they are. Such forced movement creates severe hardship for families who have to leave behind their possessions. They may find themselves in a new place where they do not speak the local language, where customs are unfamiliar, and where basic necessities, such as food, shelter, and medical care, are in short supply.

An agency of the United Nations, the Office of the High Commissioner for Refugees (UNHCR), is responsible for the safety and well-being of refugees worldwide and for protecting their rights. UNHCR works to find solutions to refugee situations through voluntary return to home countries, integration in a host country, or resettlement to another country.

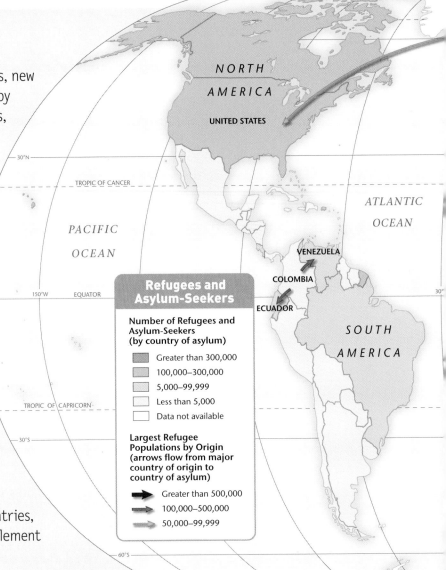

Refugees and Asylum-Seekers

Number of Refugees and Asylum-Seekers (by country of asylum)

- Greater than 300,000
- 100,000–300,000
- 5,000–99,999
- Less than 5,000
- Data not available

Largest Refugee Populations by Origin (arrows flow from major country of origin to country of asylum)

- Greater than 500,000
- 100,000–500,000
- 50,000–99,999

REFUGEE HOST COUNTRIES

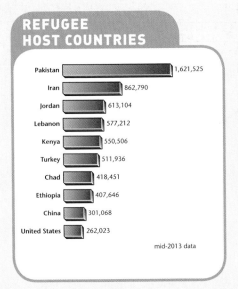

Pakistan	1,621,525
Iran	862,790
Jordan	613,104
Lebanon	577,212
Kenya	550,506
Turkey	511,936
Chad	418,451
Ethiopia	407,646
China	301,068
United States	262,023

mid-2013 data

REFUGEES fleeing hostilities in the Democratic Republic of the Congo (DRC) receive food in a transit camp in Uganda. More than two million people have been displaced—many within the DRC, others crossing into neighboring countries.

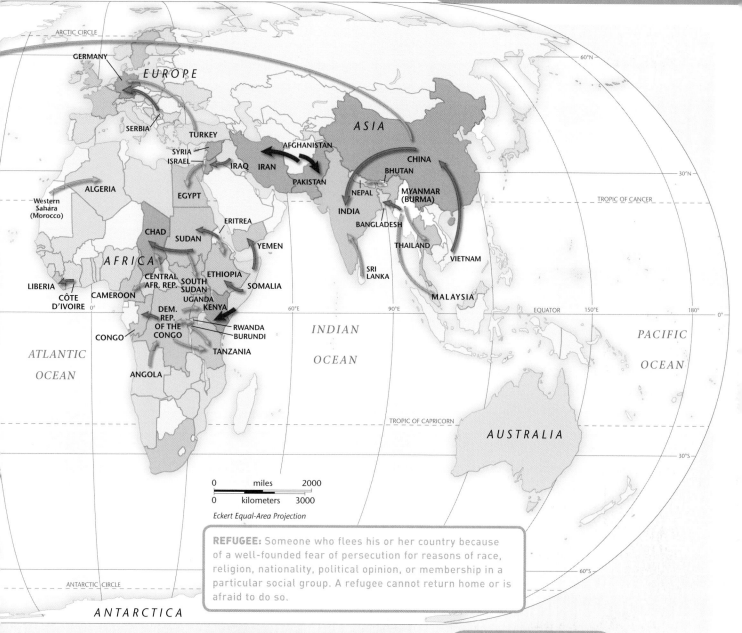

ARCTIC CIRCLE

GERMANY

EUROPE

SERBIA

TURKEY

SYRIA
ISRAEL

IRAQ IRAN

AFGHANISTAN

ASIA

CHINA

BHUTAN

ALGERIA

EGYPT

PAKISTAN

NEPAL

MYANMAR
(BURMA)

Western
Sahara
(Morocco)

ERITREA

CHAD

SUDAN

YEMEN

AFRICA

INDIA

BANGLADESH

THAILAND

VIETNAM

SRI
LANKA

LIBERIA

CENTRAL
AFR. REP.

ETHIOPIA

SOUTH
SUDAN

SOMALIA

MALAYSIA

CÔTE
D'IVOIRE

CAMEROON

UGANDA

KENYA

INDIAN

PACIFIC

CONGO

DEM.
REP.
OF THE
CONGO

RWANDA
BURUNDI

OCEAN

OCEAN

ATLANTIC

OCEAN

TANZANIA

ANGOLA

INDIAN

OCEAN

AUSTRALIA

60°N

30°N

TROPIC OF CANCER

EQUATOR

TROPIC OF CAPRICORN

30°S

60°S

ANTARCTIC CIRCLE

ANTARCTICA

| 0 | miles | 2000 |
| 0 | kilometers | 3000 |

Eckert Equal-Area Projection

REFUGEE: Someone who flees his or her country because of a well-founded fear of persecution for reasons of race, religion, nationality, political opinion, or membership in a particular social group. A refugee cannot return home or is afraid to do so.

⬤ **MANY KURDS,** a people who live mainly in Iraq and Turkey, fled to the remote mountains of northern Iraq to escape spreading hostilities. This region, referred to as Kurdistan, is the traditional homeland of these stateless people.

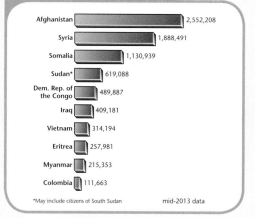

REFUGEES BY ORIGIN

Country	Refugees
Afghanistan	2,552,208
Syria	1,888,491
Somalia	1,130,939
Sudan*	619,088
Dem. Rep. of the Congo	489,887
Iraq	409,181
Vietnam	314,194
Eritrea	257,981
Myanmar	215,353
Colombia	111,663

*May include citizens of South Sudan   mid-2013 data

Quality of Life

The world's population is unevenly distributed (see map on pages 32–33), and not everyone experiences the same quality of life. The level of development in countries is often measured in economic terms, but beginning in 1990, the United Nations Development Program introduced a different and more complete way to evaluate the condition of life in the world's countries: the Human Development Index (HDI). The HDI combines both social and economic factors to rank the world's countries based on three indicators: health, education, and living standard (see map at right). Health is measured by life expectancy at birth (see map below). Education is measured by average years of schooling. And living standard is measured using gross national income per capita—the total income earned in a country each year divided by the country's population (see graph).

Human Development Index

Level of Human Development

- Very high
- High
- Medium
- Low
- No data

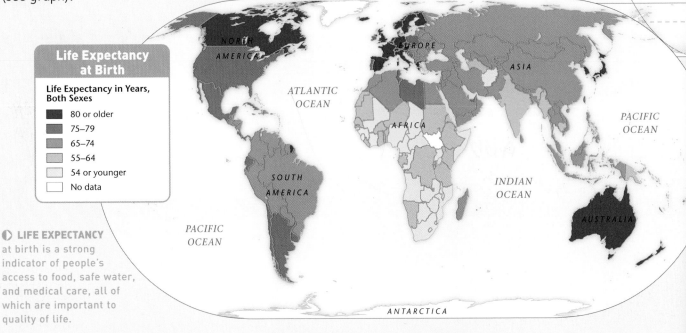

Life Expectancy at Birth

Life Expectancy in Years, Both Sexes

- 80 or older
- 75–79
- 65–74
- 55–64
- 54 or younger
- No data

◗ LIFE EXPECTANCY at birth is a strong indicator of people's access to food, safe water, and medical care, all of which are important to quality of life.

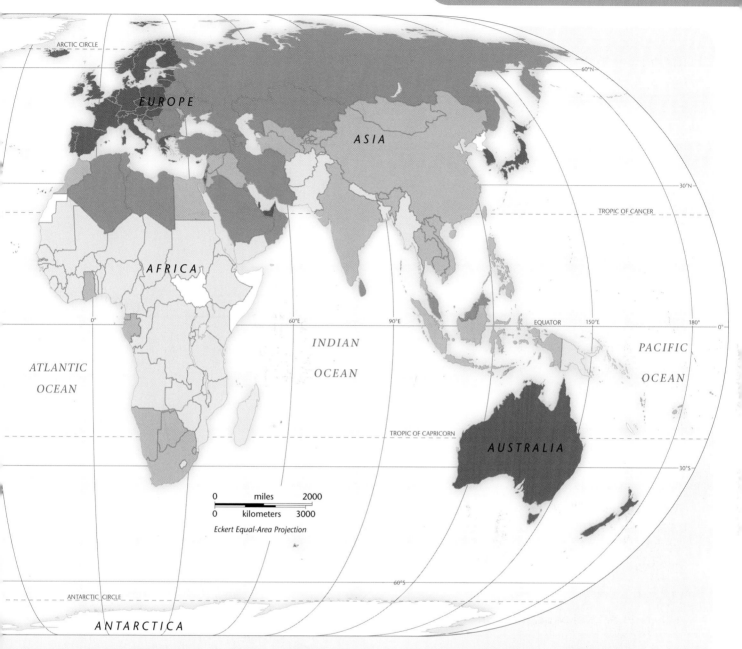

Eckert Equal-Area Projection

⬤ **THE HUMAN DEVELOPMENT INDEX** ranks countries of the world in four categories: very high, high, medium, and low human development, based on health, education, and income statistics.

◖ **EDUCATION** opens doors to employment and a better standard of living, but only 59 percent of school-age children in Mozambique are enrolled in school.

◖ **QUALITY OF LIFE,** as measured in terms of income per person, varies greatly among the world's ten most populous countries.

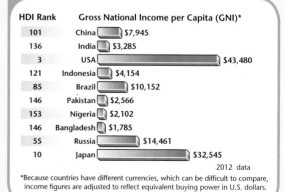

GROSS NATIONAL INCOME

HDI Rank	Gross National Income per Capita (GNI)*	
101	China	$7,945
136	India	$3,285
3	USA	$43,480
121	Indonesia	$4,154
85	Brazil	$10,152
146	Pakistan	$2,566
153	Nigeria	$2,102
146	Bangladesh	$1,785
55	Russia	$14,461
10	Japan	$32,545

2012 data

*Because countries have different currencies, which can be difficult to compare, income figures are adjusted to reflect equivalent buying power in U.S. dollars.

World Cities

Throughout most of history, people have lived spread across the land, first as hunters and gatherers, later as farmers. But urban geographers—people who study cities—have determined that today more than half of Earth's population lives in urban areas. Urban areas include one or more cities and their surrounding suburbs. People living there are employed primarily in industry or in service-related jobs. Large urban areas are sometimes called metropolitan areas. In some countries, such as Belgium, almost all the population lives in cities. But throughout much of Africa and Asia, only about 40 percent of the people live in urban areas. Even so, some of the world's fastest growing urban areas are towns and small cities in Africa and Asia.

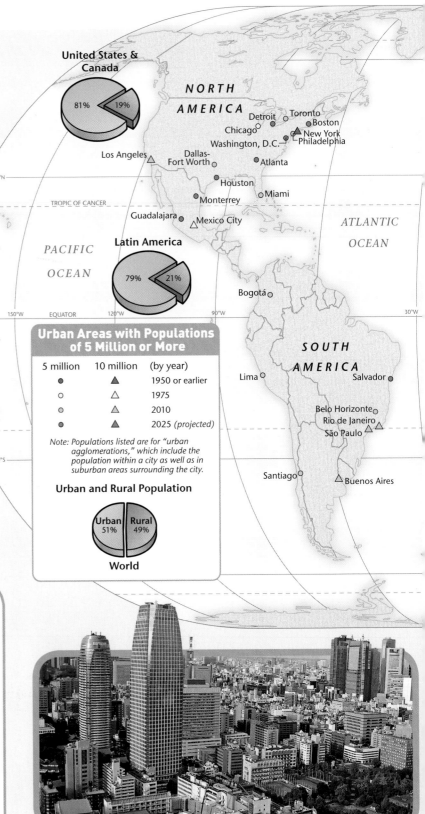

United States & Canada

81% 19%

NORTH AMERICA

Detroit Toronto Boston
Chicago New York
Washington, D.C. Philadelphia
Los Angeles Dallas-Fort Worth Atlanta

30°N

TROPIC OF CANCER

Houston
Monterrey Miami
Guadalajara Mexico City

PACIFIC OCEAN

Latin America

79% 21%

Bogotá

ATLANTIC OCEAN

150°W EQUATOR 120°W 90°W 30°W

SOUTH AMERICA

Lima Salvador

Belo Horizonte
Rio de Janeiro
São Paulo

30°S

Santiago Buenos Aires

Urban Areas with Populations of 5 Million or More

5 million	10 million	(by year)
●	▲	1950 or earlier
○	△	1975
◌	△	2010
◌	▲	2025 (projected)

Note: Populations listed are for "urban agglomerations," which include the population within a city as well as in suburban areas surrounding the city.

Urban and Rural Population

Urban 51% | Rural 49%

World

MOST POPULOUS URBAN AREAS

In 1950 New York was the larger of just two urban areas with a population of 10 million or more. By 2011, New York had dropped behind Tokyo, Delhi, and Mexico City in a list of 23 urban areas with populations of at least 10 million. By 2025, the list is projected to include 37 urban areas.

Urban areas with populations greater than 10 million for the years:

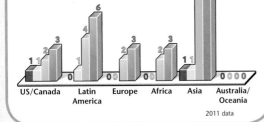
1970 1990 2011 2025

US/Canada	Latin America	Europe	Africa	Asia	Australia/Oceania

2011 data

⬡ **CENTRAL TOKYO,** viewed from high above crowded city streets, contains a mix of modern high-rise and older low-rise buildings. With more than 37 million people, Tokyo is Japan's largest and most densely populated urban area and the world's largest urban agglomeration.

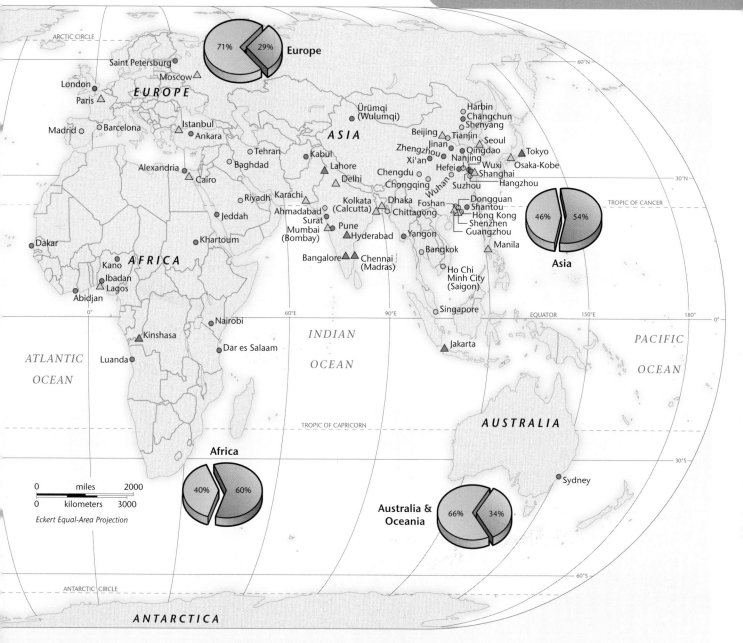

Europe
71% 29%

Asia
46% 54%

Africa
40% 60%

Australia & Oceania
66% 34%

ARCTIC CIRCLE

Saint Petersburg
Moscow
London
Paris
EUROPE
Madrid   Barcelona
Istanbul
Ankara
Alexandria
Cairo
Tehran
Baghdad
Kabul
Riyadh   Karachi
Jeddah
Ahmadabad
Surat
Mumbai
(Bombay)
Pune
Hyderabad
Bangalore
Chennai
(Madras)

ASIA
Ürümqi
(Wulumqi)
Harbin
Changchun
Shenyang
Beijing   Tianjin
Jinan   Qingdao
Zhengzhou   Seoul
Xi'an   Nanjing
Tokyo
Osaka-Kobe
Chengdu
Hefei   Wuxi
Shanghai
Chongqing   Wuhan   Hangzhou
Suzhou
Lahore
Delhi
Kolkata
(Calcutta)
Dhaka
Chittagong
Foshan
Dongguan
Shantou
Hong Kong
Shenzhen
Guangzhou
Yangon
Bangkok
Manila
Ho Chi
Minh City
(Saigon)
Singapore
Jakarta

Dakar
AFRICA
Kano
Ibadan
Lagos
Abidjan
Kinshasa
Luanda
Khartoum
Nairobi
Dar es Salaam

ATLANTIC
OCEAN

INDIAN
OCEAN

PACIFIC
OCEAN

AUSTRALIA
Sydney

ANTARCTICA

TROPIC OF CANCER
EQUATOR
TROPIC OF CAPRICORN
ANTARCTIC CIRCLE

60°N
30°N
0°
30°S
60°S

0°   60°E   90°E   150°E   180°

miles   0   2000
kilometers   0   3000
Eckert Equal-Area Projection

URBAN AREAS are home to more than half the world's people. As shown by the symbols on the map, Asia has most of the largest cities, including 13 megacities with at least 10 million people.

RAPID URBAN GROWTH in Africa overwhelms public utilities and contributes to disease, as in this urban slum in Nairobi, Kenya.

NG EXPLORER: THOMAS TAHA RASSAM CULHANE

As part of his work as an urban planner, Thomas Culhane helps developing communities survive and thrive through self-sustainability. His non-governmental organization, Solar C.I.T.I.E.S., assists the residents of Cairo's poorest neighborhoods in installing rooftop solar heaters built from recycled materials. These bring water access to families and help reduce carbon emissions. *nationalgeographic.com/explorers/bios/culhane-thomas*

World Languages

Culture is all the shared traits that make different groups of people around the world unique. For example, customs, food and clothing preferences, housing styles, and music and art forms are all a part of each group's culture. Language is one of the most defining characteristics of culture.

Language reflects what people value and the way they understand the world. It also reveals how certain groups of people may have had common roots at some point in history. For example, English and German are two very different languages, but both are part of the same Indo-European language family. This means that these two languages share certain characteristics that suggest they have evolved from a common ancestor language.

Patterns on the world language families map (right) offer clues to the diffusion, or movement, of groups of people. For example, the widespread use of English, extending from the United States to India, reflects the far-reaching effects of the British colonial empire. Today, English is the main language of the Internet.

About 5,000 languages are spoken in the world today, but experts think many may become extinct as more people become involved in global trade, communications, and travel.

⟨ **THE GOLDEN ARCHES** icon helps you identify this restaurant in Moscow even if you don't know how to read the Cyrillic alphabet of the Russian language.

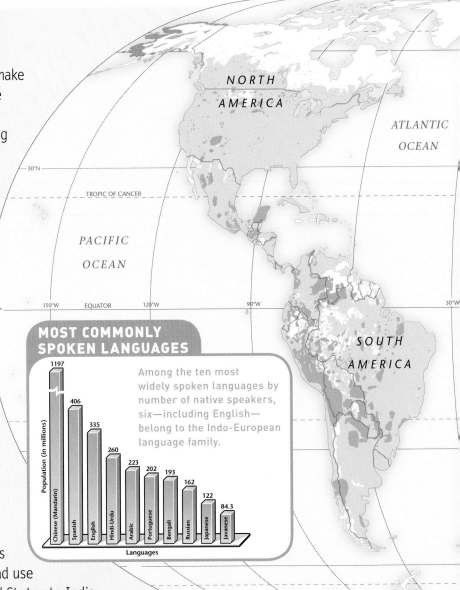

MOST COMMONLY SPOKEN LANGUAGES

Among the ten most widely spoken languages by number of native speakers, six—including English—belong to the Indo-European language family.

Population (in millions)

Language	Population
Chinese (Mandarin)	1197
Spanish	406
English	335
Hindi-Urdu	260
Arabic	223
Portuguese	202
Bengali	193
Russian	162
Japanese	122
Javanese	84.3

Languages

Макдоналдс

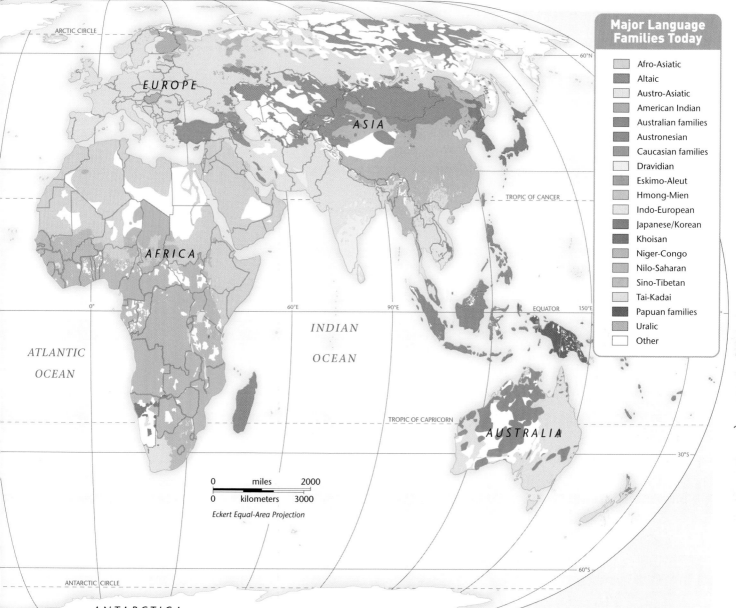

Major Language Families Today

- Afro-Asiatic
- Altaic
- Austro-Asiatic
- American Indian
- Australian families
- Austronesian
- Caucasian families
- Dravidian
- Eskimo-Aleut
- Hmong-Mien
- Indo-European
- Japanese/Korean
- Khoisan
- Niger-Congo
- Nilo-Saharan
- Sino-Tibetan
- Tai-Kadai
- Papuan families
- Uralic
- Other

ARCTIC CIRCLE

EUROPE

ASIA

TROPIC OF CANCER

AFRICA

60°N

60°E   90°E   EQUATOR   150°E

ATLANTIC
OCEAN

INDIAN

OCEAN

TROPIC OF CAPRICORN

AUSTRALIA

30°S

0   miles   2000
0   kilometers   3000

Eckert Equal-Area Projection

60°S

ANTARCTIC CIRCLE

ANTARCTICA

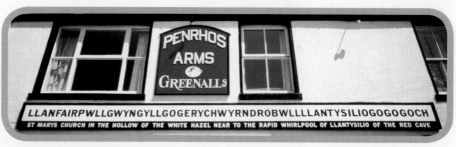

⬤ **SOME WORDS TELL A STORY,** like this place-name on the island of Anglesey in Wales. Welsh is an ancient Gaelic language. The alphabet may look familiar, but it has a few more letters than English and different pronunciations.

◖ **BENGALI,** a language derived from ancient Sanskrit, appears on the walls of a women's health clinic in Kolkata (Calcutta), India. It is just one of the many languages that make up the Indo-European language family.

World Religions

Religious beliefs are a central element of culture. Religious beliefs and practices help people deal with the unknown. But people in different places have developed a variety of belief systems.

Universalizing religions, such as Christianity, Islam, and Buddhism, seek converts. They have spread throughout the world from their origins in Asia. Other religions, including Judaism, Hinduism, and Shinto—called ethnic religions—tend to be associated with particular groups of people and are concentrated in certain places. Some groups, especially indigenous, or native, people living in the tropical forests of Africa and South America, believe that spirits inhabit all things in the natural world. Such belief systems are known as animistic religions.

Places of worship are often a distinctive part of the cultural landscape. A cathedral, mosque, or temple can reveal much about the people who live in a particular place.

There are nearly as many Jews living in the United States as there are in Israel. The United States also has almost as many Muslims as Jews, approximately five million each.

Christianity dominates in the Americas as a result of large-scale European colonization.

Dominant Religion

	Buddhism	Christianity	Hinduism	Islam (Muslim)	Judaism	Ethno-religionism	Not affiliated
90% and above							
70%–89.9%							
50%–69.9%							
Below 50%							

MOST OF HINDUISM'S 900 million followers live in India and other countries of South Asia. The goddess Durga (above) is regarded as Mother of the Universe and protector of the righteous.

JERUSALEM IS HOLY to Muslims, Christians, and Jews, a fact that has led to tension and conflict. Below, a Russian orthodox church is silhouetted against the Wailing Wall, while sunlight reflects off the Dome of the Rock, a Muslim shrine.

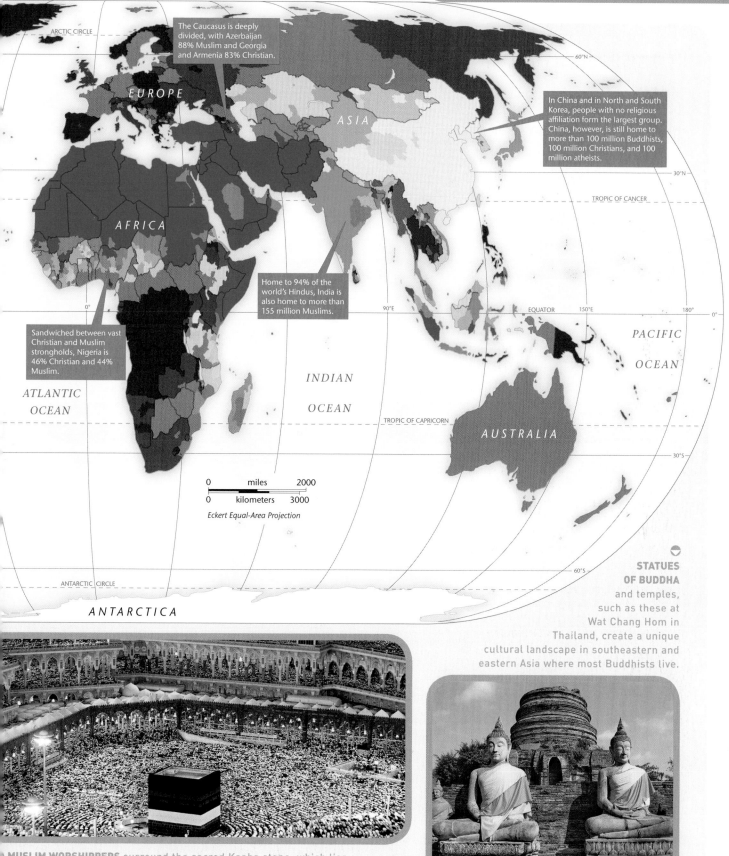

ARCTIC CIRCLE

The Caucasus is deeply divided, with Azerbaijan 88% Muslim and Georgia and Armenia 83% Christian.

EUROPE

ASIA

In China and in North and South Korea, people with no religious affiliation form the largest group. China, however, is still home to more than 100 million Buddhists, 100 million Christians, and 100 million atheists.

60°N

30°N

TROPIC OF CANCER

AFRICA

Home to 94% of the world's Hindus, India is also home to more than 155 million Muslims.

90°E

EQUATOR

150°E

180°

0°

PACIFIC OCEAN

Sandwiched between vast Christian and Muslim strongholds, Nigeria is 46% Christian and 44% Muslim.

ATLANTIC OCEAN

INDIAN OCEAN

0°

TROPIC OF CAPRICORN

AUSTRALIA

30°S

| 0 | miles | 2000 |
| 0 | kilometers | 3000 |

Eckert Equal-Area Projection

60°S

ANTARCTIC CIRCLE

ANTARCTICA

STATUES OF BUDDHA and temples, such as these at Wat Chang Hom in Thailand, create a unique cultural landscape in southeastern and eastern Asia where most Buddhists live.

MUSLIM WORSHIPPERS surround the sacred Kaaba stone, which lies shrouded in black cloth at the center of the Grand Mosque in Mecca. Each year two million Muslims make a hajj, or pilgrimage, here to Islam's holiest shrine.

Predominant World Economies

Economic activities are the many different ways that people generate income to meet their needs and wants. Long ago most people lived by hunting and gathering. Today, most engage in a variety of activities that can be grouped into three categories, or sectors: agriculture, as well as other primary activities such as fishing and forestry; industry, which includes manufacturing and processing activities; and services that range from banking and medicine to information exchange and e-commerce—buying and selling over the Internet. Services and industry, which generate higher incomes, are predominant in more developed countries, while many less developed countries still rely on agriculture.

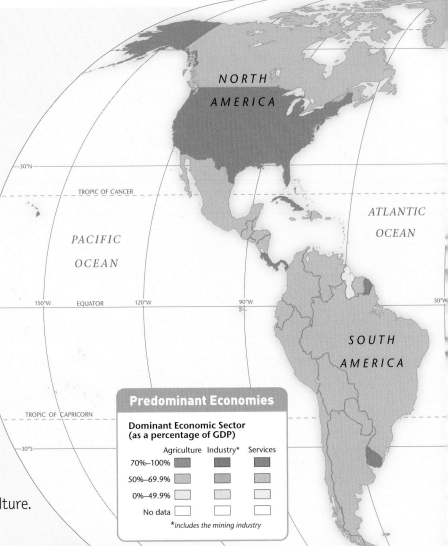

NORTH AMERICA

ATLANTIC OCEAN

PACIFIC OCEAN

SOUTH AMERICA

30°N

TROPIC OF CANCER

150°W   EQUATOR   120°W   90°W   30°W

0°

TROPIC OF CAPRICORN

30°S

60°S

Predominant Economies

Dominant Economic Sector
(as a percentage of GDP)

	Agriculture	Industry*	Services
70%–100%			
50%–69.9%			
0%–49.9%			
No data			

*includes the mining industry

⊙ **SUBSISTENCE AGRICULTURE.** Many people in developing countries, such as these farmers in Bhutan, use traditional methods to grow crops for their daily food requirements rather than for commercial sale.

◐ **LOGGING.** Workers ready logs to float down the Columbia River in Washington State. Processing plants will turn the logs into paper products or cut them into lumber for the construction industry.

◑ **FISHING.** Tuna is one of the chief commercial fishes as well as a favorite among big game fishermen. Japan is the world's leading harvester of tuna. Albacore, shown here, is one of the top commercial varieties.

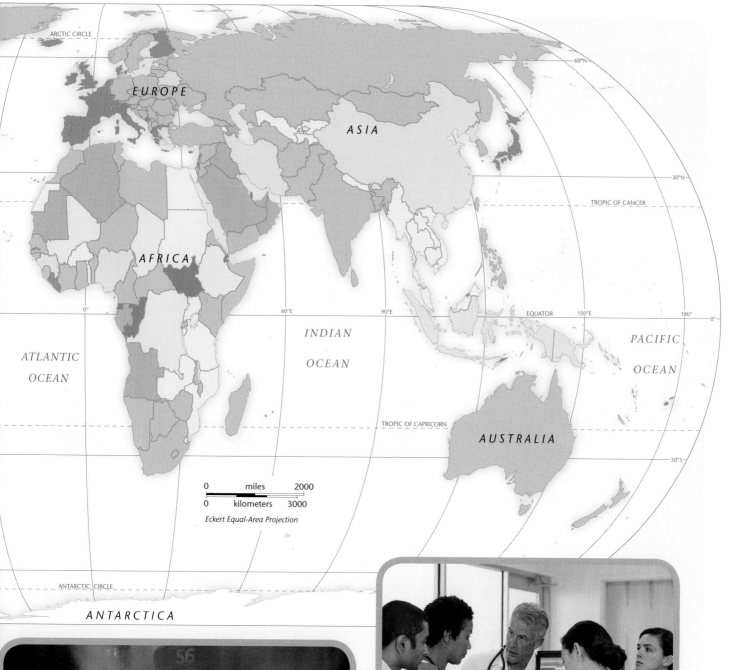

ARCTIC CIRCLE

60°N

EUROPE

ASIA

30°N

TROPIC OF CANCER

AFRICA

0°   60°E   90°E   EQUATOR   150°E   180°   0°

ATLANTIC
OCEAN

INDIAN

OCEAN

PACIFIC

OCEAN

TROPIC OF CAPRICORN

AUSTRALIA

30°S

0   miles   2000
0   kilometers   3000
Eckert Equal-Area Projection

ANTARCTIC CIRCLE

ANTARCTICA

⬭ **MANUFACTURING.** This mill in Slovakia processes raw materials—coal and iron ore—to make steel, which in turn is used by other industries to produce cars, machinery, and other manufactured goods.

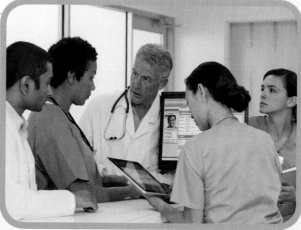

⬭ **COMMUNICATIONS AND TECHNOLOGY.** Medical professionals use computers as they consult about patient treatment. The Internet and advanced technologies have introduced new ways of exchanging information and accessing the latest research in order to solve problems. E-mail connects people in places near and far, while e-commerce makes possible buying and selling from home or office.

World Food

In mid-2013, the world's population reached 7.2 billion people—all needing to be fed. However, the productive potential of Earth's surface varies greatly from place to place. Some areas are good for growing crops; some are better for grazing animals; others have little or no agricultural potential. Grains, such as rice, corn, and wheat, are main sources of food calories, while meat, poultry, and fish are sources of protein.

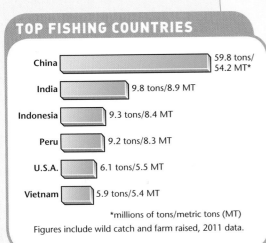

TOP FISHING COUNTRIES

China	59.8 tons/54.2 MT*
India	9.8 tons/8.9 MT
Indonesia	9.3 tons/8.4 MT
Peru	9.2 tons/8.3 MT
U.S.A.	6.1 tons/5.5 MT
Vietnam	5.9 tons/5.4 MT

*millions of tons/metric tons (MT)
Figures include wild catch and farm raised, 2011 data.

🌐 **FEEDING THE WORLD.** Fish and other seafood are important in the diets of much of the world's population. But rising demand has raised concerns that this important food source is at risk due to overharvesting.

GEOGRAPHY CAREERS
NG EXPLORER: BARTON SEAVER

Barton Seaver is a chef who has dedicated his career to restoring the ocean's fragile ecosystems. Barton pursues solutions to overfishing through innovations in sustainability and education, and works to promote the concept of seafood sustainability. He also is involved in promoting healthier eating lifestyles, and works with various organizations in the fight against hunger. *nationalgeographic.com/explorers/bios/ barton-seaver*

🌐 **WHEAT,** the world's leading export grain, is a r ingredient in bread and pasta and is grown on eve inhabited continent. Each year, trade in this grain exceeds 143 million tons (130 million MT).

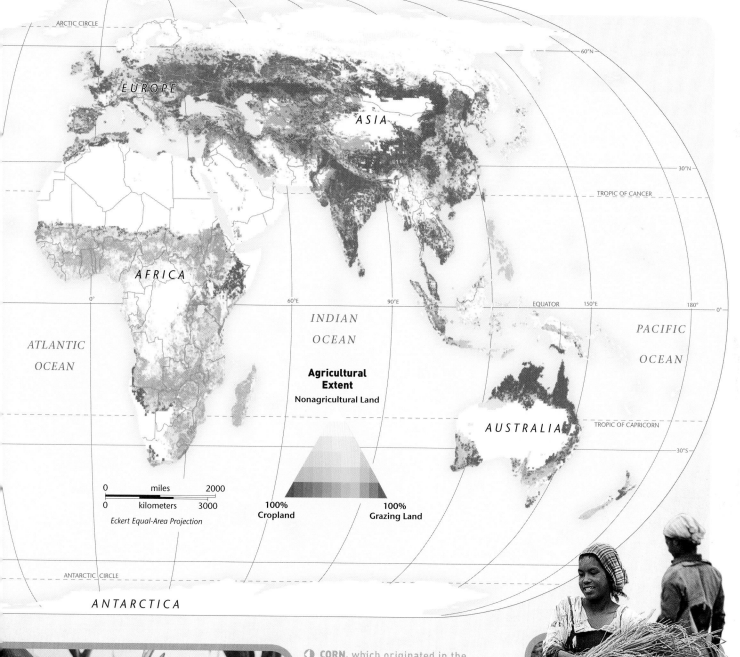

ARCTIC CIRCLE

60°N

EUROPE

ASIA

30°N

TROPIC OF CANCER

AFRICA

0°

60°E

90°E

EQUATOR

150°E

180°

0°

INDIAN

OCEAN

ATLANTIC

OCEAN

PACIFIC

OCEAN

Agricultural Extent

Nonagricultural Land

AUSTRALIA

TROPIC OF CAPRICORN

30°S

| 0 | miles | 2000 |
| 0 | kilometers | 3000 |

Eckert Equal-Area Projection

100%
Cropland

100%
Grazing Land

ANTARCTIC CIRCLE

ANTARCTICA

CORN, which originated in the Americas, is an important food grain for both people and livestock. Corn is also used to make ethanol, which is added to gasoline to make a cleaner fuel.

RICE is an important staple food crop, especially in eastern and southern Asia. Although China produces about one-third of the world's rice, it is also a major importer of rice to feed its population of more than a billion people.

World Energy & Mineral Resources

Beginning in the 19th century, as the Industrial Revolution spread across Europe and around the world, the demand for energy and non-fuel mineral resources skyrocketed. Fossil fuels—first coal, then oil and natural gas—have provided the energy that keeps the wheels of industry turning. Non-fuel minerals such as iron ore (essential for steel production) and copper (for electrical wiring) have become increasingly important.

Energy and non-fuel minerals, like all nonrenewable resources, are in limited supply and are unevenly distributed. Exporting countries with major deposits can influence both supply and prices of these resources, thus playing an important role in the global economy.

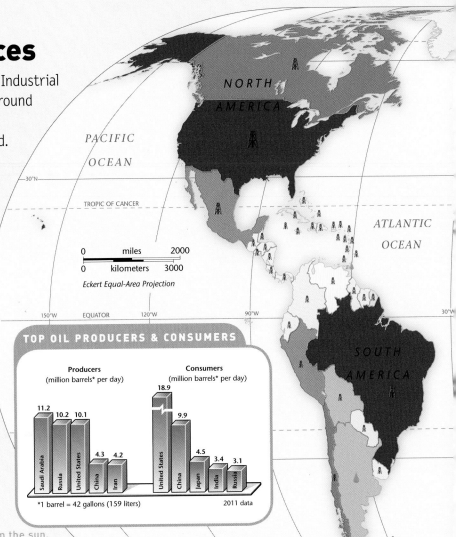

TOP OIL PRODUCERS & CONSUMERS

Producers (million barrels* per day)
- Saudi Arabia 11.2
- Russia 10.2
- United States 10.1
- China 4.3
- Iran 4.2

Consumers (million barrels* per day)
- United States 18.9
- China 9.9
- Japan 4.5
- India 3.4
- Russia 3.1

*1 barrel = 42 gallons (159 liters)   2011 data

RENEWABLE ENERGY, including energy from the sun, wind, running water, and heat from within Earth, is an important alternative to fossil fuels, supplies of which are rapidly being depleted. (Numbers on the map correspond to numbers on the photographs on page 49.)

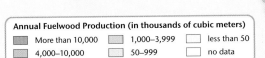

Renewable Energy

Major Power Plant
- ■ Selected hydroelectric plant (greater than 2,000 megawatts)
- ▲ Selected geothermal plant (greater than 20 megawatts)
- ✿ Selected solar plant (greater than 2 megawatts)

Potential Geothermal Resources
- ◉ High temperature geothermal regions

Annual Fuelwood Production (in thousands of cubic meters)
- More than 10,000
- 4,000–10,000
- 1,000–3,999
- 50–999
- less than 50
- no data

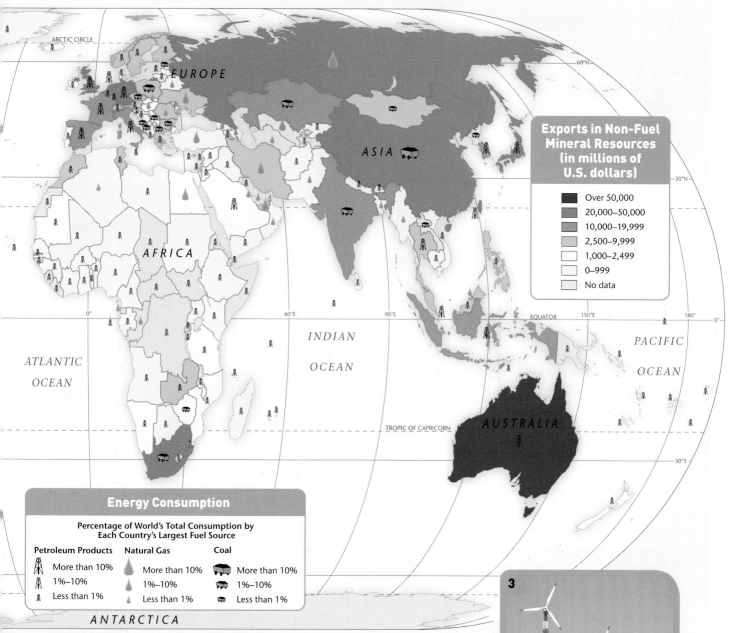

Exports in Non-Fuel Mineral Resources (in millions of U.S. dollars)

- Over 50,000
- 20,000–50,000
- 10,000–19,999
- 2,500–9,999
- 1,000–2,499
- 0–999
- No data

ARCTIC CIRCLE

EUROPE

ASIA

AFRICA

ATLANTIC OCEAN

INDIAN OCEAN

PACIFIC OCEAN

EQUATOR

TROPIC OF CAPRICORN

AUSTRALIA

ANTARCTICA

Energy Consumption

Percentage of World's Total Consumption by Each Country's Largest Fuel Source

Petroleum Products	Natural Gas	Coal
More than 10%	More than 10%	More than 10%
1%–10%	1%–10%	1%–10%
Less than 1%	Less than 1%	Less than 1%

1 **NUCLEAR REACTORS AND SOLAR PANELS** near Sacramento produce renewable energy for California's power-hungry population.

2

WINDMILLS rising above ancient temples near Jaisalmer, India, generate electricity by capturing the energy of winds blowing off the Indian Ocean.

A GEOTHERMAL POWER PLANT, fueled by heat from deep within Earth, produces energy to heat homes in Iceland. Runoff creates a warm pool for bathers.

3

Globalization

The close of the 20th century saw a technology revolution that changed the way people and countries relate to each other. This revolution in technology is part of a process known as globalization.

Globalization refers to the complex network of interconnections linking people, companies, and places together without regard for national boundaries. Although it began when some countries became increasingly active in international trade, the process of globalization has gained momentum in recent years, expanding to include political and social interactions, but not all countries are major players in the global arena.

Improvements in communications and transportation have enabled companies to employ workers in distant countries. Some workers make clothing; some perform accounting tasks; and others work in call centers answering inquiries about products or services. Technology also allows banking transactions to take place faster and over greater distances than ever before. Companies that conduct business in multiple countries around the world are called transnational companies.

An important part of today's global communications system is the Internet, a vast system of computer networks that allows people to access information around the world in seconds. Ideas and images now travel over the Internet, introducing change and making places more and more alike.

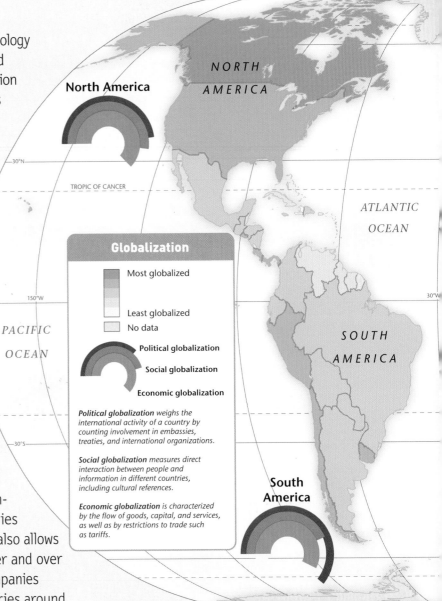

North America

NORTH AMERICA

30°N

TROPIC OF CANCER

ATLANTIC OCEAN

150°W

0°

PACIFIC OCEAN

30°S

SOUTH AMERICA

30°W

South America

Globalization

Most globalized

Least globalized

No data

Political globalization

Social globalization

Economic globalization

Political globalization weighs the international activity of a country by counting involvement in embassies, treaties, and international organizations.

Social globalization measures direct interaction between people and information in different countries, including cultural references.

Economic globalization is characterized by the flow of goods, capital, and services, as well as by restrictions to trade such as tariffs.

◗ **MAQUILADORAS,** foreign-owned assembly plants located in Mexico, import parts and materials duty-free to produce finished goods for consumers in the U.S. and around the world. Maquiladoras, such as this one in Ciudad Juárez, employ a large workforce.

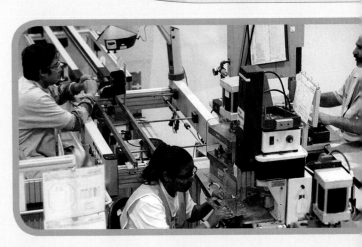

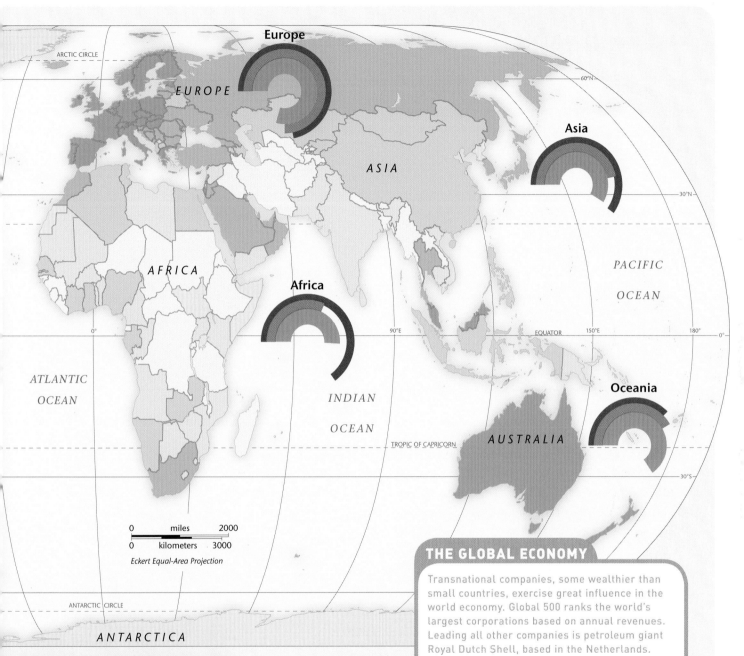

Europe

EUROPE

ARCTIC CIRCLE

60°N

Asia

ASIA

30°N

AFRICA

Africa

PACIFIC

OCEAN

0°

90°E

EQUATOR

150°E

180°

0°

ATLANTIC

OCEAN

INDIAN

OCEAN

Oceania

AUSTRALIA

TROPIC OF CAPRICORN

30°S

| 0 | miles | 2000 |
| 0 | kilometers | 3000 |

Eckert Equal-Area Projection

ANTARCTIC CIRCLE

ANTARCTICA

◔ **OLD MEETS NEW** as a Miao woman, wearing traditional garments, takes a photo of herself using a cell phone camera. The Miao, who live in southwestern China, are one of the country's largest ethnic minorities.

THE GLOBAL ECONOMY

Transnational companies, some wealthier than small countries, exercise great influence in the world economy. Global 500 ranks the world's largest corporations based on annual revenues. Leading all other companies is petroleum giant Royal Dutch Shell, based in the Netherlands.

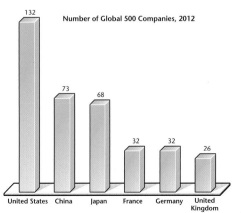

Number of Global 500 Companies, 2012

United States	China	Japan	France	Germany	United Kingdom
132	73	68	32	32	26

Cultural Diffusion

In the past, when groups of people lived in relative isolation, cultures varied widely from place to place. Customs, styles, and preferences were handed down from one generation to the next.

Today, as a result of globalization, cultures all around the world are encountering and adopting new ideas. New customs, clothing and music trends, food habits, and lifestyles are being introduced into cultures everywhere at almost the same time. Some people are concerned that this trend in popular culture may result in a loss of cultural distinctiveness that makes places unique. For example, fast food chains once found only in the United States can now be seen in major cities around the world. And denim jeans, once a distinctively American clothing style, are worn by young people everywhere in place of more traditional clothing.

An important key to the spread, or diffusion, of popular culture is the increasing contact between people and places around the world. Cellular telephones, satellite television, and cybercafés have opened the world to styles and trends popular in Western countries. And tourists, traveling to places that were once considered remote and isolated, carry with them new ideas and fashions that become catalysts for bringing about cultural change.

International Tourism

International Tourist Arrivals

- More than 25,000,000
- 5,000,000–25,000,000
- 500,000–4,999,999
- 100,000–499,999
- Less than 100,000
- No data

◗ **THE INFLUENCE OF IMMIGRANT CULTURES** on the American landscape is evident in ethnic communities such as Chinatown in the heart of New York City.

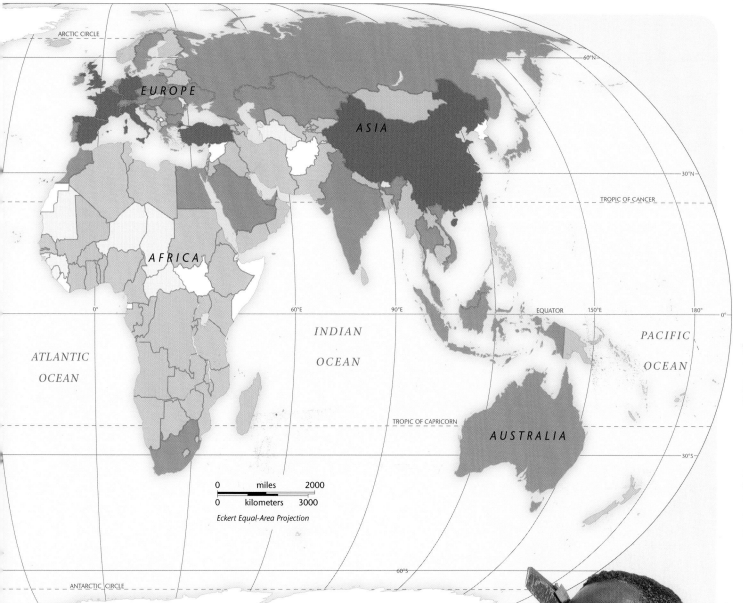

ARCTIC CIRCLE

60°N

EUROPE

ASIA

30°N

TROPIC OF CANCER

AFRICA

0°   60°E   90°E   EQUATOR   150°E   180°   0°

ATLANTIC
OCEAN

INDIAN
OCEAN

PACIFIC
OCEAN

TROPIC OF CAPRICORN

AUSTRALIA

30°S

```
0        miles      2000
0     kilometers   3000
```
Eckert Equal-Area Projection

60°S

ANTARCTIC CIRCLE

ANTARCTICA

◗ **A COUPLE IN TRADITIONAL ROBES** strolls through a modern shopping mall in Doha, Qatar. Stores and movie theaters bring Western fashions, technologies, and ideas into contact with long-established Arab culture and values.

◗ **TAKING A BREAK** from a tribal ceremony, a Maasai warrior in Kenya enjoys a soft drink that was once uniquely American.

North America:
A View From Space

Viewed from high above, North America stretches from the frozen expanses of the Arctic Ocean and Greenland to the lush green of Panama's tropical forests. Hudson Bay and the Great Lakes, fingerprints of long-departed glaciers, dominate the continent's east, while the brown landscapes of the west and southwest tell of dry lands where water is scarce.

North America

PHYSICAL			POLITICAL		
Land area 9,449,000 sq mi (24,474,000 sq km)	**Lowest point** Death Valley, California -282 ft (-86 m)	**Largest lake** Lake Superior, U.S.-Canada 31,700 sq mi (82,100 sq km)	**Population** 556,558,000 **Number of** **independent** **countries** 23	**Largest country** Canada 3,855,101 sq mi (9,984,670 sq km) **Smallest country** St. Kitts and Nevis 104 sq mi (269 sq km)	**Most populous country** United States Pop. 316,158,000 **Least populous country** St. Kitts and Nevis Pop. 55,000
Highest point Mount McKinley (Denali), Alaska 20,320 ft (6,194 m)	**Longest river** Mississippi-Missouri, United States 3,710 mi (5,970 km)				

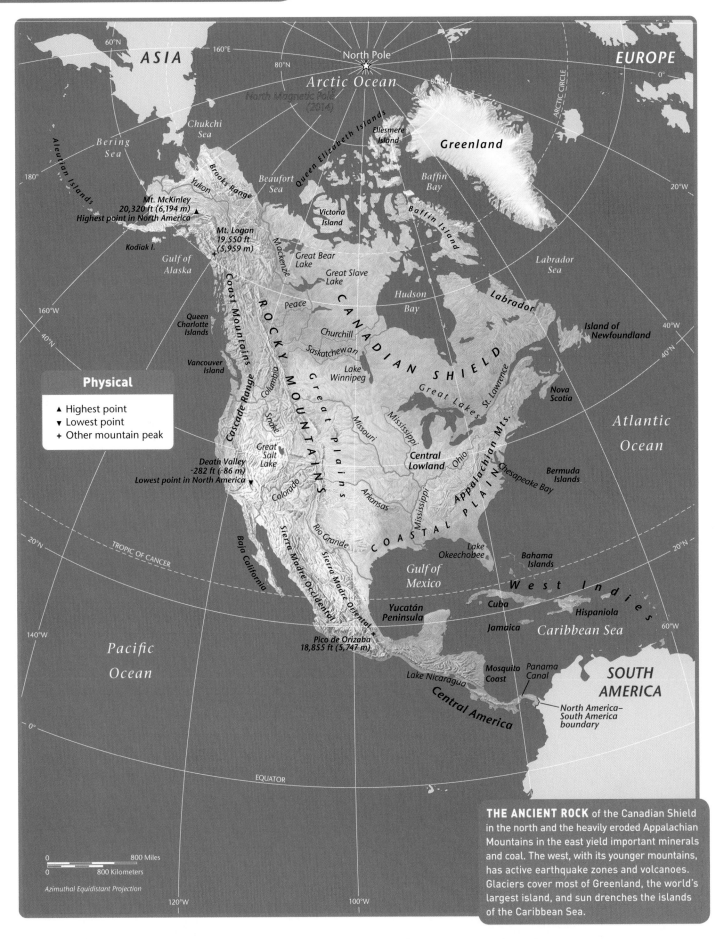

ASIA

60°N

160°E

80°N

North Pole

EUROPE

0°

Arctic Ocean

North Magnetic Pole (2014)

ARCTIC CIRCLE

20°W

Chukchi Sea

Queen Elizabeth Islands

Ellesmere Island

Greenland

180°

Bering Sea

Brooks Range

Beaufort Sea

Baffin Bay

Aleutian Islands

Yukon

Mt. McKinley
20,320 ft (6,194 m)
Highest point in North America ▲

Mt. Logan
19,550 ft
+ (5,959 m)

Mackenzie

Victoria Island

Baffin Island

Labrador Sea

40°W

Kodiak I.

Gulf of Alaska

Great Bear Lake

Great Slave Lake

Hudson Bay

Labrador

Island of Newfoundland

160°W

40°N

Peace

C A N A D I A N   S H I E L D

40°N

Coast Mountains

Churchill

Saskatchewan

Atlantic Ocean

Queen Charlotte Islands

R O C K Y   M O U N T A I N S

Lake Winnipeg

Great Lakes

St. Lawrence

Nova Scotia

Vancouver Island

Great Plains

Mississippi

Missouri

Columbia

Cascade Range

Snake

Central Lowland

Ohio

Appalachian Mts.

Chesapeake Bay

Bermuda Islands

Great Salt Lake

Death Valley
-282 ft (-86 m)
Lowest point in North America ▼

Colorado

Arkansas

Mississippi

C O A S T A L   P L A I N

20°N

TROPIC OF CANCER

Baja California

Sierra Madre Occidental

Rio Grande

Sierra Madre Oriental

Gulf of Mexico

Lake Okeechobee

Bahama Islands

W e s t   I n d i e s

20°N

140°W

Pacific Ocean

Yucatán Peninsula

Cuba

Hispaniola

60°W

Pico de Orizaba
18,855 ft (5,747 m)

Jamaica

Caribbean Sea

Lake Nicaragua

Mosquito Coast

Panama Canal

SOUTH AMERICA

North America–South America boundary

C e n t r a l   A m e r i c a

0°

EQUATOR

0

800 Miles

0

800 Kilometers

Azimuthal Equidistant Projection

120°W

100°W

THE ANCIENT ROCK of the Canadian Shield in the north and the heavily eroded Appalachian Mountains in the east yield important minerals and coal. The west, with its younger mountains, has active earthquake zones and volcanoes. Glaciers cover most of Greenland, the world's largest island, and sun drenches the islands of the Caribbean Sea.

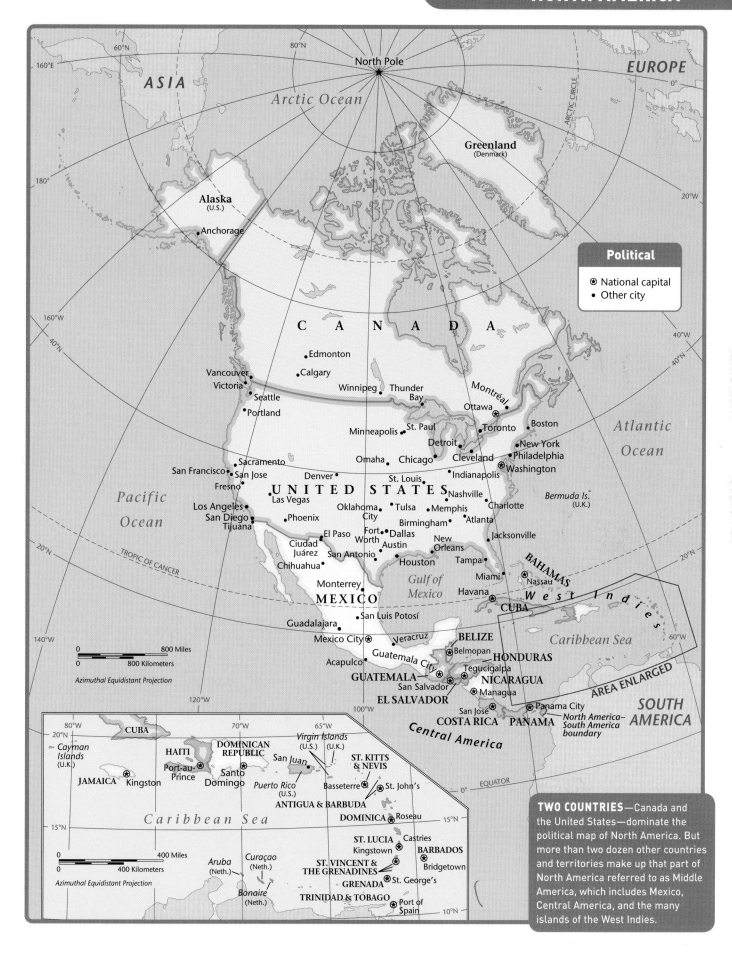

ASIA

EUROPE

Arctic Ocean

North Pole

Greenland
(Denmark)

Alaska
(U.S.)

Anchorage

ARCTIC CIRCLE

Political
⊗ National capital
• Other city

C A N A D A

Edmonton
Calgary

Vancouver
Victoria
Seattle
Portland

Winnipeg   Thunder
Bay

Montréal

Ottawa ⊗

Toronto   Boston

Minneapolis   St. Paul

Detroit

New York
Cleveland   Philadelphia

⊗ Washington

*Atlantic
Ocean*

Sacramento

San Francisco
San Jose
Fresno

U N I T E D   S T A T E S

Las Vegas

Los Angeles
San Diego
Tijuana

Phoenix

El Paso
Fort
Worth

Ciudad
Juárez

Chihuahua

San Antonio

Omaha   Chicago

Denver

St. Louis   Indianapolis

Nashville

Oklahoma   Tulsa   Memphis
City

Birmingham

Dallas
Austin

New
Orleans

Houston

Charlotte

Atlanta

Jacksonville

Bermuda Is.
(U.K.)

*Pacific

Ocean*

TROPIC OF CANCER

Monterrey

MEXICO

San Luis Potosí

*Gulf of
Mexico*

Tampa

Miami

Havana ⊗

CUBA

Nassau

BAHAMAS

W e s t   I n d i e s

Caribbean Sea

AREA ENLARGED

Guadalajara

Mexico City ⊗   Veracruz

Acapulco   Guatemala City

BELIZE
⊗ Belmopan

HONDURAS
Tegucigalpa ⊗

GUATEMALA
San Salvador ⊗

EL SALVADOR

Managua ⊗

NICARAGUA

San José ⊗   Panama City ⊗

COSTA RICA   **PANAMA**

*North America–
South America
boundary*

Central America

**SOUTH
AMERICA**

0   800 Miles
0   800 Kilometers

Azimuthal Equidistant Projection

EQUATOR

CUBA

*Cayman
Islands*
(U.K.)

HAITI

**DOMINICAN
REPUBLIC**

San Juan

Virgin Islands
(U.S.)   (U.K.)

**ST. KITTS
& NEVIS**

JAMAICA
Port-au-
Prince ⊗   Santo
Domingo ⊗

Kingston ⊗

Puerto Rico
(U.S.)

Basseterre ⊗   St. John's ⊗

ANTIGUA & BARBUDA

Caribbean   Sea

DOMINICA   Roseau ⊗

ST. LUCIA   Castries ⊗

Kingstown ⊗

BARBADOS
⊗ Bridgetown

0   400 Miles
0   400 Kilometers

Azimuthal Equidistant Projection

Aruba
(Neth.)

Curaçao
(Neth.)

**ST. VINCENT &
THE GRENADINES**

GRENADA   ⊗ St. George's

Bonaire
(Neth.)

TRINIDAD & TOBAGO

⊗ Port of
Spain

TWO COUNTRIES—Canada and
the United States—dominate the
political map of North America. But
more than two dozen other countries
and territories make up that part of
North America referred to as Middle
America, which includes Mexico,
Central America, and the many
islands of the West Indies.

THE CONTINENT:
NORTH AMERICA

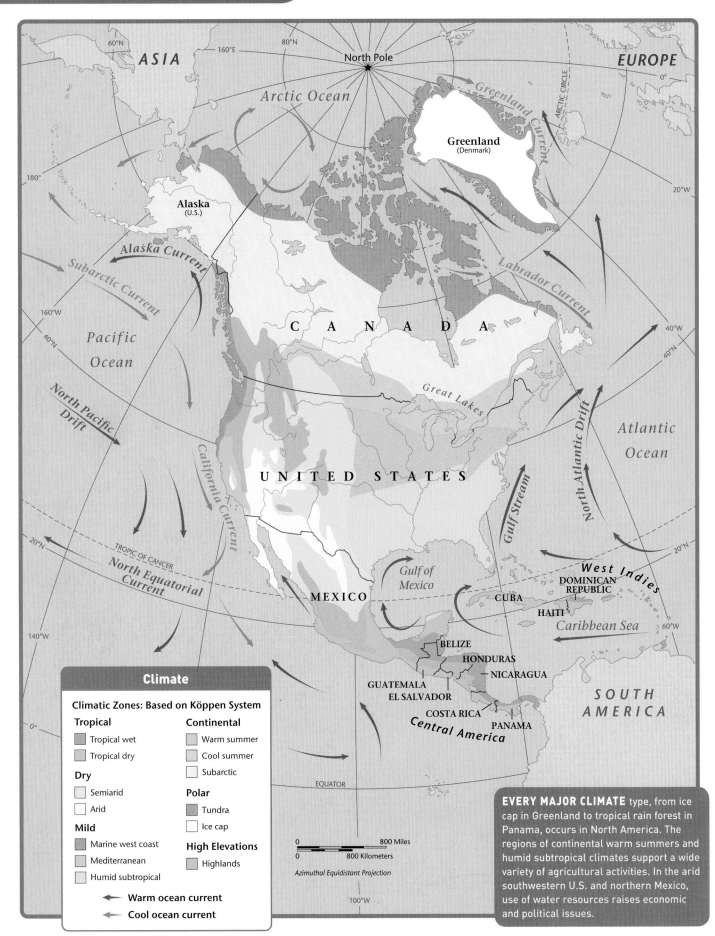

ASIA

EUROPE

North Pole

Arctic Ocean

Greenland Current

Greenland
(Denmark)

ARCTIC CIRCLE

60°N

160°E

80°N

0°

Alaska
(U.S.)

180°

20°W

Alaska Current

Subarctic Current

Labrador Current

C A N A D A

160°W

40°W

*Pacific
Ocean*

*North Pacific
Drift*

40°N

40°N

Great Lakes

*Atlantic
Ocean*

California Current

U N I T E D   S T A T E S

North Atlantic Drift

Gulf Stream

20°N

TROPIC OF CANCER

*North Equatorial
Current*

*Gulf of
Mexico*

West Indies

20°N

140°W

DOMINICAN
REPUBLIC

MEXICO

CUBA

HAITI

Caribbean Sea

60°W

BELIZE

HONDURAS

0°

NICARAGUA

GUATEMALA
EL SALVADOR

*S O U T H
A M E R I C A*

COSTA RICA

PANAMA

Central America

Climate

Climatic Zones: Based on Köppen System

Tropical
- Tropical wet
- Tropical dry

Dry
- Semiarid
- Arid

Mild
- Marine west coast
- Mediterranean
- Humid subtropical

Continental
- Warm summer
- Cool summer
- Subarctic

Polar
- Tundra
- Ice cap

High Elevations
- Highlands

EQUATOR

800 Miles
0
0
800 Kilometers

Azimuthal Equidistant Projection

100°W

← Warm ocean current
← Cool ocean current

EVERY MAJOR CLIMATE type, from ice cap in Greenland to tropical rain forest in Panama, occurs in North America. The regions of continental warm summers and humid subtropical climates support a wide variety of agricultural activities. In the arid southwestern U.S. and northern Mexico, use of water resources raises economic and political issues.

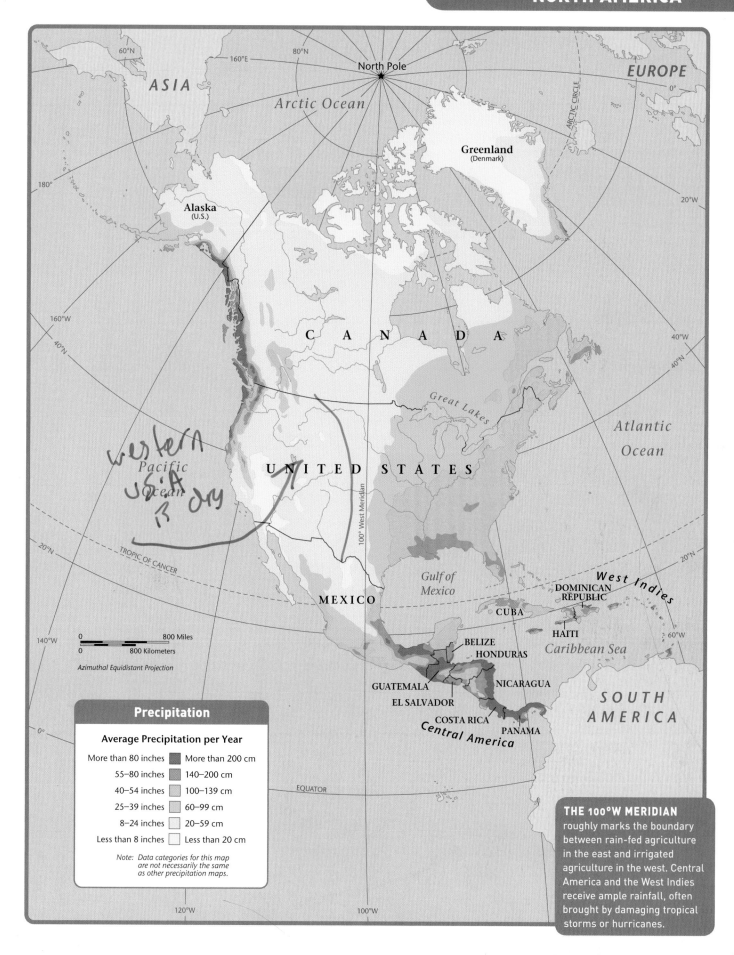

ASIA

Arctic Ocean

North Pole

EUROPE

Greenland
(Denmark)

Alaska
(U.S.)

C A N A D A

Great Lakes

Atlantic
Ocean

western
USA is dry

Pacific
Ocean

U N I T E D   S T A T E S

100° West Meridian

MEXICO

Gulf of
Mexico

West Indies

DOMINICAN
REPUBLIC

CUBA

HAITI

Caribbean Sea

TROPIC OF CANCER

0   800 Miles
0   800 Kilometers

Azimuthal Equidistant Projection

BELIZE
HONDURAS

GUATEMALA

NICARAGUA

SOUTH
AMERICA

EL SALVADOR

COSTA RICA

PANAMA

Central America

EQUATOR

Precipitation

Average Precipitation per Year

More than 80 inches	More than 200 cm
55–80 inches	140–200 cm
40–54 inches	100–139 cm
25–39 inches	60–99 cm
8–24 inches	20–59 cm
Less than 8 inches	Less than 20 cm

*Note: Data categories for this map
are not necessarily the same
as other precipitation maps.*

THE 100°W MERIDIAN
roughly marks the boundary
between rain-fed agriculture
in the east and irrigated
agriculture in the west. Central
America and the West Indies
receive ample rainfall, often
brought by damaging tropical
storms or hurricanes.

THE CONTINENT:
NORTH AMERICA

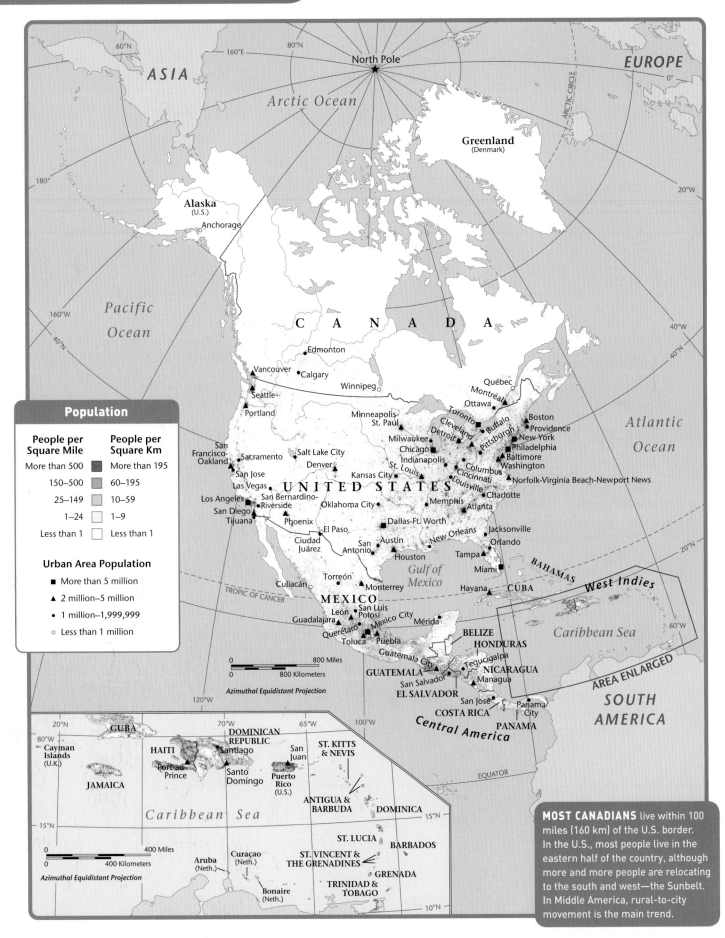

ASIA

Arctic Ocean

North Pole

160°E

80°N

60°N

EUROPE

0°

ARCTIC CIRCLE

Greenland
(Denmark)

20°W

180°

Alaska
(U.S.)

Anchorage

Pacific
Ocean

160°W

40°N

C A N A D A

40°W

40°N

Edmonton

Vancouver · Calgary

Winnipeg

Seattle

Portland

Québec
Montréal
Ottawa

Boston
Providence

Atlantic
Ocean

Population

People per Square Mile / People per Square Km

People per Square Mile	People per Square Km
More than 500	More than 195
150–500	60–195
25–149	10–59
1–24	1–9
Less than 1	Less than 1

Urban Area Population

- ■ More than 5 million
- ▲ 2 million–5 million
- • 1 million–1,999,999
- ○ Less than 1 million

Minneapolis-
St. Paul

Toronto
Cleveland Buffalo
Detroit Pittsburgh
Milwaukee
Chicago

New York
Philadelphia
Baltimore
Washington

San
Francisco-
Oakland · Sacramento

San Jose

Las Vegas

Los Angeles
San Bernardino-
Riverside
San Diego
Tijuana

Salt Lake City

Denver

U N I T E D   S T A T E S

Phoenix

El Paso

Ciudad
Juárez

Kansas City

Indianapolis
St. Louis
Louisville
Cincinnati
Columbus

Oklahoma City

Dallas-Ft. Worth

San
Antonio

Austin

Houston

Memphis

New Orleans

Norfolk-Virginia Beach-Newport News

Charlotte

Atlanta

Jacksonville

Orlando

Tampa

Miami

BAHAMAS

West Indies

60°W

20°N

Culiacán

TROPIC OF CANCER

Torreón

Monterrey

Gulf of
Mexico

Havana   CUBA

Caribbean Sea

AREA ENLARGED

M E X I C O

León   San Luis
Potosí
Guadalajara   Mexico City
Querétaro
Toluca   Puebla

Mérida

BELIZE
HONDURAS

Tegucigalpa

GUATEMALA
Guatemala City

San Salvador
EL SALVADOR

San José
COSTA RICA

NICARAGUA
Managua

Panama
City

PANAMA

SOUTH
AMERICA

Central America

0   800 Miles
0   800 Kilometers
Azimuthal Equidistant Projection

120°W

100°W

EQUATOR

20°N
80°W

CUBA

Cayman
Islands
(U.K.)

JAMAICA

Caribbean   Sea

15°N

0   400 Miles
0   400 Kilometers
Azimuthal Equidistant Projection

70°W

65°W

DOMINICAN
REPUBLIC

HAITI   Santiago

Port-au-
Prince   Santo
Domingo

San
Juan

Puerto
Rico
(U.S.)

ST. KITTS
& NEVIS

ANTIGUA &
BARBUDA

DOMINICA

ST. LUCIA

BARBADOS

ST. VINCENT &
THE GRENADINES

GRENADA

TRINIDAD &
TOBAGO

Aruba
(Neth.)

Curaçao
(Neth.)

Bonaire
(Neth.)

15°N

10°N

MOST CANADIANS live within 100 miles (160 km) of the U.S. border. In the U.S., most people live in the eastern half of the country, although more and more people are relocating to the south and west—the Sunbelt. In Middle America, rural-to-city movement is the main trend.

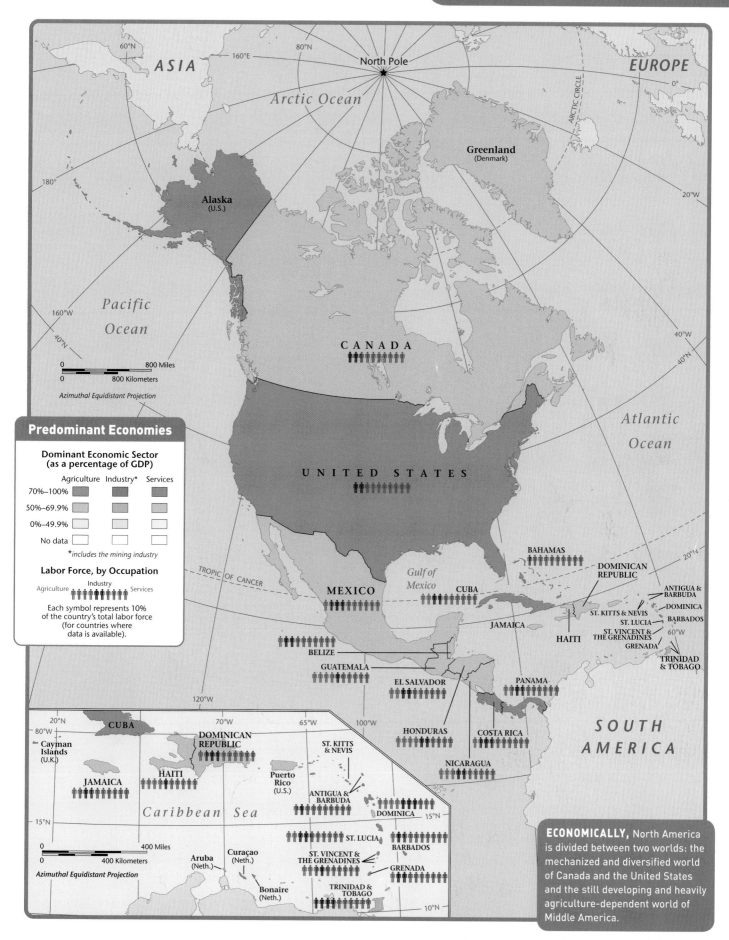

Predominant Economies

Dominant Economic Sector
(as a percentage of GDP)

Agriculture Industry* Services

70%–100%
50%–69.9%
0%–49.9%
No data

*includes the mining industry

Labor Force, by Occupation

Agriculture · Industry · Services

Each symbol represents 10%
of the country's total labor force
(for countries where
data is available).

ASIA

EUROPE

North Pole

Arctic Ocean

Greenland
(Denmark)

Alaska
(U.S.)

Pacific
Ocean

CANADA

Atlantic
Ocean

UNITED STATES

TROPIC OF CANCER

Gulf of
Mexico

BAHAMAS

DOMINICAN
REPUBLIC

MEXICO

CUBA

ANTIGUA &
BARBUDA
DOMINICA

JAMAICA

ST. KITTS & NEVIS
ST. LUCIA
BARBADOS
ST. VINCENT &
THE GRENADINES
GRENADA

HAITI

BELIZE

TRINIDAD
& TOBAGO

GUATEMALA

EL SALVADOR

PANAMA

HONDURAS

COSTA RICA

SOUTH
AMERICA

NICARAGUA

CUBA

Cayman
Islands
(U.K.)

DOMINICAN
REPUBLIC

ST. KITTS
& NEVIS

JAMAICA

HAITI

Puerto
Rico
(U.S.)

ANTIGUA &
BARBUDA

Caribbean   Sea

DOMINICA

ST. LUCIA

BARBADOS

Aruba
(Neth.)

Curaçao
(Neth.)

ST. VINCENT &
THE GRENADINES

GRENADA

Bonaire
(Neth.)

TRINIDAD &
TOBAGO

ECONOMICALLY, North America
is divided between two worlds: the
mechanized and diversified world
of Canada and the United States
and the still developing and heavily
agriculture-dependent world of
Middle America.

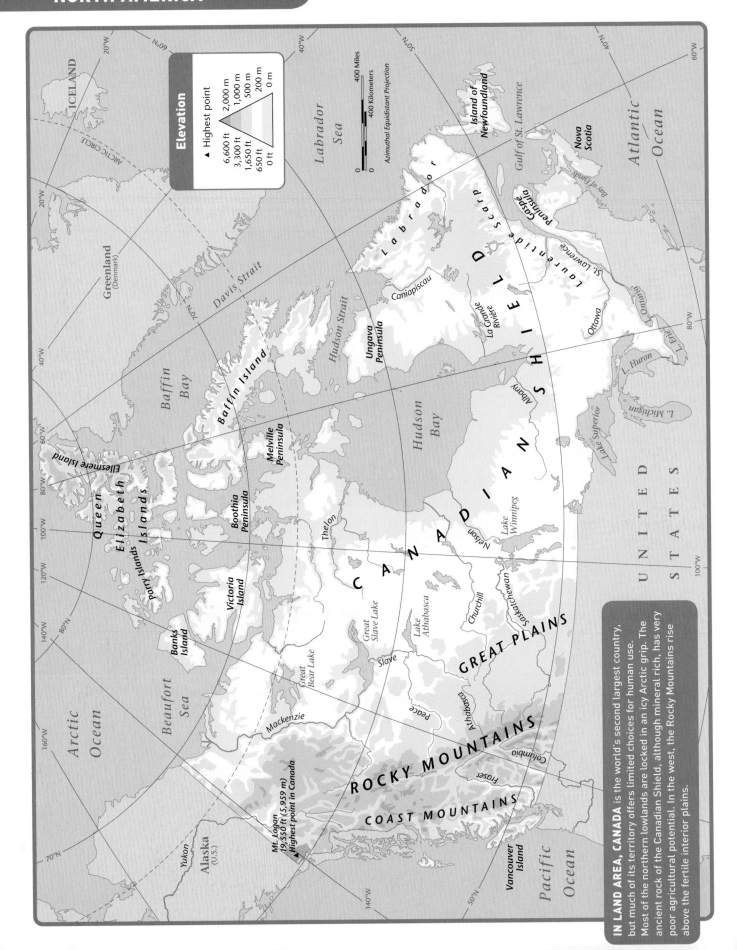

Elevation

▲ Highest point

6,600 ft   2,000 m
3,300 ft   1,000 m
1,650 ft   500 m
650 ft   200 m
0 ft   0 m

400 Miles
400 Kilometers
Azimuthal Equidistant Projection

ICELAND

ARCTIC CIRCLE

Greenland
(Denmark)

Davis Strait

Baffin
Bay

Labrador
Sea

Island of
Newfoundland

Gulf of St. Lawrence

Nova
Scotia

Atlantic
Ocean

Labrador

Gaspé
Peninsula

St. Lawrence

Bay of Fundy

Laurentide Scarp

Caniapiscau

La Grande
Rivière

Ottawa

L. Erie

L. Ontario

Ellesmere Island

Queen
Elizabeth
Islands

Parry Islands

Baffin Island

Hudson Strait

Ungava
Peninsula

C A N A D I A N   S H I E L D

Albany

Hudson
Bay

Lake Superior

L. Huron

L. Michigan

Melville
Peninsula

Boothia
Peninsula

Thelon

Lake
Winnipeg

Nelson

U N I T E D

S T A T E S

Victoria
Island

Banks
Island

Great
Slave Lake

Great
Bear Lake

Lake
Athabasca

Churchill

Saskatchewan

GREAT PLAINS

Beaufort
Sea

Arctic
Ocean

Slave

Athabasca

Peace

Mackenzie

ROCKY MOUNTAINS

Columbia

Fraser

COAST MOUNTAINS

Mt. Logan
19,550 ft (5,959 m)
▲ Highest point in Canada

Yukon

Alaska
(U.S.)

Vancouver
Island

Pacific
Ocean

IN LAND AREA, CANADA is the world's second largest country, but much of its territory offers limited choices for human use. Most of the northern lowlands are locked in an icy Arctic grip. The ancient rock of the Canadian Shield, although mineral rich, has very poor agricultural potential. In the west, the Rocky Mountains rise above the fertile interior plains.

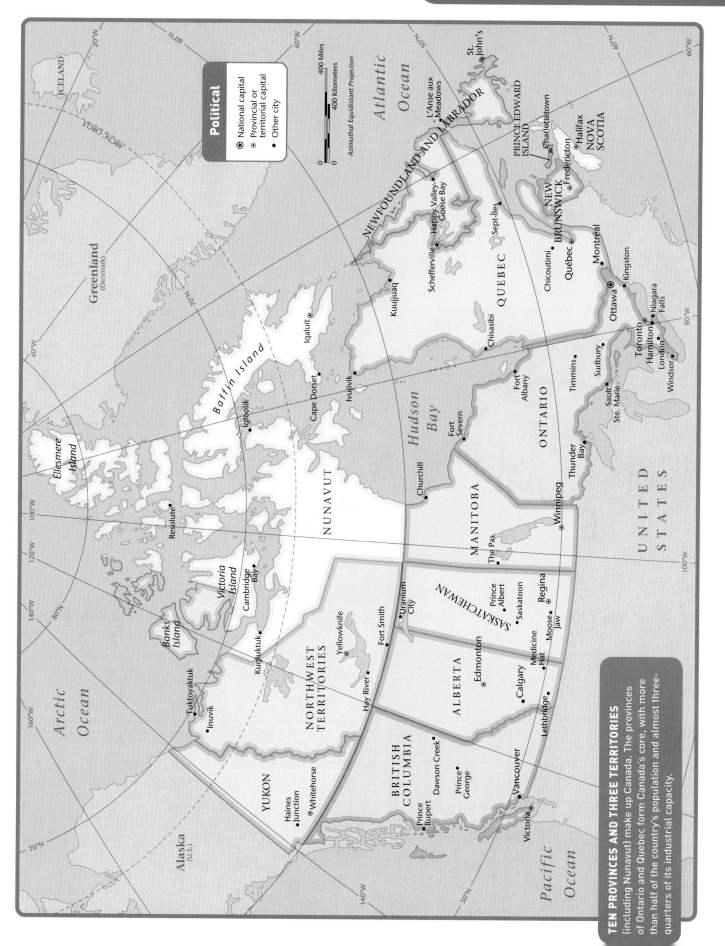

Political
- ⊛ National capital
- ◉ Provincial or territorial capital
- • Other city

400 Miles
400 Kilometers
Azimuthal Equidistant Projection

TEN PROVINCES AND THREE TERRITORIES
(including Nunavut) make up Canada. The provinces of Ontario and Quebec form Canada's core, with more than half of the country's population and almost three-quarters of its industrial capacity.

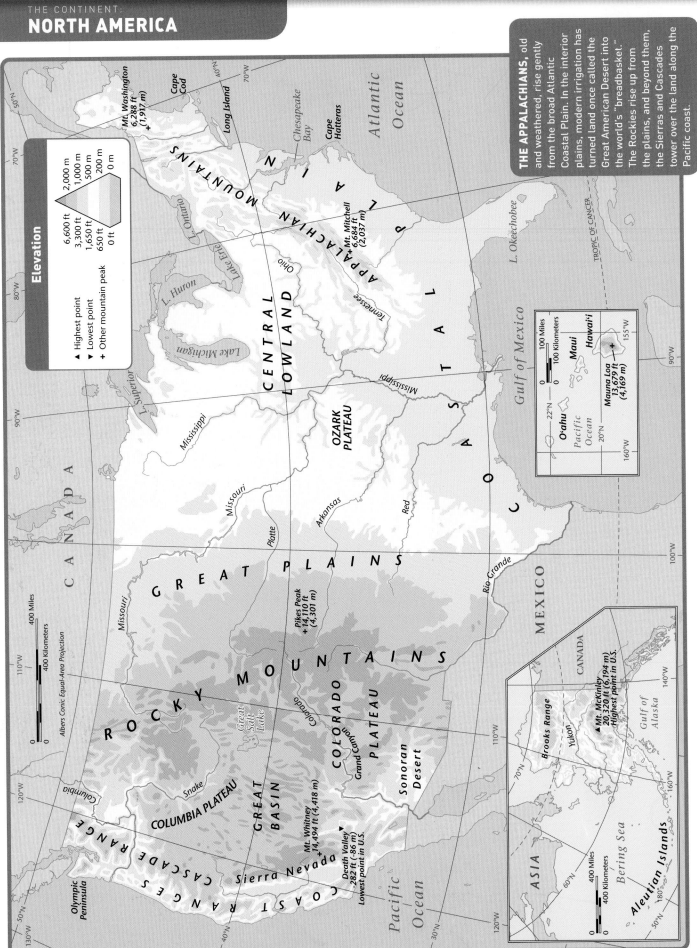

THE CONTINENT:
NORTH AMERICA

THE APPALACHIANS, old and weathered, rise gently from the broad Atlantic Coastal Plain. In the interior plains, modern irrigation has turned land once called the Great American Desert into the world's "breadbasket." The Rockies rise up from the plains, and beyond them, the Sierras and Cascades tower over the land along the Pacific coast.

Elevation

2,000 m	6,600 ft
1,000 m	3,300 ft
500 m	1,650 ft
200 m	650 ft
0 m	0 ft

▲ Highest point
▼ Lowest point
+ Other mountain peak

Mt. Washington
6,288 ft
(1,917 m)

Cape Cod

Long Island

L. Ontario

Lake Erie

L. Huron

Lake Michigan

L. Superior

Chesapeake Bay

Cape Hatteras

Atlantic Ocean

APPALACHIAN MOUNTAINS

+ Mt. Mitchell
6,684 ft
(2,037 m)

Ohio

Tennessee

CENTRAL LOWLAND

COASTAL PLAIN

Mississippi

OZARK PLATEAU

Mississippi

Missouri

Arkansas

Red

Rio Grande

Gulf of Mexico

L. Okeechobee

TROPIC OF CANCER

MEXICO

CANADA

GREAT PLAINS

Pikes Peak
+ 14,110 ft
(4,301 m)

Platte

Missouri

ROCKY MOUNTAINS

Great Salt Lake

Colorado

COLORADO PLATEAU

Grand Canyon

Sonoran Desert

Snake

COLUMBIA PLATEAU

GREAT BASIN

Mt. Whitney +
14,494 ft (4,418 m)

Sierra Nevada

Death Valley
–282 ft (–86 m)
Lowest point in U.S.

COAST RANGES

CASCADE RANGE

Olympic Peninsula

Columbia

Pacific Ocean

400 Miles
400 Kilometers
Albers Conic Equal-Area Projection

Hawai'i

100 Miles
100 Kilometers

O'ahu

Maui

Mauna Loa
13,679 ft
(4,169 m)

Pacific Ocean

Alaska inset:

Mt. McKinley ▲
20,320 ft (6,194 m)
Highest point in U.S.

Brooks Range

Yukon

CANADA

Gulf of Alaska

ASIA

Bering Sea

Aleutian Islands

400 Miles
400 Kilometers

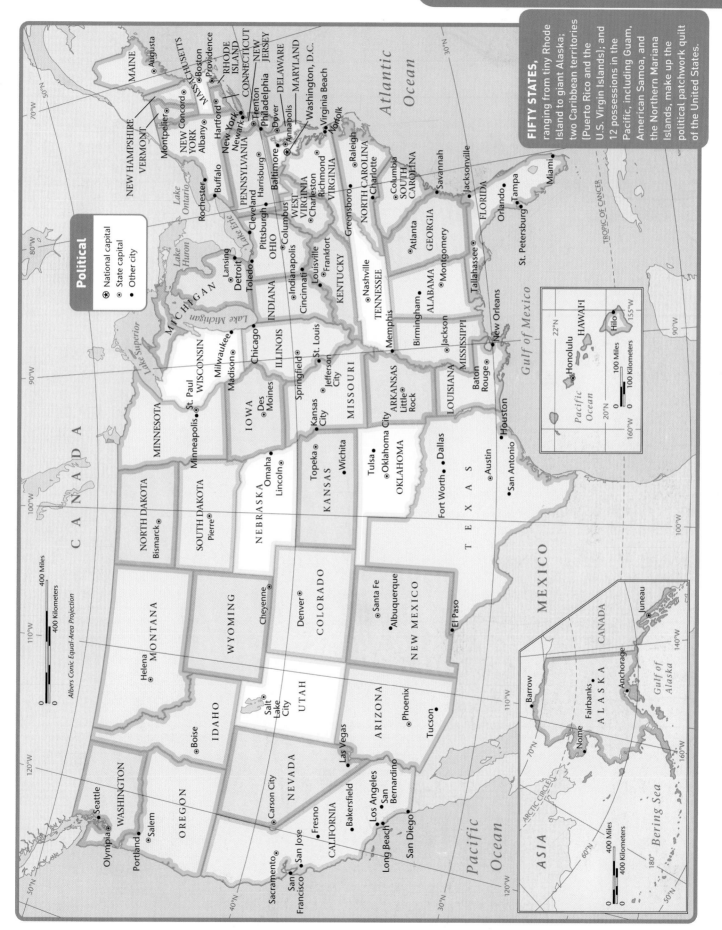

Political
⊛ National capital
◎ State capital
• Other city

Atlantic Ocean

Pacific Ocean

Gulf of Mexico

Bering Sea

C A N A D A

M E X I C O

A S I A

TROPIC OF CANCER

ARCTIC CIRCLE

Albers Conic Equal-Area Projection

400 Miles
400 Kilometers

MAINE
Augusta ◎
NEW HAMPSHIRE
VERMONT
Montpelier ◎
Concord ◎
MASSACHUSETTS
Boston ◎
Providence ◎
RHODE ISLAND
CONNECTICUT
NEW YORK
Albany ◎
Hartford ◎
New York
Newark •
Trenton ◎
NEW JERSEY
DELAWARE
Dover ◎
Philadelphia •
MARYLAND
Washington, D.C. ⊛
Annapolis ◎
Baltimore •
Virginia Beach
Norfolk •

PENNSYLVANIA
Harrisburg ◎
Buffalo •
Rochester •
Pittsburgh •
WEST VIRGINIA
Charleston ◎
Richmond ◎
VIRGINIA
Raleigh ◎
NORTH CAROLINA
Charlotte •
Greensboro •
Columbia ◎
SOUTH CAROLINA
Savannah •
Jacksonville •
FLORIDA
Orlando •
Tampa •
St. Petersburg •
Miami •

Lake Ontario
Lake Erie
Lake Huron
Lake Superior
Lake Michigan

MICHIGAN
Lansing ◎
Detroit •
Toledo •
Cleveland •
Columbus ◎
OHIO
Cincinnati •
INDIANA
Indianapolis ◎
Louisville •
Frankfort ◎
KENTUCKY
Nashville ◎
TENNESSEE
Memphis •
Atlanta ◎
GEORGIA
Montgomery ◎
ALABAMA
Birmingham •
Tallahassee ◎
MISSISSIPPI
Jackson ◎
New Orleans •
LOUISIANA
Baton Rouge ◎

WISCONSIN
Madison ◎
Milwaukee •
St. Paul ◎
Minneapolis •
MINNESOTA
Chicago •
ILLINOIS
Springfield ◎
St. Louis •
IOWA
Des Moines ◎
MISSOURI
Jefferson City ◎
Kansas City •
Topeka ◎
KANSAS
Wichita •
ARKANSAS
Little Rock ◎
Tulsa •
Oklahoma City ◎
OKLAHOMA

NORTH DAKOTA
Bismarck ◎
SOUTH DAKOTA
Pierre ◎
NEBRASKA
Lincoln ◎
Omaha •

WYOMING
Cheyenne ◎
COLORADO
Denver ◎
Santa Fe ◎
Albuquerque •
NEW MEXICO
El Paso •

MONTANA
Helena ◎
IDAHO
Boise •
UTAH
Salt Lake City ◎
ARIZONA
Phoenix ◎
Tucson •

WASHINGTON
Olympia ◎
Seattle •
Portland •
Salem ◎
OREGON
Sacramento ◎
San Francisco •
San Jose •
CALIFORNIA
Fresno •
Bakersfield •
Los Angeles •
Long Beach •
San Bernardino •
San Diego •
Las Vegas •
NEVADA
Carson City ◎

T E X A S
Dallas •
Fort Worth •
Austin ◎
San Antonio •
Houston •

Pacific Ocean
Gulf of Alaska
HAWAI'I
Honolulu ◎
Hilo •
22°N
20°N
100 Miles
100 Kilometers
160°W
155°W

A L A S K A
Juneau ◎
Anchorage •
Fairbanks •
Nome •
Barrow •
CANADA
70°N
60°N
400 Miles
400 Kilometers
180°
160°W
140°W

80°W
70°W
90°W
100°W
110°W
120°W
30°N
40°N
50°N

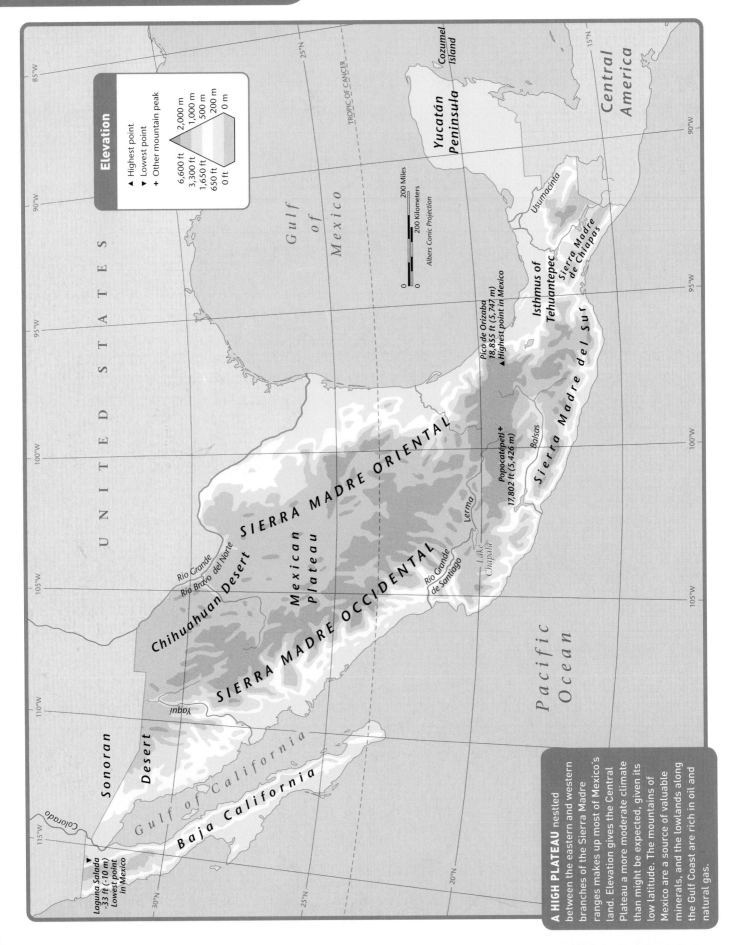

Elevation

▲ Highest point
▼ Lowest point
+ Other mountain peak

2,000 m 1,000 m 500 m 200 m 0 m
6,600 ft 3,300 ft 1,650 ft 650 ft 0 ft

TROPIC OF CANCER

Cozumel Island

Yucatán Peninsula

Central America

200 Miles

200 Kilometers

Albers Conic Projection

Usumacinta

Sierra Madre de Chiapas

Isthmus of Tehuantepec

Pico de Orizaba
18,855 ft (5,747 m)
▲Highest point in Mexico

Sierra Madre del Sur

Popocatépetl +
17,802 ft (5,426 m)

Balsas

G u l f   o f   M e x i c o

Lerma

S I E R R A   M A D R E   O R I E N T A L

M e x i c a n   P l a t e a u

Lake Chapala

Rio Grande de Santiago

U N I T E D   S T A T E S

Rio Grande

Rio Bravo del Norte

Chihuahuan Desert

S I E R R A   M A D R E   O C C I D E N T A L

Yaqui

P a c i f i c   O c e a n

S o n o r a n   D e s e r t

G u l f   o f   C a l i f o r n i a

B a j a   C a l i f o r n i a

Colorado

▲ Laguna Salada
-33 ft (-10 m)
Lowest point in Mexico

A HIGH PLATEAU nestled between the eastern and western branches of the Sierra Madre ranges makes up most of Mexico's land. Elevation gives the Central Plateau a more moderate climate than might be expected, given its low latitude. The mountains of Mexico are a source of valuable minerals, and the lowlands along the Gulf Coast are rich in oil and natural gas.

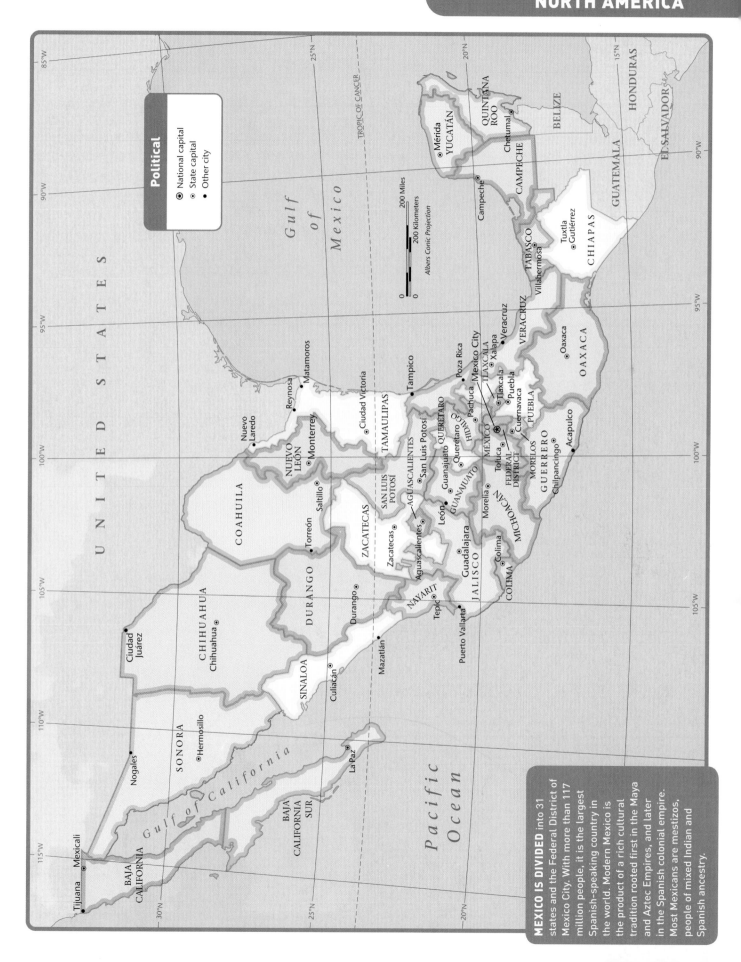

Political
- ⊛ National capital
- ⊙ State capital
- • Other city

UNITED STATES

Gulf of Mexico

Pacific Ocean

Gulf of California

200 Miles
200 Kilometers
Albers Conic Projection

TROPIC OF CANCER

BAJA CALIFORNIA
Tijuana
Mexicali
Nogales

SONORA
Hermosillo

BAJA CALIFORNIA SUR
La Paz

CHIHUAHUA
Ciudad Juárez
Chihuahua

SINALOA
Culiacán
Mazatlán

COAHUILA
Torreón
Saltillo

DURANGO
Durango

ZACATECAS
Zacatecas

NUEVO LEÓN
Monterrey
Nuevo Laredo

TAMAULIPAS
Reynosa
Matamoros
Ciudad Victoria
Tampico

SAN LUIS POTOSÍ
San Luis Potosí

NAYARIT
Tepic

AGUASCALIENTES
Aguascalientes

GUANAJUATO
Guanajuato
León

JALISCO
Guadalajara
Puerto Vallarta

COLIMA
Colima

MICHOACÁN
Morelia

QUERÉTARO
Querétaro

HIDALGO
Pachuca

MEXICO
Toluca

FEDERAL DISTRICT
Mexico City

TLAXCALA
Tlaxcala

PUEBLA
Puebla
Cuernavaca

MORELOS

GUERRERO
Chilpancingo
Acapulco

VERACRUZ
Poza Rica
Veracruz
Xalapa

OAXACA
Oaxaca

TABASCO
Villahermosa

CHIAPAS
Tuxtla Gutiérrez

CAMPECHE
Campeche

YUCATÁN
Mérida

QUINTANA ROO
Chetumal

GUATEMALA
BELIZE
HONDURAS
EL SALVADOR

MEXICO IS DIVIDED into 31 states and the Federal District of Mexico City. With more than 117 million people, it is the largest Spanish-speaking country in the world. Modern Mexico is the product of a rich cultural tradition rooted first in the Maya and Aztec Empires, and later in the Spanish colonial empire. Most Mexicans are mestizos, people of mixed Indian and Spanish ancestry.

NATURAL HAZARDS: SELECTED STATISTICS

HURRICANES

This list names North America's eight most intense hurricanes (based on barometric pressure) since 1950. Average sea-level pressure is 1,013.25 millibars (mbr), or 29.92 inches.

1968	Camille	909 mbr/26.84 in
2005	Katrina	920 mbr/27.17 in
1992	Andrew	922 mbr/27.23 in
1960	Donna	930 mbr/27.46 in
1961	Carla	931 mbr/27.49 in
1989	Hugo	934 mbr/27.58 in
2005	Rita	937 mbr/27.67 in
1954	Hazel	938 mbr/27.70 in

TORNADOES

The following states had the highest average annual number of tornadoes from 1981 to 2010.

Texas: 150
Kansas: 78
Oklahoma: 57
Florida: 52
Nebraska: 51
Iowa: 48

EARTHQUAKES

This list shows the number of earthquakes in North America since 1900 that had a magnitude of 8.0 or greater on the Richter scale.

Alaska (U.S.): 6
Mexico: 4
British Columbia (Canada): 1
Dominican Republic: 1 (see inset map p. 57)

VOLCANOES

This list shows major volcanic eruptions in the U.S. since 1980.

Mount St. Helens (WA): 1980–1986
Kilauea (HI): 1983–ongoing
Mauna Loa (HI): 1984
Augustine (AK): 1986
Redoubt (AK): 1989–1990

Natural Hazards

The forces of nature inspire awe. They can also bring damage and destruction, especially when people locate homes and businesses in places that are at risk of experiencing violent storms, earthquakes, volcanoes, floods, wildfires, or other natural hazards. Tornadoes—violent, swirling storms with winds that can exceed 200 miles (300 km) per hour—strike the U.S. more than 800 times each year. Hurricanes, massive low-pressure storms that form over warm ocean waters, bring destructive winds and rain primarily to the Gulf of Mexico and the southeastern mainland. Melting spring snows and heavy rains trigger flooding; periods of drought make other regions vulnerable to wildfires. These and other hazards of nature are not limited to this continent. Natural hazards pose serious threats to lives and property wherever people live.

VOLCANOES. From deep inside Earth, molten rock, called magma, rises and breaks through the surface, sometimes quietly, but more often violently, shooting billowing ash clouds, as shown here at Mount St. Helens, in Washington State.

WILDFIRES. Putting lives and property at great risk, wildfires destroy millions of acres (ha) of forest each year. At the same time, fires help renew ecosystems by removing debris and encouraging seedling growth.

FLOODS. Towns located along New Jersey's coastline experienced widespread flooding as a result of the storm surge and heavy rains associated with Hurricane Sandy in October 2012.

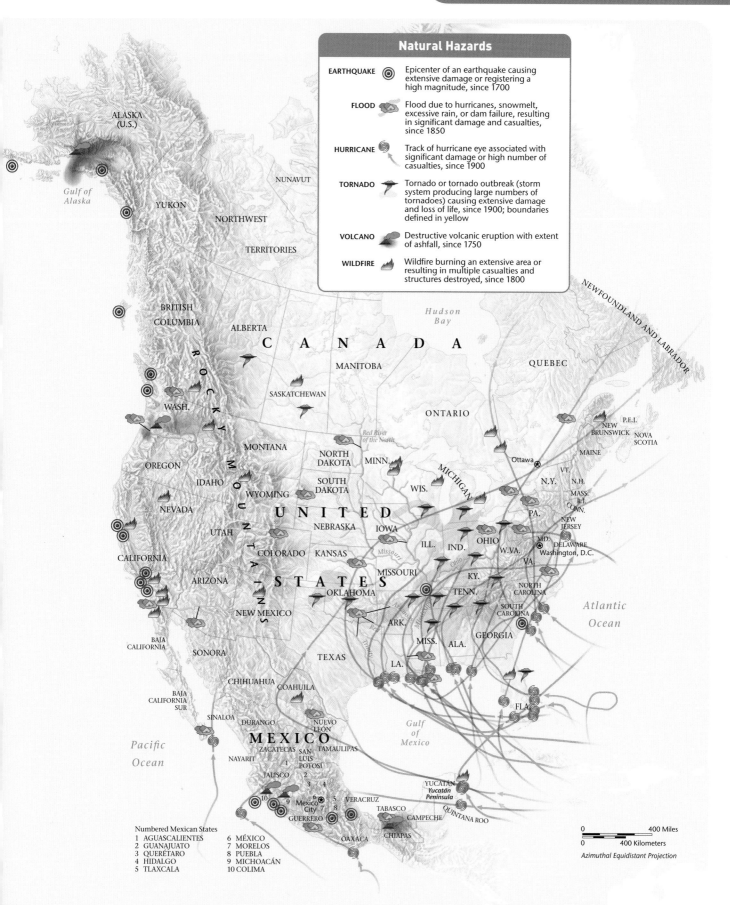

Natural Hazards

EARTHQUAKE Epicenter of an earthquake causing extensive damage or registering a high magnitude, since 1700

FLOOD Flood due to hurricanes, snowmelt, excessive rain, or dam failure, resulting in significant damage and casualties, since 1850

HURRICANE Track of hurricane eye associated with significant damage or high number of casualties, since 1900

TORNADO Tornado or tornado outbreak (storm system producing large numbers of tornadoes) causing extensive damage and loss of life, since 1900; boundaries defined in yellow

VOLCANO Destructive volcanic eruption with extent of ashfall, since 1750

WILDFIRE Wildfire burning an extensive area or resulting in multiple casualties and structures destroyed, since 1800

ALASKA (U.S.)

Gulf of Alaska

YUKON

NUNAVUT

NORTHWEST TERRITORIES

BRITISH COLUMBIA

ALBERTA

NEWFOUNDLAND AND LABRADOR

Hudson Bay

C A N A D A

MANITOBA

SASKATCHEWAN

QUEBEC

ONTARIO

P.E.I.
NEW BRUNSWICK
NOVA SCOTIA

WASH.

ROCKY MOUNTAINS

MONTANA

NORTH DAKOTA

Red River of the North

MINN.

MAINE

Ottawa

OREGON

IDAHO

WYOMING

SOUTH DAKOTA

WIS.

MICHIGAN

VT.
N.H.
N.Y.
MASS.
CONN. R.I.

NEVADA

UTAH

NEBRASKA

IOWA

ILL.

IND.

OHIO

PA.

NEW JERSEY

Missouri

CALIFORNIA

COLORADO

KANSAS

MISSOURI

MD.
DELAWARE
Washington, D.C.
W.VA.
VA.

ARIZONA

U N I T E D   S T A T E S

OKLAHOMA

Ohio

KY.

TENN.

NORTH CAROLINA

NEW MEXICO

ARK.

SOUTH CAROLINA

Atlantic Ocean

BAJA CALIFORNIA

SONORA

TEXAS

MISS.

ALA.

GEORGIA

LA.

BAJA CALIFORNIA SUR

CHIHUAHUA

COAHUILA

FLA.

SINALOA

DURANGO

NUEVO LEÓN

Gulf of Mexico

Pacific Ocean

M E X I C O

ZACATECAS

SAN LUIS POTOSÍ

TAMAULIPAS

NAYARIT

1

JALISCO

2

3

4

5

VERACRUZ

YUCATÁN
Yucatán Peninsula

6

Mexico City

7

8

TABASCO

CAMPECHE

QUINTANA ROO

9

10

GUERRERO

OAXACA

CHIAPAS

Numbered Mexican States
1 AGUASCALIENTES
2 GUANAJUATO
3 QUERÉTARO
4 HIDALGO
5 TLAXCALA
6 MÉXICO
7 MORELOS
8 PUEBLA
9 MICHOACÁN
10 COLIMA

0   400 Miles
0   400 Kilometers

Azimuthal Equidistant Projection

South America:
A View From Space

From the towering, snow-capped Andes in the west to the steamy rain forest of the Amazon Basin in the north, and from the fertile grasslands of the Pampas to the arid Atacama Desert along the Pacific coast, South America is a continent of extremes. North to south, the continent extends from the tropical waters of the Caribbean Sea to the wind-swept islands of Tierra del Fuego. Its longest river, the Amazon, carries more water than any other river in the world.

Snow- and ice-covered Mount Fitzroy rises above Los Glaciares National Park in Patagonia, Argentina.

South America

PHYSICAL

Land area
6,880,000 sq mi
(17,819,000 sq km)

Highest point
Cerro Aconcagua,
Argentina
22,831 ft (6,959 m)

Lowest point
Laguna del Carbón, Argentina
-344 ft (-105 m)

Longest river
Amazon
4,150 mi (6,679 km)

Largest lake
Lake Titicaca,
Bolivia-Peru
3,200 sq mi
(8,290 sq km)

POLITICAL

Population
401,139,000

**Number of
independent
countries**
12

Largest country
Brazil
3,300,169 sq mi (8,547,403 sq km)

Smallest country
Suriname
63,037 sq mi (163,265 sq km)

Most populous country
Brazil
Pop. 195,527,000

Least populous country
Suriname
Pop. 558,000

THE CONTINENT:
SOUTH AMERICA

TWO PHYSICAL FEATURES dominate South America's landscape—the rugged Andes that stretch north to south from Colombia to Tierra del Fuego, and the Amazon Basin, the drainage area of the Amazon River and site of the world's largest tropical forest.

Central America

Caribbean Sea

80°W

70°W

60°W

50°W

Lake Maracaibo

Orinoco

Llanos

GUIANA HIGHLANDS

Angel Falls

South America–North America boundary

Malpelo I.

A N D E S

Negro

EQUATOR

Amazon

Marajó I.

0°

A M A Z O N

Amazon

0°

B A S I N

Tapajós

Xingu

Purus

Madeira

Tocantins

Ucayali

10°S

São Francisca

10°S

Lake Titicaca

BRAZILIAN

HIGHLANDS

A N D E S

Atacama Desert

20°S

Gran Chaco

Paraguay

Iguazú Falls

TROPIC OF CAPRICORN

20°S

San Félix I.   San Ambrosio I.

Ojos del Salado 22,572 ft (6,880 m)

Paraná

Atlantic Ocean

Cerro Aconcagua 22,831 ft (6,959 m) Highest point in South America

P A M P A S

Uruguay

30°S

Juan Fernández Is.

Rio de la Plata

30°S

Pacific Ocean

Colorado

Physical

▲ Highest point
▼ Lowest point
+ Other mountain peak

Isla Grande de Chiloé

40°S

P A T A G O N I A

A N D E S

40°S

Gulf of San Jorge

Laguna del Carbón -344 ft (-105 m) Lowest point in South America

0   600 Miles

0   600 Kilometers

Azimuthal Equidistant Projection

Falkland Islands

Strait of Magellan

50°S

Tierra del Fuego

South Georgia

50°S

Cape Horn

100°W   90°W   80°W   70°W   60°W   50°W   40°W   30°W   20°W

THE CONTINENT:
SOUTH AMERICA

TWELVE COUNTRIES and one French territory (French Guiana) make up South America. The continent was under mainly Spanish and Portuguese control from the 16th century to the 19th century. Colonial influence is still evident in the use of Spanish and Portuguese languages and in the widespread presence of the Roman Catholic church.

Central America

Caribbean Sea

80°W
70°W
60°W
50°W

Barranquilla
Maracaibo
Caracás
Barquisimeto
Valencia

VENEZUELA

Georgetown
Paramaribo
Cayenne
French Guiana (France)

GUYANA
SURINAME

South America–North America boundary

Medellín
Bogotá
Cali

COLOMBIA

EQUATOR
0°
Quito
ECUADOR
Guayaquil

Manaus

Belém

EQUATOR
0°

Fortaleza
Natal
Recife

P E R U

Trujillo

B R A Z I L

10°S

Lima
Cusco

Salvador (Bahia)

B O L I V I A
La Paz

Goiânia
Brasília

Santa Cruz
Sucre

Belo Horizonte

PARAGUAY

20°S

Nova Iguaçu
São Paulo
Rio de Janeiro
Santos
Curitiba

TROPIC OF CAPRICORN

Asunción

San Miguel de Tucumán

A R G E N T I N A

C H I L E

Atlantic Ocean

Porto Alegre

Córdoba
Santa Fe
Rosario

URUGUAY

30°S

Valparaíso
Santiago
Buenos Aires
La Plata
Montevideo

Pacific Ocean

Mar del Plata

Political
⊛ National capital
• Other city

40°S

0   600 Miles
0   600 Kilometers

Azimuthal Equidistant Projection

Stanley
Falkland Islands (U.K.)

Punta Arenas

South Georgia (U.K.)

50°S

100°W
90°W
80°W
70°W
60°W
50°W
40°W
30°W
20°W

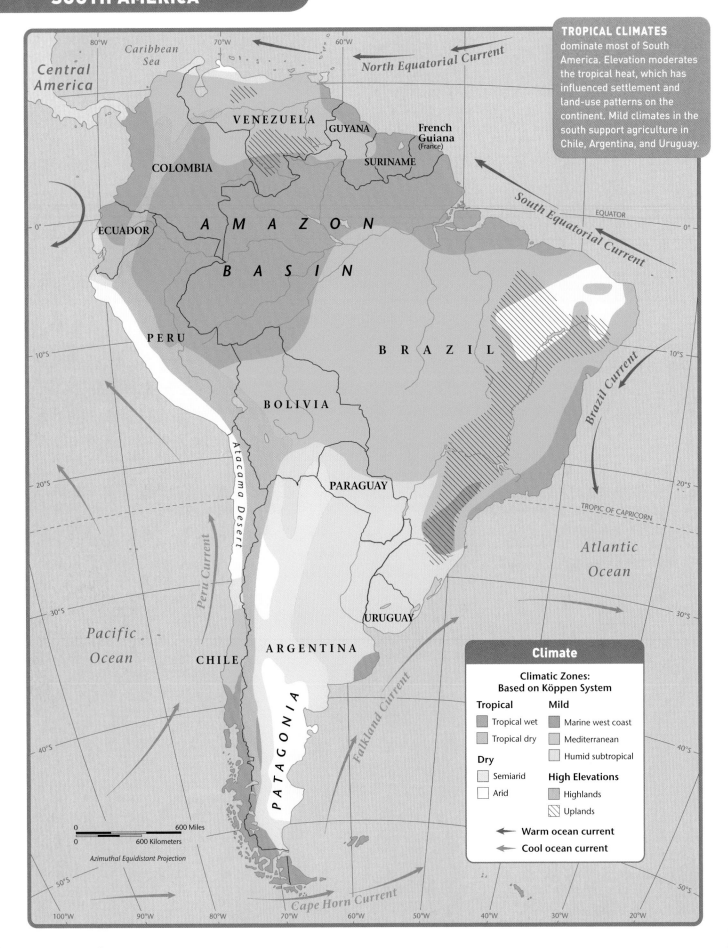

Caribbean Sea

Central America

North Equatorial Current

VENEZUELA
GUYANA
French Guiana (France)
COLOMBIA
SURINAME

South Equatorial Current

EQUATOR

A M A Z O N

ECUADOR

B A S I N

PERU

B R A Z I L

Brazil Current

BOLIVIA

Atacama Desert

Peru Current

PARAGUAY

TROPIC OF CAPRICORN

Atlantic Ocean

URUGUAY

Pacific Ocean

ARGENTINA

CHILE

Falkland Current

P A T A G O N I A

0   600 Miles
0   600 Kilometers

Azimuthal Equidistant Projection

Cape Horn Current

Climate

**Climatic Zones:
Based on Köppen System**

Tropical
- Tropical wet
- Tropical dry

Dry
- Semiarid
- Arid

Mild
- Marine west coast
- Mediterranean
- Humid subtropical

High Elevations
- Highlands
- Uplands

← Warm ocean current
← Cool ocean current

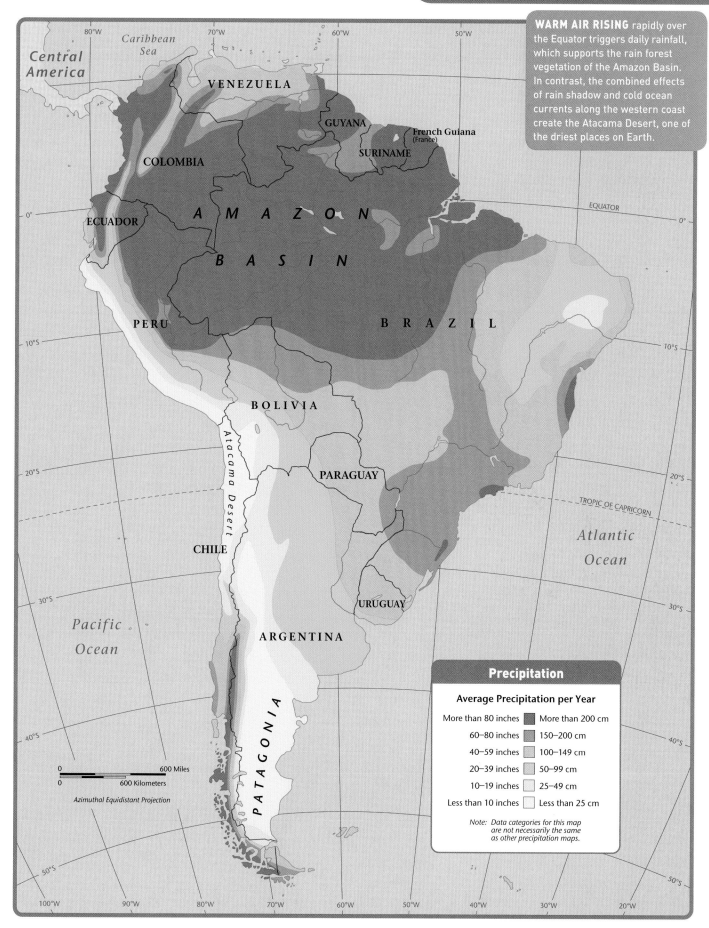

WARM AIR RISING rapidly over the Equator triggers daily rainfall, which supports the rain forest vegetation of the Amazon Basin. In contrast, the combined effects of rain shadow and cold ocean currents along the western coast create the Atacama Desert, one of the driest places on Earth.

Caribbean Sea

Central America

VENEZUELA

GUYANA

French Guiana
(France)

COLOMBIA

SURINAME

ECUADOR

A M A Z O N

B A S I N

EQUATOR

PERU

B R A Z I L

BOLIVIA

Atacama Desert

PARAGUAY

TROPIC OF CAPRICORN

CHILE

Atlantic Ocean

URUGUAY

Pacific Ocean

ARGENTINA

PATAGONIA

600 Miles
0
0
600 Kilometers

Azimuthal Equidistant Projection

Precipitation

Average Precipitation per Year

More than 80 inches	More than 200 cm
60–80 inches	150–200 cm
40–59 inches	100–149 cm
20–39 inches	50–99 cm
10–19 inches	25–49 cm
Less than 10 inches	Less than 25 cm

Note: Data categories for this map are not necessarily the same as other precipitation maps.

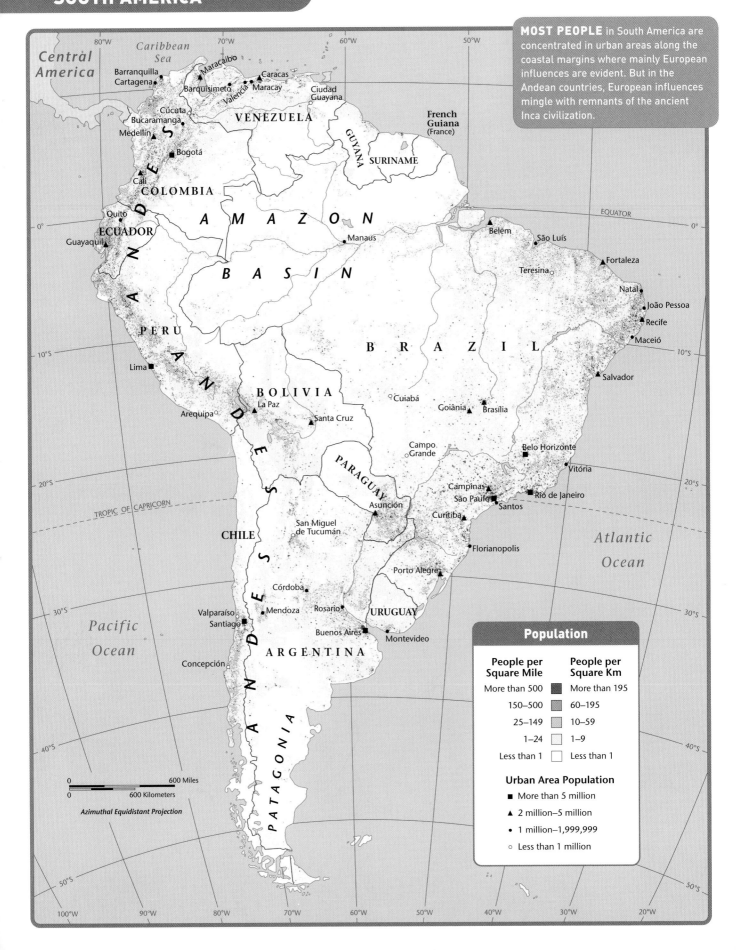

MOST PEOPLE in South America are concentrated in urban areas along the coastal margins where mainly European influences are evident. But in the Andean countries, European influences mingle with remnants of the ancient Inca civilization.

Central America

Caribbean Sea

Barranquilla
Cartagena
Maracaibo
Caracas
Barquisimeto
Valencia Maracay
Ciudad Guayana
Cúcuta
Bucaramanga
Medellín
Bogotá
Cali
COLOMBIA
VENEZUELA
GUYANA
SURINAME
French Guiana (France)

Quito
ECUADOR
Guayaquil

AMAZON

BASIN

Manaus

Belém
São Luís
Fortaleza
Teresina
Natal
João Pessoa
Recife
Maceió

EQUATOR

PERU

Lima

BOLIVIA
La Paz
Arequipa
Santa Cruz

BRAZIL

Salvador

Cuiabá

Goiânia Brasília

Campo Grande

Belo Horizonte
Vitória

PARAGUAY
Asunción

Campinas
São Paulo
Santos
Curitiba
Rio de Janeiro

Florianopolis

San Miguel de Tucumán

CHILE

Porto Alegre

Córdoba
Mendoza
Rosario
URUGUAY

Valparaíso
Santiago
Buenos Aires
Montevideo

Concepción
ARGENTINA

PATAGONIA

ANDES

Pacific Ocean

Atlantic Ocean

0   600 Miles
0   600 Kilometers
Azimuthal Equidistant Projection

TROPIC OF CAPRICORN

Population

People per Square Mile	People per Square Km
More than 500	More than 195
150–500	60–195
25–149	10–59
1–24	1–9
Less than 1	Less than 1

Urban Area Population

■ More than 5 million

▲ 2 million–5 million

• 1 million–1,999,999

○ Less than 1 million

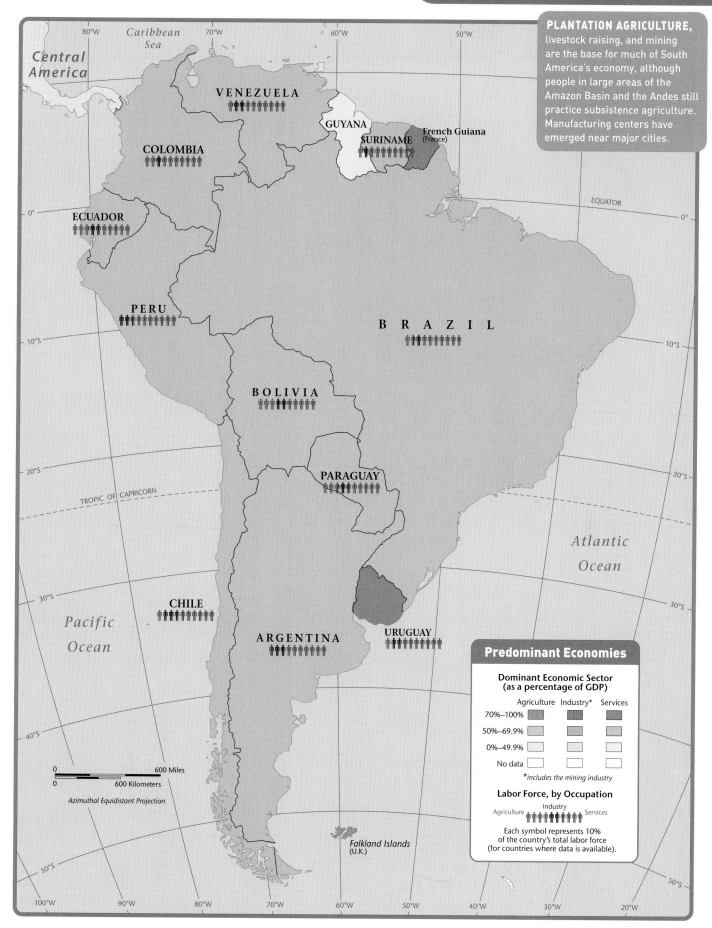

PLANTATION AGRICULTURE, livestock raising, and mining are the base for much of South America's economy, although people in large areas of the Amazon Basin and the Andes still practice subsistence agriculture. Manufacturing centers have emerged near major cities.

Predominant Economies

Dominant Economic Sector
(as a percentage of GDP)

	Agriculture	Industry*	Services
70%–100%			
50%–69.9%			
0%–49.9%			
No data			

*includes the mining industry

Labor Force, by Occupation

Agriculture — Industry — Services

Each symbol represents 10% of the country's total labor force (for countries where data is available).

0   600 Miles
0   600 Kilometers

Azimuthal Equidistant Projection

TROPICAL RAIN FORESTS:

FACTS & FIGURES

- Tropical rain forests cover 6 percent of Earth's surface, but are home to half of Earth's species.
- Average monthly temperature is 68° to 82°F (20° to 28°C).
- Total annual rainfall averages 5 to 33 feet (1.5 to 10 m).
- Trees in tropical rain forests can grow up to 200 feet (60 m) in height.
- Most nutrients in tropical rain forests are stored in the vegetation rather than in the soil, which is very poor.
- Some of Earth's most valuable woods, such as teak, mahogany, rosewood, and sandalwood, grow in tropical rain forests.
- Up to 25 percent of all medicines include products originating in tropical rain forests.
- Tropical rain forests absorb carbon dioxide and release oxygen.
- Deforestation of tropical rain forests contributes to climate change.
- Almost half of all forest loss in the period 2000–2010 occurred in tropical forests.
- Brazil and Indonesia had the highest net loss of forest in the 1990s but have significantly reduced their rates of loss.

Amazon Rain Forest

The Amazon rain forest, which covers approximately 2.7 million square miles (7 million sq km), is the world's largest tropical forest. Located mainly in Brazil, the Amazon rain forest accounts for more than 20 percent of all the world's tropical forests. Known in Brazil as the selva, the rain forest is a vast storehouse of biological diversity, filled with plants and animals both familiar and exotic. According to estimates, at least half of all terrestrial species are found in tropical forests, but many of these species have not yet been identified.

Tropical forests contain many valuable resources, including cacao (chocolate), nuts, spices, rare hardwoods, and plant extracts used to make medicines. Some drugs used in treating cancer and heart disease come from plants found only in tropical forests. But human intervention—logging, mining, and clearing land for crops and grazing—has put tropical forests at great risk. In Brazil, roads cut into the rain forest have opened the way for settlers, who clear away the forest only to discover soil too poor in nutrients to sustain agriculture for more than a few years. Land usually is cleared by a method called slash-and-burn, which contributes to global warming by releasing great amounts of carbon dioxide into the atmosphere.

SLOW-MOVING, this three-toed sloth spends most of its life in the treetops. It is one of the many unusual species of animals that make their homes in the forests of the Amazon Basin.

DENSE CANOPY OF THE RAIN FOREST stands in sharp contrast to the silt-laden waters of one of the Amazon's many tributaries. Although seemingly endless, the forest in Brazil is decreasing in size due to mining, farming, ranching, and logging.

SLASH-AND-BURN is a method used in the tropics for clearing land for farms. But the soil is poor in nutrients, and good yields are short-lived.

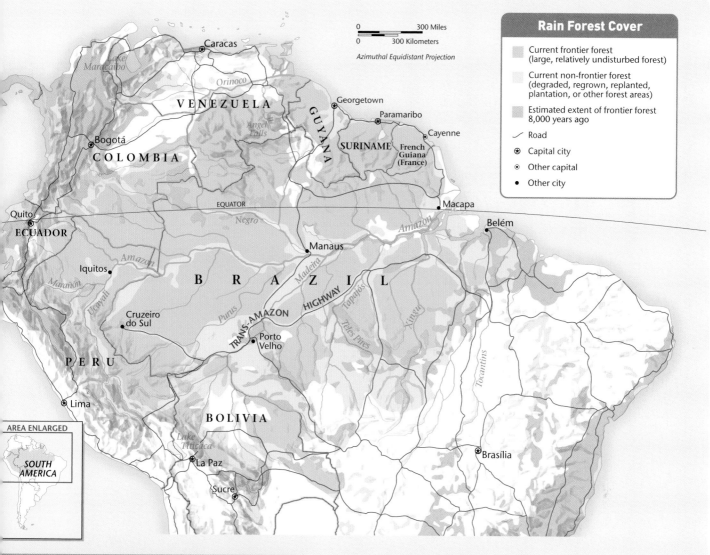

0   300 Miles
0   300 Kilometers
Azimuthal Equidistant Projection

Rain Forest Cover

- Current frontier forest (large, relatively undisturbed forest)
- Current non-frontier forest (degraded, regrown, replanted, plantation, or other forest areas)
- Estimated extent of frontier forest 8,000 years ago
- ⁄ Road
- ⊛ Capital city
- ⊙ Other capital
- • Other city

Caracas

VENEZUELA

Lake Maracaibo

Orinoco

GUYANA

Georgetown

Paramaribo

SURINAME

Cayenne

French Guiana (France)

Bogotá

COLOMBIA

Angel Falls

EQUATOR

Quito

ECUADOR

Negro

Amazon

Macapa

Belém

Manaus

Iquitos

BRAZIL

Amazon

Marañón

Madeira

Ucayali

Purus

TRANS-AMAZON HIGHWAY

Tapajós

Teles Pires

Xingu

Cruzeiro do Sul

Porto Velho

PERU

Tocantins

Lima

BOLIVIA

Lake Titicaca

Brasília

La Paz

Sucre

AREA ENLARGED

SOUTH AMERICA

◖ **MINING OPERATIONS,** such as this tin mine, remove forests to gain access to mineral deposits.

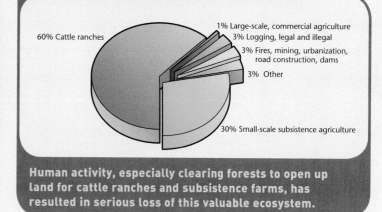

CAUSES OF DEFORESTATION IN THE AMAZON

60% Cattle ranches

1% Large-scale, commercial agriculture
3% Logging, legal and illegal
3% Fires, mining, urbanization, road construction, dams
3% Other

30% Small-scale subsistence agriculture

Human activity, especially clearing forests to open up land for cattle ranches and subsistence farms, has resulted in serious loss of this valuable ecosystem.

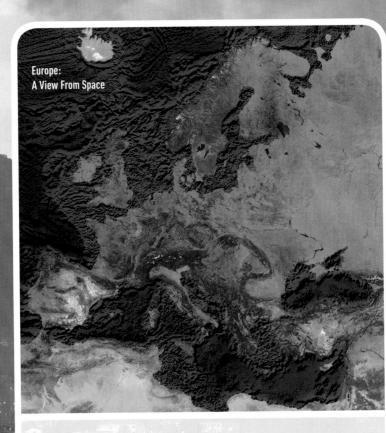

Europe:
A View From Space

Smaller than every other continent except Australia, Europe is a mosaic of islands and peninsulas. In fact, Europe itself is one big peninsula, jutting westward from the huge landmass of Asia and nearly touching Africa to the south. Europe's ragged coastline measures more than one and a half times the length of the Equator—38,279 miles (61,603 km) to be exact—giving 32 of its 46 countries direct access to the sea.

The Cathedral of Santa Maria del Fiore dominates the skyline of Florence, Italy.

Europe

PHYSICAL

Land area 3,841,000 sq mi (9,947,000 sq km)	**Lowest point** Caspian Sea -92 ft (-28 m)	**Largest lake entirely in Europe** Ladoga, Russia 6,853 sq mi (17,703 sq km)
Highest point El'brus, Russia 18,510 ft (5,642 m)	**Longest river** Volga, Russia 2,294 mi (3,692 km)	

POLITICAL

Population 739,517,000	**Largest country entirely in Europe** Ukraine 233,090 sq mi (603,700 sq km)	**Most populous country entirely in Europe** Germany Pop. 80,572,000
Number of independent countries 46 (including Russia)	**Smallest country** Vatican City 0.2 sq mi (0.4 sq km)	**Least populous country** Vatican City Pop. 798

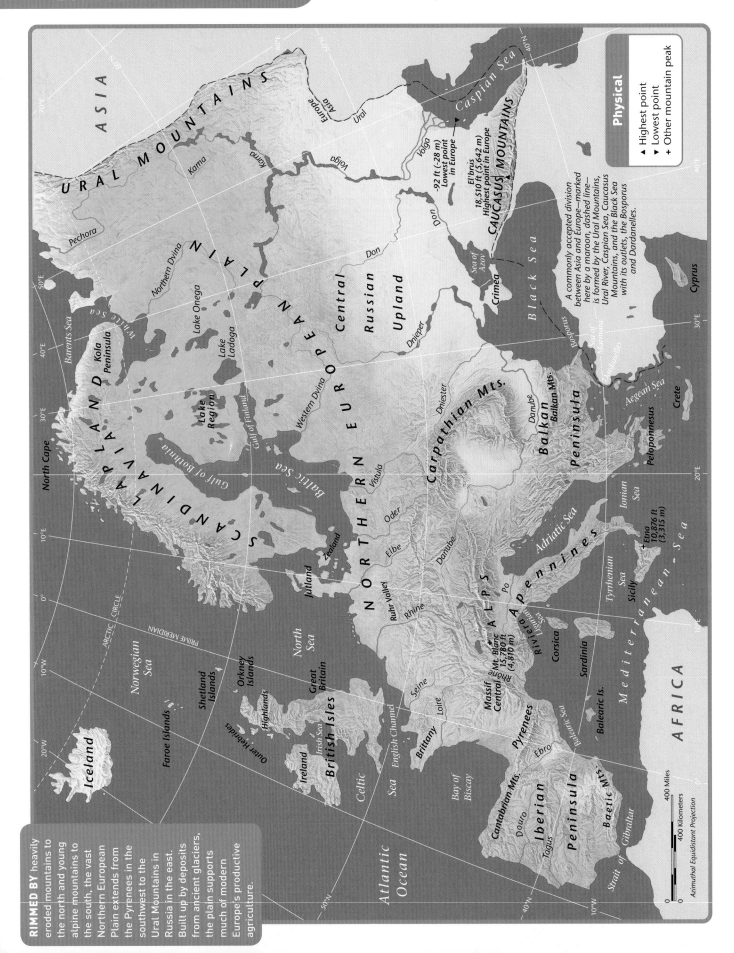

Physical

◄ Highest point
► Lowest point
+ Other mountain peak

A commonly accepted division between Asia and Europe—marked here by a maroon, dashed line—is formed by the Ural Mountains, Ural River, Caspian Sea, Caucasus Mountains, and the Black Sea with its outlets, the Bosporus and Dardanelles.

-92 ft (-28 m)
Lowest point in Europe

El'brus
18,510 ft (5,642 m)
Highest point in Europe

Etna
10,876 ft
(3,315 m)

Massif
Central

Mt. Blanc
15,780 ft
(4,810 m)

ASIA

URAL MOUNTAINS

Pechora

Kama

Kama

Ural

Volga

Europe
Asia

Volga

Don

Caspian Sea

CAUCASUS MOUNTAINS

Barents Sea

White Sea

Northern Dvina

Lake Onega

Lake Ladoga

Central Russian Upland

Sea of Azov

Crimea

Black Sea

Sea of Marmara

Bosporus

Dardanelles

Cyprus

North Cape

Kola Peninsula

SCANDINAVIAN PLAIN

Lake Region

Gulf of Finland

Western Dvina

NORTHERN EUROPEAN PLAIN

Dniepr

Dniester

Carpathian Mts.

Danube

Balkan Mts.

Balkan Peninsula

Aegean Sea

Crete

Peloponnesus

Gulf of Bothnia

Baltic Sea

Vistula

Oder

Elbe

Danube

Adriatic Sea

Apennines

Ionian Sea

ALPS

Po

Tyrrhenian Sea

Sicily

Mediterranean Sea

Norwegian Sea

Shetland Islands

Orkney Islands

Highlands

Outer Hebrides

Faroe Islands

Iceland

Ireland

Irish Sea

Great Britain

British Isles

Celtic Sea

North Sea

Jutland

Zealand

Ruhr Valley

Rhine

Rhône

Riviera

Ligurian Sea

Corsica

Sardinia

Balearic Sea

Balearic Is.

AFRICA

ARCTIC CIRCLE

PRIME MERIDIAN

Atlantic Ocean

English Channel

Brittany

Seine

Loire

Bay of Biscay

Pyrenees

Ebro

Cantabrian Mts.

Douro

Tagus

Iberian Peninsula

Baetic Mts.

Strait of Gibraltar

400 Miles
400 Kilometers
Azimuthal Equidistant Projection

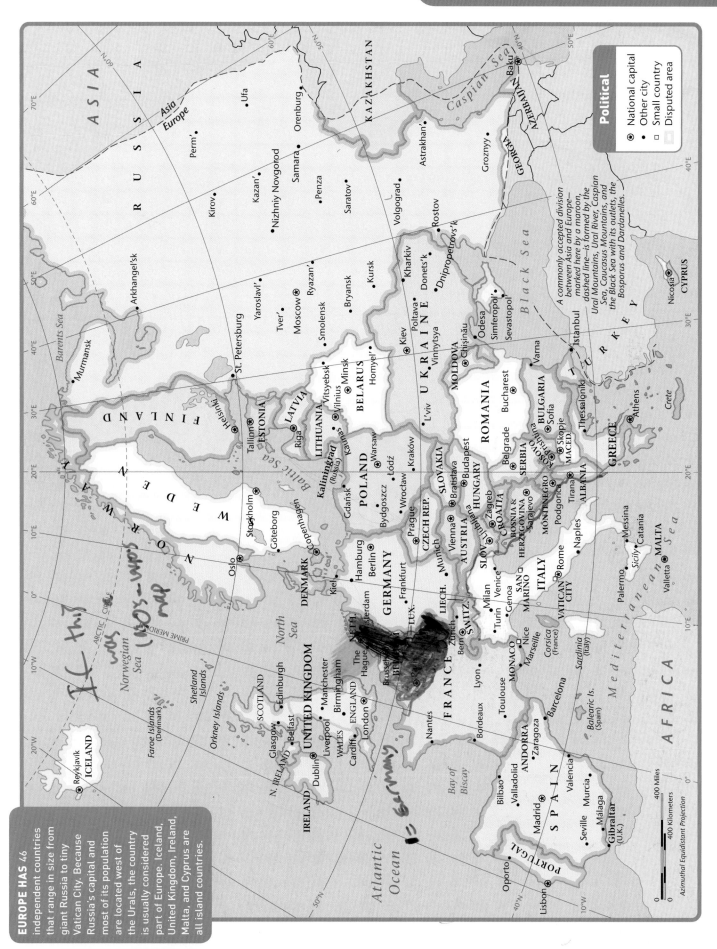

A commonly accepted division
between Asia and Europe—
marked here by a maroon,
dashed line—is formed by the
Ural Mountains, Ural River, Caspian
Sea, Caucasus Mountains, and
the Black Sea with its outlets, the
Bosporus and Dardanelles.

EUROPE HAS *46*
independent countries
that range in size from
giant Russia to tiny
Vatican City. Because
Russia's capital and
most of its population
are located west of
the Urals, the country
is usually considered
part of Europe. Iceland,
United Kingdom, Ireland,
Malta, and Cyprus are
all island countries.

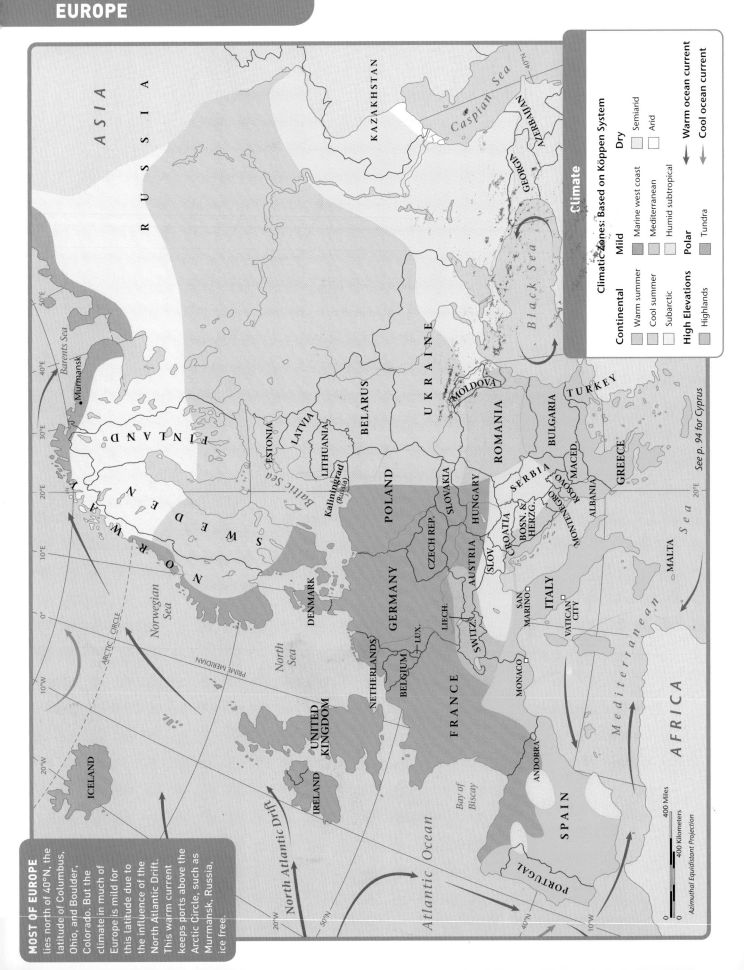

See p. 94 for Cyprus

Climate

Climatic Zones: Based on Köppen System

Continental
- Warm summer
- Cool summer
- Subarctic

Mild
- Marine west coast
- Mediterranean
- Humid subtropical

Dry
- Semiarid
- Arid

Polar
- Tundra

High Elevations
- Highlands

→ Warm ocean current
→ Cool ocean current

MOST OF EUROPE lies north of 40°N, the latitude of Columbus, Ohio, and Boulder, Colorado. But the climate in much of Europe is mild for this latitude due to the influence of the North Atlantic Drift. This warm current keeps ports above the Arctic Circle, such as Murmansk, Russia, ice free.

400 Miles

400 Kilometers

Azimuthal Equidistant Projection

Precipitation

Average Precipitation per Year

More than 80 inches — More than 200 cm
60–80 inches — 150–200 cm
40–59 inches — 100–149 cm
20–39 inches — 50–99 cm
10–19 inches — 25–49 cm
Less than 10 inches — Less than 25 cm

Note: Data categories for this map are not necessarily the same as other precipitation maps.

WESTERLY WINDS blowing off the Atlantic Ocean bring ample rainfall to Europe. This precipitation, combined with mild temperatures, supports a wide variety of agriculture. In the Mediterranean area, hot, dry summers favor orchards and vineyards.

Azimuthal Equidistant Projection

400 Miles
400 Kilometers

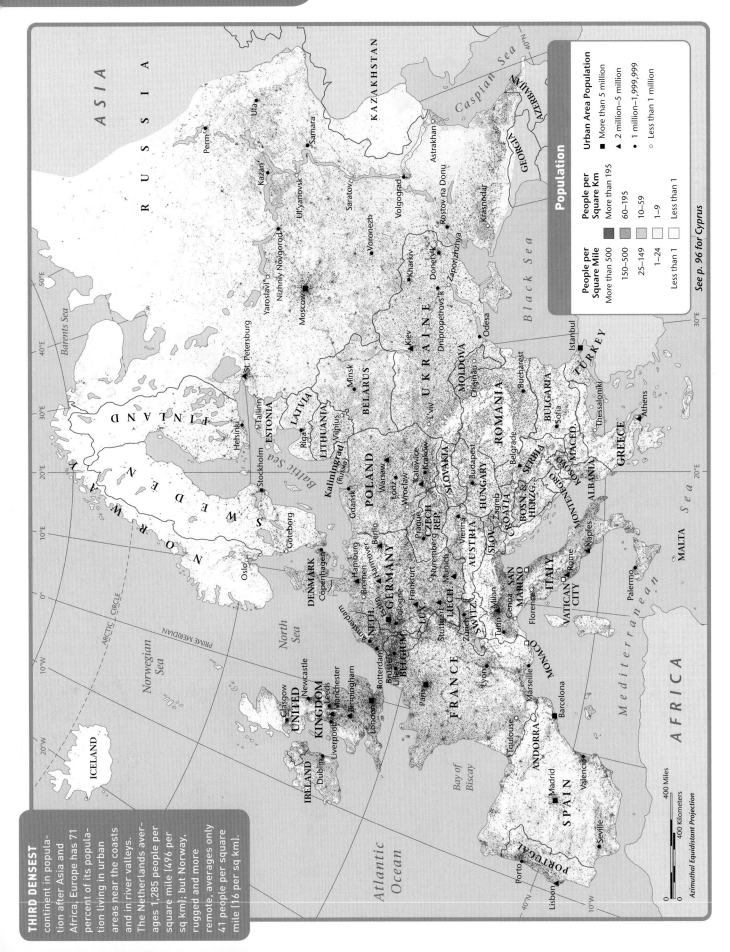

Population

People per Square Mile

	More than 500
	150–500
	25–149
	1–24
	Less than 1

People per Square Km

	More than 195
	60–195
	10–59
	1–9
	Less than 1

Urban Area Population

■ More than 5 million
▲ 2 million–5 million
● 1 million–1,999,999
○ Less than 1 million

See p. 96 for Cyprus

Azimuthal Equidistant Projection

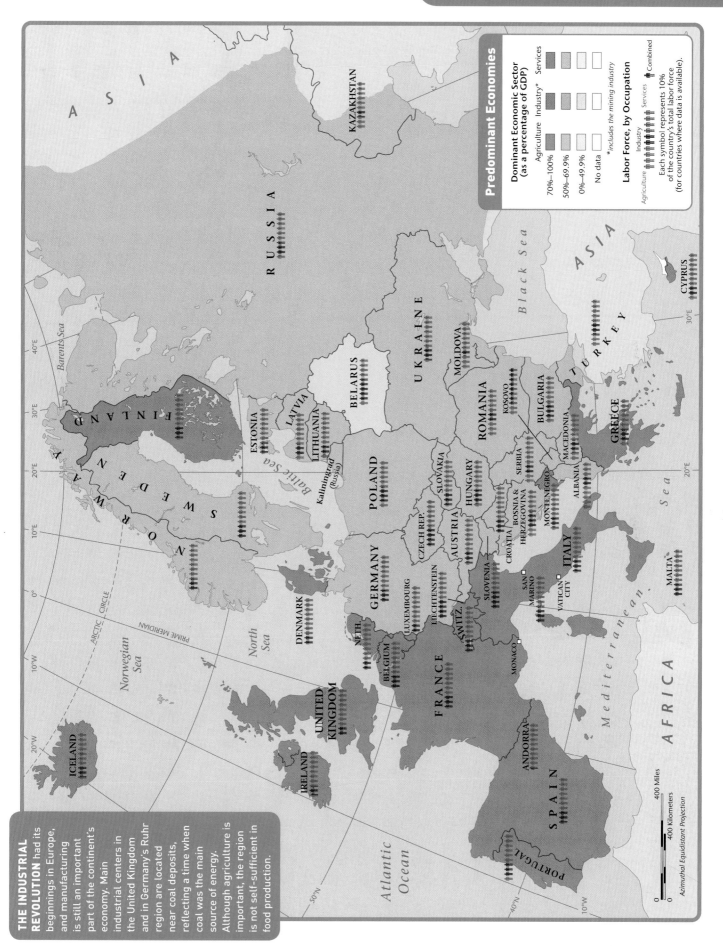

Predominant Economies

Dominant Economic Sector
(as a percentage of GDP)

Agriculture Industry* Services

70%–100%

50%–69.9%

0%–49.9%

No data

*includes the mining industry

Labor Force, by Occupation

Agriculture   Services   ♦Combined
      Industry

Each symbol represents 10%
of the country's total labor force
(for countries where data is available).

ASIA

A S I A

R U S S I A

KAZAKHSTAN

Barents Sea

BELARUS

U K R A I N E

MOLDOVA

ESTONIA

LATVIA

LITHUANIA

Kaliningrad
(Russia)

Baltic Sea

POLAND

Black Sea

A S I A

T U R K E Y

KOSOVO

BULGARIA

ROMANIA

MACEDONIA

GREECE

SERBIA

HUNGARY

ALBANIA

SLOVAKIA

MONTENEGRO

BOSNIA &
HERZEGOVINA

CROATIA

AUSTRIA

CZECH REP.

SLOVENIA

ITALY

SAN
MARINO

VATICAN
CITY

F I N L A N D

30°E

40°E

N O R W A Y

S W E D E N

GERMANY

LIECHTENSTEIN

LUXEMBOURG

SWITZ.

NETH.

DENMARK

BELGIUM

North
Sea

FRANCE

MONACO

MALTA

Mediterranean Sea

Sea

20°E

10°E

PRIME MERIDIAN

ARCTIC CIRCLE

Norwegian
Sea

UNITED
KINGDOM

IRELAND

ANDORRA

S P A I N

PORTUGAL

A F R I C A

ICELAND

Atlantic
Ocean

10°W

20°W

50°N

40°N

30°E

20°E

10°W

400 Miles

400 Kilometers

Azimuthal Equidistant Projection

0

0

**THE INDUSTRIAL
REVOLUTION** had its
beginnings in Europe,
and manufacturing
is still an important
part of the continent's
economy. Main
industrial centers in
the United Kingdom
and in Germany's Ruhr
region are located
near coal deposits,
reflecting a time when
coal was the main
source of energy.
Although agriculture is
important, the region
is not self-sufficient in
food production.

European Waterways

The physical landscape of Europe is crossed by many rivers that link the countries, people, and economies to the seas that border the continent. Fourteen of Europe's countries are landlocked (have no direct access to open waters), but the rivers and canals that make up Europe's network of waterways give even these countries access to global shipping routes.

Among these many waterways, the Rhine-Main-Danube system supports commercial and recreational traffic all the way from Rotterdam on the North Sea to Constanta on the Black Sea. Rotterdam, Europe's largest port as well as a major world port, handles 495 million tons (450 million MT) of goods each year. And Constanta is the largest port on the Black Sea.

The Rhine-Main-Danube waterway boasts a rich historical and cultural tradition. During Roman times, the rivers were used to transport supplies to armies along the northern border of the empire. Cities, such as Cologne, Vienna, and Budapest, emerged as cultural centers with churches, cathedrals, opera houses, and palaces that today attract tourists from around the world. And the Middle Rhine is famous for castles perched high above the banks of the river, where traders were once required to pay tolls to travel on the waterways.

HEIDELBURG CASTLE stands above the Rhine River in Germany, attracting millions of tourists each year.

◁ **COLOGNE CATHEDRAL,** begun in 1248, rises above the city of Cologne, Germany, on the banks of the Rhine River.

SELECTED EUROPEAN RIVERS

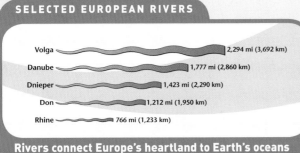

Volga — 2,294 mi (3,692 km)
Danube — 1,777 mi (2,860 km)
Dnieper — 1,423 mi (2,290 km)
Don — 1,212 mi (1,950 km)
Rhine — 766 mi (1,233 km)

Rivers connect Europe's heartland to Earth's oceans and seas, linking people, cities, and commerce to the global economy.

◯ **IRON GATE:** The face of the Dacian king Decebalus is carved into the rocks above the Iron Gates gorges on the Danube River between Romania and Serbia.

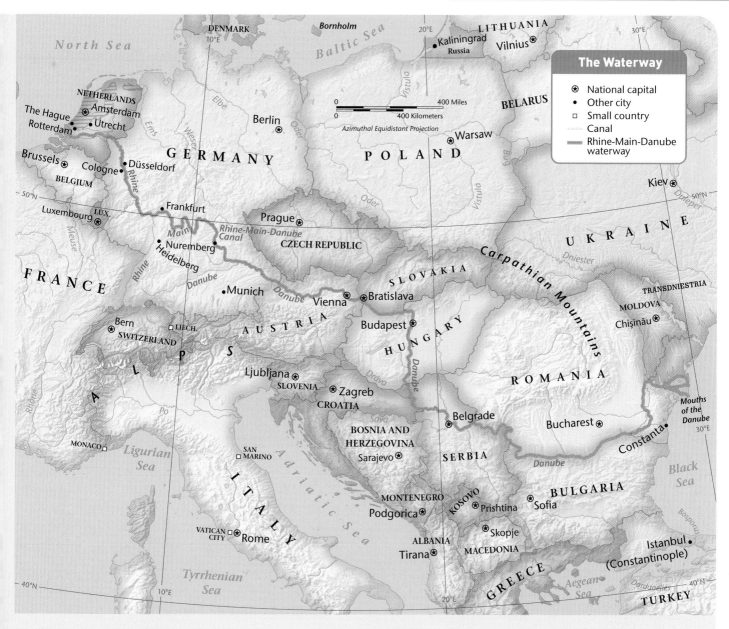

Azimuthal Equidistant Projection

The Waterway
- ⊛ National capital
- • Other city
- ☐ Small country
- ⋯ Canal
- ▬ Rhine-Main-Danube waterway

⬭ **THE RHINE-MAIN-DANUBE CANAL,** completed in 1992, connects the Rhine, Main, and Danube Rivers to create a continuous waterway from the North Sea to the Black Sea, which gives access to Turkey's Dardanelles and to the ports of Asia. The canal is 106 miles (171 km) long and makes navigation by large barges and riverboats possible for the full length of the waterway.

◖ **A CITY DIVIDED,** Budapest, Hungary, lies on both sides of the Danube River. Once two separate towns, Buda and Pest were united in 1872. The country's Parliament Building, an important city landmark, stretches 880 feet (268 m) along the Pest side of the river.

Asia:
A View From Space

From the frozen shores of the Arctic Ocean to the equatorial islands of Indonesia, Asia stretches across 90 degrees of latitude. From the Ural Mountains to the Pacific Ocean, it covers more than 150 degrees of longitude. Here, three of history's great culture hearths emerged in the valleys of the Tigris and Euphrates, the Indus, and the Yellow (Huang) Rivers. Today, Asia is home to 60 percent of Earth's people and some of the world's fastest growing economies.

The Taj Mahal in Agra, India

Asia

PHYSICAL

Land area 17,208,000 sq mi (44,570,000 sq km)	**Lowest point** Dead Sea, Israel-Jordan -1,385 ft (-422 m)	**Largest lake entirely in Asia** Lake Baikal 12,200 sq mi (31,500 sq km)
Highest point Mount Everest, China-Nepal 29,035 ft (8,850 m)	**Longest river** Yangtze (Chang), China 3,880 mi (6,244 km)	

POLITICAL

Population 4,302,088,000 **Number of independent countries** 46 (excluding Russia)	**Largest country entirely in Asia** China 3,705,405 sq mi (9,596,960 sq km) **Smallest country** Maldives 115 sq mi (298 sq km)	**Most populous country** China Pop. 1,357,372,000 **Least populous country** Maldives Pop. 360,000

THE CONTINENT:
ASIA

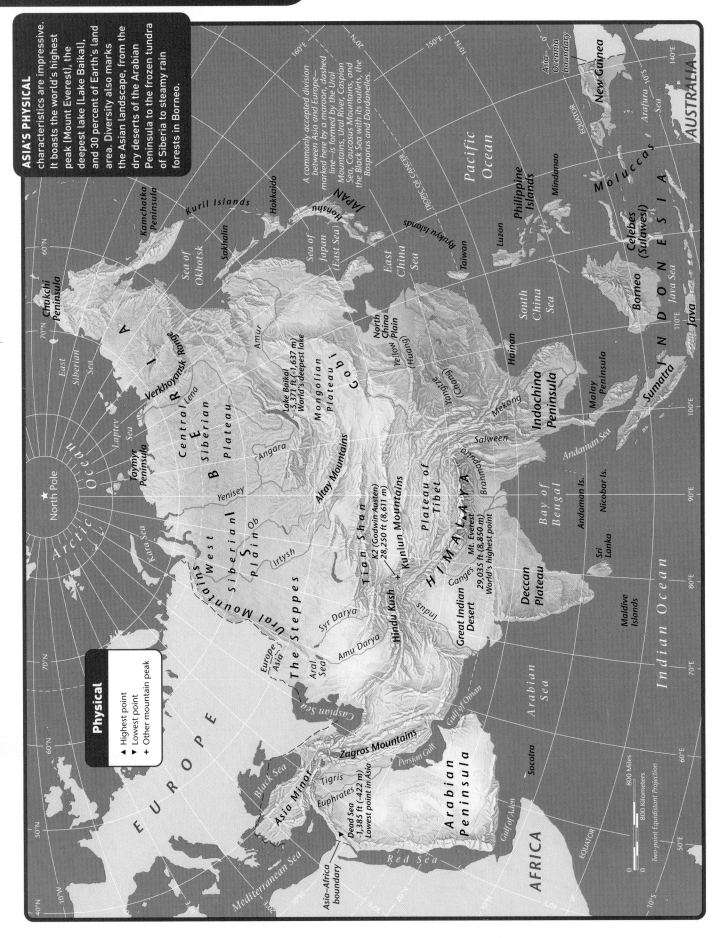

A commonly accepted division between Asia and Europe—marked here by a maroon, dashed line—is formed by the Ural Mountains, Ural River, Caspian Sea, Caucasus Mountains, and the Black Sea with its outlets, the Bosporus and Dardanelles.

Physical

▲ Highest point
▼ Lowest point
+ Other mountain peak

North Pole

Arctic Ocean

Chukchi Peninsula

Kamchatka Peninsula

Kuril Islands

Hokkaido

Sakhalin

Sea of Okhotsk

East Siberian Sea

Laptev Sea

Kara Sea

Taymyr Peninsula

Verkhoyansk Range

Lena

Central Siberian Plateau

Amur

Sea of Japan (East Sea)

Honshu

JAPAN

Ryukyu Islands

Pacific Ocean

TROPIC OF CANCER

Philippine Islands

Mindanao

New Guinea

Asia–Oceania boundary

AUSTRALIA

Arafura Sea

Moluccas

Celebes (Sulawesi)

Java

Sumatra

INDONESIA

Borneo

Java Sea

Malay Peninsula

Hainan

South China Sea

East China Sea

Taiwan

Luzon

North China Plain

Yellow Plain (Huang)

Yangtze (Chang)

Gobi

Mongolian Plateau

Lake Baikal -5,371 ft (-1,637 m) World's deepest lake

Angara

Yenisey

West Siberian Plain

Ob

Irtysh

Altay Mountains

Tian Shan

K2 (Godwin Austen) 28,250 ft (8,611 m)

+ Kunlun Mountains

Plateau of Tibet

Indochina Peninsula

Mekong

Salween

Brahmaputra

Andaman Sea

H I M A L A Y A

Mt. Everest 29,035 ft (8,850 m) World's highest point

Ganges

Indus

Deccan Plateau

Bay of Bengal

Andaman Is.

Nicobar Is.

Sri Lanka

Maldive Islands

Indian Ocean

Hindu Kush

The Steppes

Ural Mountains

Europe | Asia

Aral Sea

Syr Darya

Amu Darya

Great Indian Desert

Arabian Sea

EUROPE

Black Sea

Caspian Sea

Asia Minor

Zagros Mountains

Tigris

Euphrates

Dead Sea -1,385 ft (-422 m) Lowest point in Asia

Asia–Africa boundary

Mediterranean Sea

Red Sea

Persian Gulf

Gulf of Oman

Arabian Peninsula

Socotra

Gulf of Aden

AFRICA

EQUATOR

800 Miles

800 Kilometers

Two-point Equidistant Projection

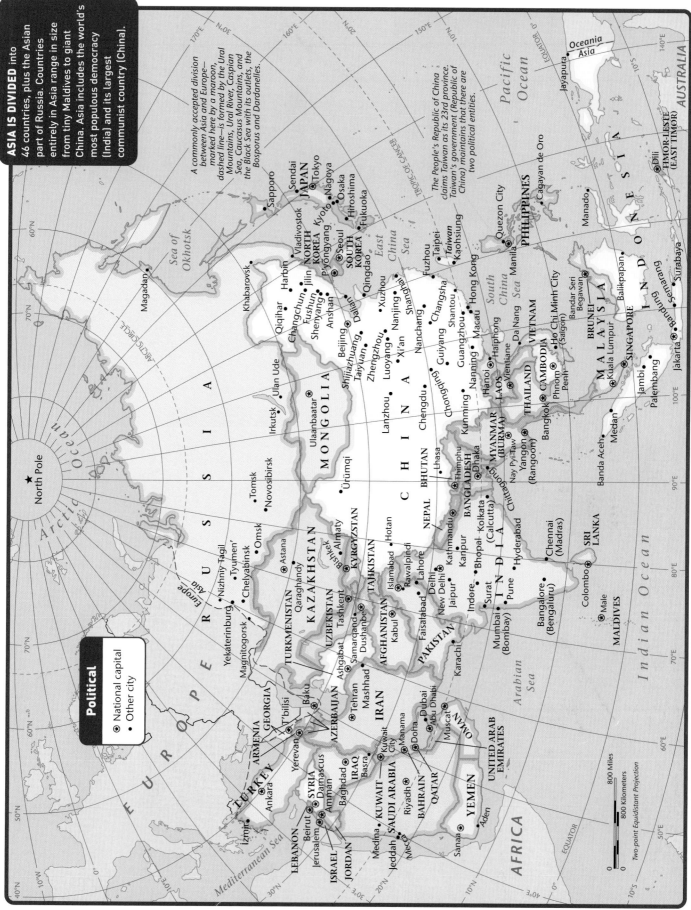

ASIA IS DIVIDED into 46 countries, plus the Asian part of Russia. Countries entirely in Asia range in size from tiny Maldives to giant China. Asia includes the world's most populous democracy (India) and its largest communist country (China).

A commonly accepted division between Asia and Europe—marked here by a maroon, dashed line—is formed by the Ural Mountains, Ural River, Caspian Sea, Caucasus Mountains, and the Black Sea with its outlets, the Bosporus and Dardanelles.

The People's Republic of China claims Taiwan as its 23rd province. Taiwan's government (Republic of China) maintains that there are two political entities.

Political
- ⊛ National capital
- • Other city

800 Miles
800 Kilometers
Two-point Equidistant Projection

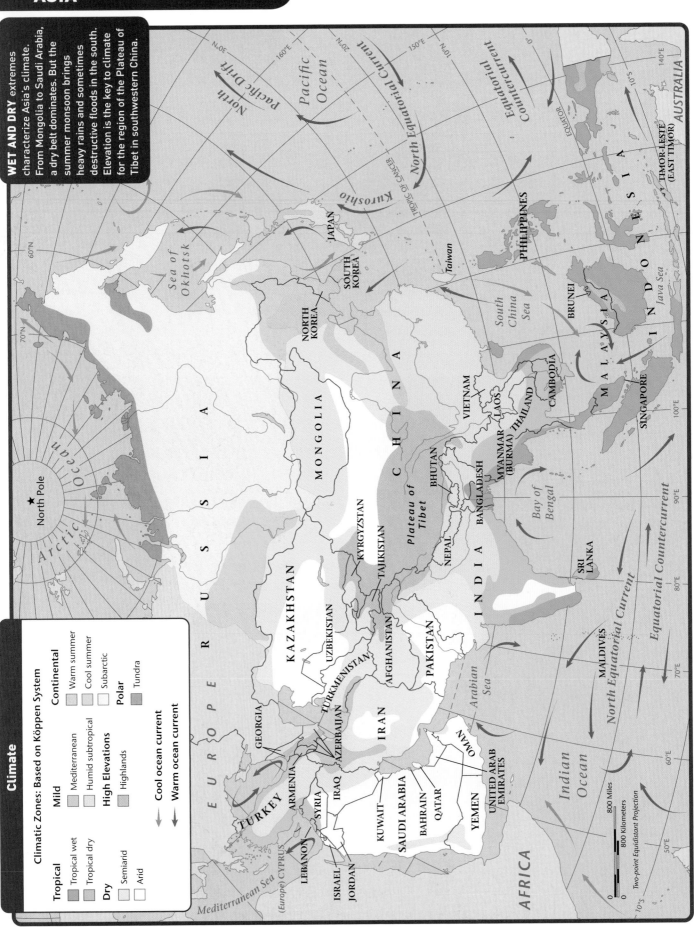

WET AND DRY extremes characterize Asia's climate. From Mongolia to Saudi Arabia, a dry belt dominates. But the summer monsoon brings heavy rains and sometimes destructive floods in the south. Elevation is the key to climate for the region of the Plateau of Tibet in southwestern China.

Climate

Climatic Zones: Based on Köppen System

Tropical
- Tropical wet
- Tropical dry

Dry
- Semiarid
- Arid

Mild
- Mediterranean
- Humid subtropical

High Elevations
- Highlands

Continental
- Warm summer
- Cool summer
- Subarctic

Polar
- Tundra

→ Cool ocean current
→ Warm ocean current

Two-point Equidistant Projection

800 Miles
800 Kilometers

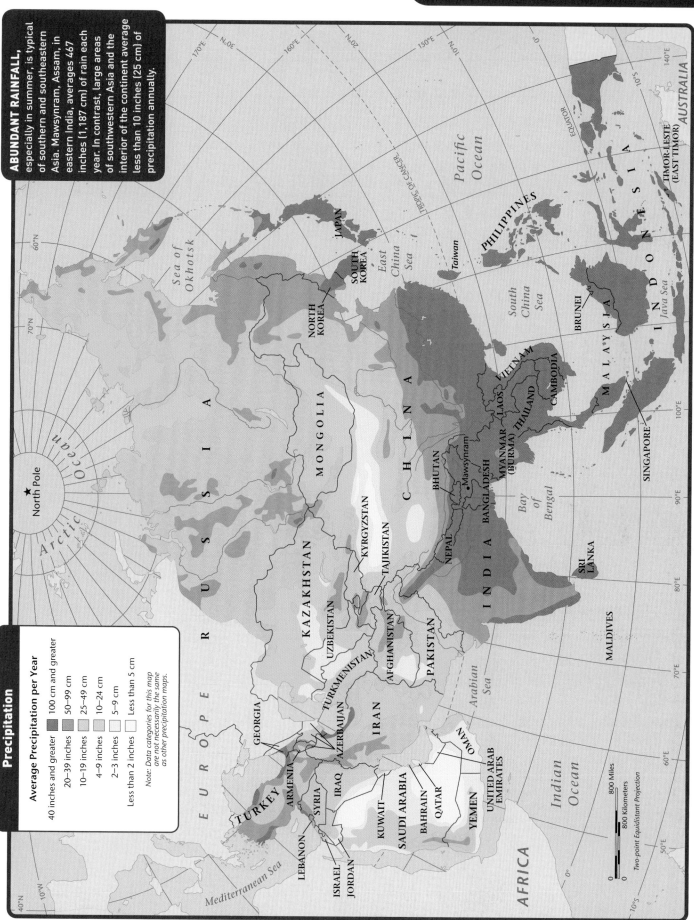

Precipitation

Average Precipitation per Year

- 40 inches and greater — 100 cm and greater
- 20–39 inches — 50–99 cm
- 10–19 inches — 25–49 cm
- 4–9 inches — 10–24 cm
- 2–3 inches — 5–9 cm
- Less than 2 inches — Less than 5 cm

Note: Data categories for this map are not necessarily the same as other precipitation maps.

ABUNDANT RAINFALL, especially in summer, is typical of southern and southeastern Asia. Mawsynram, Assam, in eastern India, averages 467 inches (1,187 cm) of rain each year. In contrast, large areas of southwestern Asia and the interior of the continent average less than 10 inches (25 cm) of precipitation annually.

North Pole

Arctic Ocean

EUROPE

RUSSIA

Sea of Okhotsk

MONGOLIA

KAZAKHSTAN

UZBEKISTAN

TURKMENISTAN

KYRGYZSTAN

TAJIKISTAN

AFGHANISTAN

PAKISTAN

GEORGIA

ARMENIA

AZERBAIJAN

TURKEY

IRAN

IRAQ

SYRIA

LEBANON

ISRAEL

JORDAN

KUWAIT

SAUDI ARABIA

BAHRAIN

QATAR

YEMEN

OMAN

UNITED ARAB EMIRATES

Mediterranean Sea

AFRICA

Arabian Sea

Indian Ocean

CHINA

NORTH KOREA

SOUTH KOREA

JAPAN

East China Sea

Taiwan

Pacific Ocean

TROPIC OF CANCER

EQUATOR

NEPAL

BHUTAN

BANGLADESH

Mawsynram

INDIA

MYANMAR (BURMA)

LAOS

THAILAND

VIETNAM

CAMBODIA

Bay of Bengal

SRI LANKA

MALDIVES

South China Sea

PHILIPPINES

BRUNEI

MALAYSIA

SINGAPORE

INDONESIA

Java Sea

TIMOR-LESTE (EAST TIMOR)

AUSTRALIA

800 Miles

800 Kilometers

Two-point Equidistant Projection

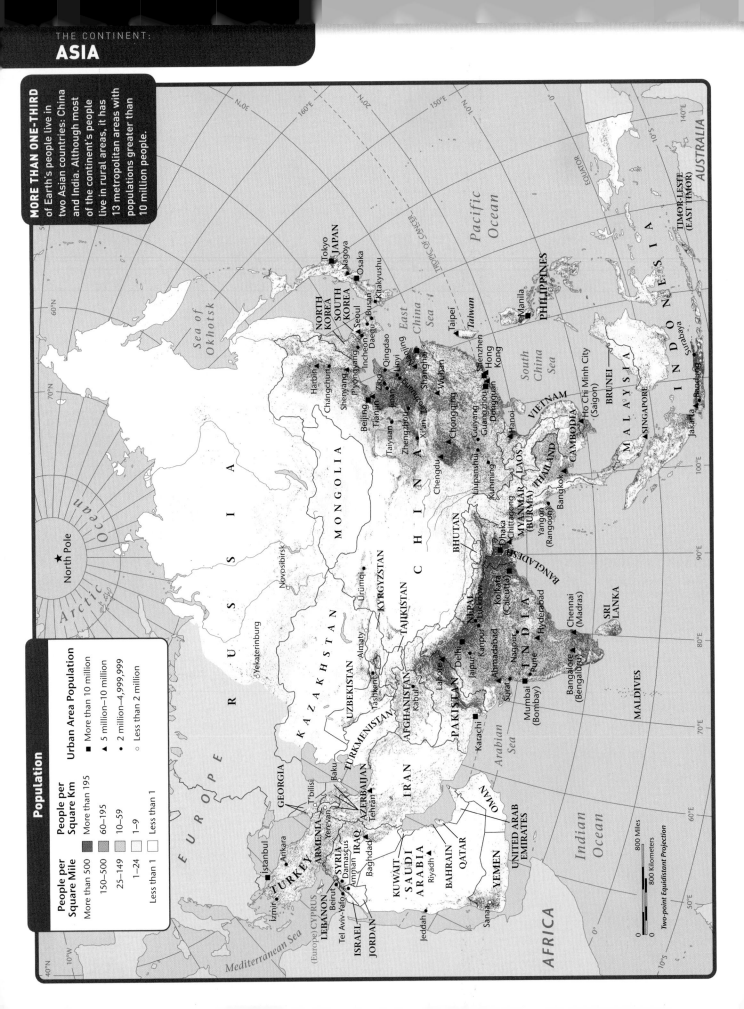

MORE THAN ONE-THIRD of Earth's people live in two Asian countries: China and India. Although most of the continent's people live in rural areas, it has 13 metropolitan areas with populations greater than 10 million people.

Population

People per Square Mile	People per Square Km
More than 500	More than 195
150–500	60–195
25–149	10–59
1–24	1–9
Less than 1	Less than 1

Urban Area Population
- ■ More than 10 million
- ▲ 5 million–10 million
- ● 2 million–4,999,999
- ○ Less than 2 million

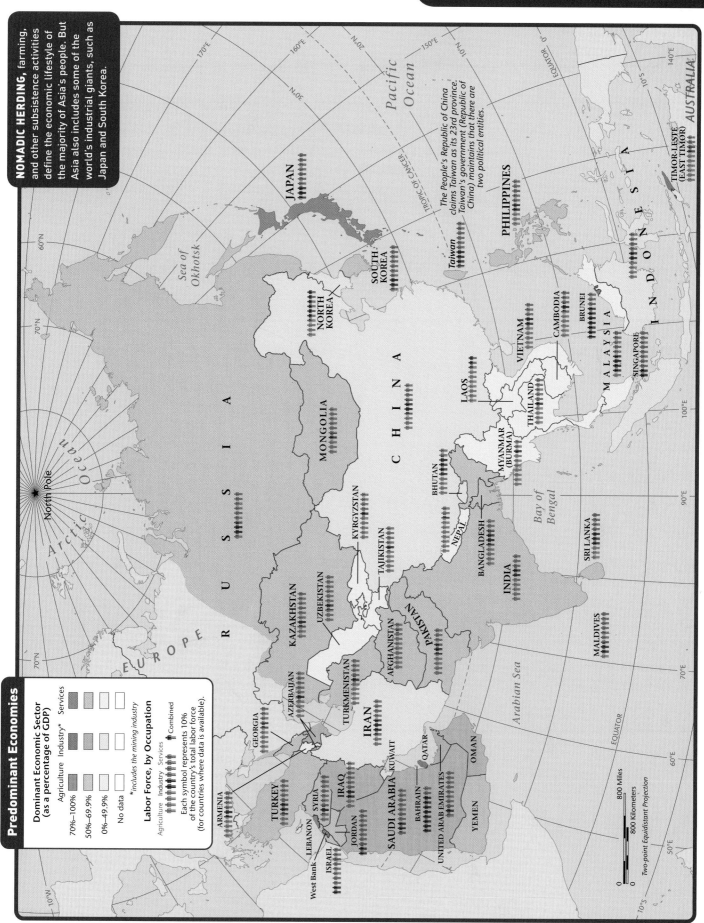

NOMADIC HERDING, farming, and other subsistence activities define the economic lifestyle of the majority of Asia's people. But Asia also includes some of the world's industrial giants, such as Japan and South Korea.

Predominant Economies

Dominant Economic Sector
(as a percentage of GDP)

Agriculture   Industry*   Services

70%–100%

50%–69.9%

0%–49.9%

No data

*includes the mining industry

Labor Force, by Occupation

Agriculture   Industry   Services   Combined

Each symbol represents 10%
of the country's total labor force
(for countries where data is available).

The People's Republic of China claims Taiwan as its 23rd province. Taiwan's government (Republic of China) maintains that there are two political entities.

Pacific Ocean

Arctic Ocean

North Pole

Sea of Okhotsk

EUROPE

R U S S I A

MONGOLIA

KAZAKHSTAN

UZBEKISTAN

KYRGYZSTAN

TAJIKISTAN

TURKMENISTAN

C H I N A

NORTH KOREA

SOUTH KOREA

JAPAN

Taiwan

PHILIPPINES

AFGHANISTAN

PAKISTAN

NEPAL

BHUTAN

INDIA

BANGLADESH

MYANMAR (BURMA)

LAOS

THAILAND

VIETNAM

CAMBODIA

BRUNEI

MALAYSIA

SINGAPORE

I N D O N E S I A

TIMOR-LESTE (EAST TIMOR)

AUSTRALIA

SRI LANKA

MALDIVES

Bay of Bengal

Arabian Sea

IRAN

IRAQ

SYRIA

TURKEY

GEORGIA

ARMENIA

AZERBAIJAN

LEBANON

West Bank

ISRAEL

JORDAN

SAUDI ARABIA

KUWAIT

BAHRAIN

QATAR

UNITED ARAB EMIRATES

OMAN

YEMEN

EQUATOR

TROPIC OF CANCER

800 Miles

800 Kilometers

Two-point Equidistant Projection

GLOBAL CONTAINER PORTS:

FACTS & FIGURES

Largest World Container Ports
(by volume – million tons; 2011 data)

Shanghai	590.4 MT
Singapore	531.2 FT
Tianjin	459.9 MT
Rotterdam	434.6 MT
Guangzhou	431.0 MT
Qingdao	372.0 MT
Ningbo	348.9 MT
Qinhuangdao	284.6 MT
Busan	281.5 RT

MT=Metric Ton; FT=Freight Ton; RT=Revenue Ton

Leading U.S. Waterborne Trade
Partners (exports by volume – metric
tons; 2012 data)

China	92,451,000
Japan	42,019,000
Mexico	38,962,000
Netherlands	28,514,000
Brazil	25,382,000
South Korea	23,514,000
Canada	22,092,000
Turkey	19,255,000
United Kingdom	16,772,000

Leading U.S. Waterborne Trade
Partners (imports by volume – metric
tons; 2012 data)

Saudi Arabia	69,519,000
Mexico	66,362,000
Venezuela	56,989,000
China	54,799,000
Canada	50,561,000
Russia	34,514,000
Brazil	31,660,000
Colombia	31,187,000

Largest Container Shipping Companies
(by world market share, 2013 data)

APM-Maersk (Denmark)	14.6%
Mediterranean Shipping Co. (Italy)	13.3%
CMA CGM (France)	8.5%
Evergreen Line (Taiwan)	4.8%
COSCO Container (China)	4.4%
Hapag-Lloyd (Germany)	4.1%
American Presidential Lines (USA)	3.6%
Hanjin Shipping (Korea/Germany)	3.5%
China Shipping Container Line	3.3%

East Asia Ports

Since the mid-20th century the world's economy has expanded to a truly global scale, made possible, in large part, by the growth of containerized shipping. The first container ship, a converted oil tanker, set sail from Newark, New Jersey, in 1956 carrying 58 containers. Today, almost 5,000 container vessels move manufactured goods cheaply and efficiently among ports around the world.

Container ships range in size up to 1,300 feet (396 m) long and 180 feet (55 m) wide—bigger than four football fields. The capacity of a container ship is measured in TEUs—a unit of measure equivalent to a 20-foot (6-m) standard container. A large container vessel can carry more than 10,000 20-foot containers, each loaded with as much as 100 tons (91 MT) of cargo. Container ports are equipped with giant cranes, more than 400 feet (122 m) tall and weighing as much as 2,000 tons (1,814 MT), that can move 30 to 40 containers on and off a ship each hour. With eight of the world's busiest container ports, containerized shipping has played an important role in Asia's economic boom.

WAIGAOQIAO TERMINAL, Shanghai Port's largest container terminal, appears as a colorful mosaic when viewed from above. Shanghai leads all container ports in tonnage handled, moving some 650 million tons (590 million MT) of goods and material each year.

SHIPPING CONTAINERS are stacked high above trucks moving through the busy port of Busan, which opened in 2004, 280 miles (450 km) southeast of Seoul, South Korea.

OLD MEETS NEW in the harbor of Ho Chi Minh City, Vietnam. Vendors steer their tradition sampan near a giant container vessel in this newly built Southeast Asian container port.

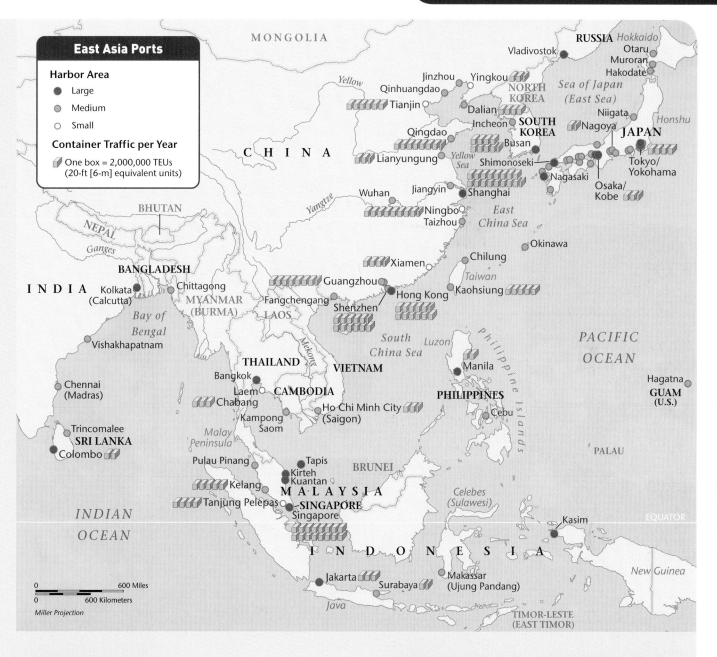

East Asia Ports

Harbor Area

- ● Large
- ● Medium
- ○ Small

Container Traffic per Year

▱ One box = 2,000,000 TEUs
(20-ft [6-m] equivalent units)

MONGOLIA

RUSSIA *Hokkaido*

Vladivostok

Otaru
Muroran
Hakodate

Jinzhou Yingkou

Qinhuangdao

NORTH
KOREA

*Sea of Japan
(East Sea)*

Niigata

Honshu

Tianjin

Dalian

Incheon SOUTH
KOREA

Nagoya JAPAN

Qingdao

Yellow

*Yellow
Sea*

Busan

Shimonoseki

Tokyo/
Yokohama

C H I N A

Lianyungung

Nagasaki

Osaka/
Kobe

Wuhan

Jiangyin

Shanghai

*East
China Sea*

BHUTAN

Yangtze

Ningbo

Taizhou

Okinawa

NEPAL

Ganges

Chilung

BANGLADESH

Xiamen

Taiwan

I N D I A Kolkata
(Calcutta)

Chittagong

MYANMAR
(BURMA)

Fangchengang

Guangzhou

Kaohsiung

Hong Kong

LAOS

Shenzhen

*Bay of
Bengal*

*South
China Sea*

Luzon

PACIFIC
OCEAN

Vishakhapatnam

Philippine Islands

Chennai
(Madras)

THAILAND

Bangkok

VIETNAM

Manila

Hagatna
GUAM
(U.S.)

Laem
Chabang

CAMBODIA

PHILIPPINES

Trincomalee
SRI LANKA

Kampong
Saom

Ho Chi Minh City
(Saigon)

Cebu

PALAU

Colombo

Pulau Pinang

Tapis
Kirteh
Kuantan

BRUNEI

*Celebes
(Sulawesi)*

Kelang

M A L A Y S I A

Kasim

EQUATOR

*INDIAN
OCEAN*

Tanjung Pelepas

SINGAPORE

Singapore

*Malay
Peninsula*

I N D O N E S I A

New Guinea

0   600 Miles
0   600 Kilometers

Miller Projection

Jakarta

Surabaya

Makassar
(Ujung Pandang)

Java

TIMOR-LESTE
(EAST TIMOR)

CONTAINER TRAFFIC

Cargo Volume, 2011
(million TEUs)

Port	TEUs
Shanghai, China	31.7
Singapore, Singapore	29.9
Hong Kong, China	24.4
Shenzhen, China	22.6
Busan, South Korea	16.2
Ningbo-Zhoushan, China	14.7
Guangzhou Harbor, China	14.3
Qingdao, China	13.0
Jebel Ali, Dubai, U.A.E.	13.0
Rotterdam, Netherlands	11.9

Asian ports dominate all others in container traffic. Shanghai alone handles more than 30 million TEUs (20-foot-/6-meter-equivalent units) of cargo each year.

◔ **CONTAINER CRANES** line this waterway in Hong Kong, one of the world's busiest international container ports.

Africa:
A View From Space

From space, Africa appears divided into three regions: the north, dominated by the Sahara, the largest hot desert in the world; a central green band of rain forests and tropical grasslands; and more dry land to the south. Africa may actually be dividing: the Great Rift Valley, running from the Red Sea through the volcanic Afar Triangle to the southern lake district, may split apart the continent.

PHYSICAL			POLITICAL		
Land area 11,608,000 sq mi (30,065,000 sq km)	Lowest point Lake Assai, Djibouti -512 ft (-156 m)	Largest lake Victoria 26,800 sq mi (69,500 sq km)	Population 1,099,579,000 Number of independent countries 54	Largest country Algeria 919,595 sq mi (2,381,741 sq km)	Most populous country Nigeria Pop. 173,615,000
Highest point Kilimanjaro, Tanzania 19,340 ft (5,895 m)	Longest river Nile 4,160 mi (6,695 km)			Smallest country Seychelles 176 sq mi (455 sq km)	Least populous country Seychelles Pop. 93,000

Africa

An elephant and calf walk in Amboseli National Park, Kenya.

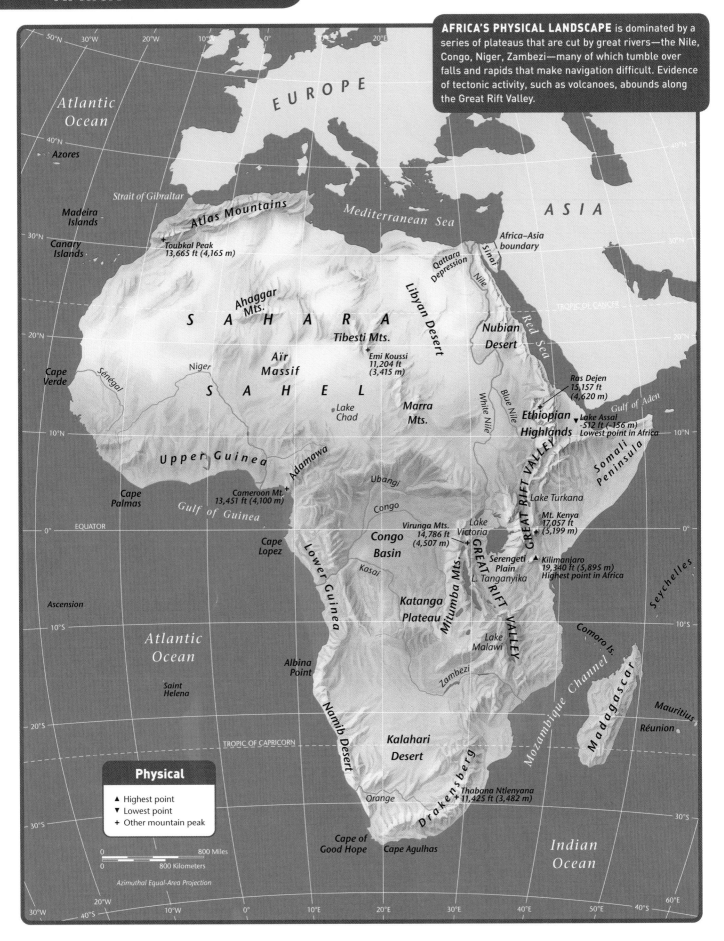

AFRICA'S PHYSICAL LANDSCAPE is dominated by a series of plateaus that are cut by great rivers—the Nile, Congo, Niger, Zambezi—many of which tumble over falls and rapids that make navigation difficult. Evidence of tectonic activity, such as volcanoes, abounds along the Great Rift Valley.

EUROPE

ASIA

Atlantic
Ocean

Azores

Madeira
Islands

Canary
Islands

Strait of Gibraltar

Atlas Mountains

Toubkal Peak
13,665 ft (4,165 m)

Mediterranean Sea

Africa–Asia
boundary

Sinai

Qattara
Depression

Nile

Red Sea

TROPIC OF CANCER

Ahaggar
Mts.

S A H A R A

Libyan Desert

Nubian
Desert

Tibesti Mts.

Emi Koussi
11,204 ft
(3,415 m)

Aïr
Massif

S A H E L

Cape
Verde

Sénégal

Niger

Lake
Chad

Marra
Mts.

White Nile

Blue Nile

Ras Dejen
15,157 ft
(4,620 m)

Gulf of Aden

Ethiopian
Highlands

Lake Assal
-512 ft (-156 m)
Lowest point in Africa

Upper Guinea

Adamawa

Cameroon Mt.
13,451 ft (4,100 m)

Cape
Palmas

Gulf of Guinea

Ubangi

Congo

Somali
Peninsula

Lake Turkana

Mt. Kenya
17,057 ft
(5,199 m)

EQUATOR

Cape
Lopez

Virunga Mts.
14,786 ft
(4,507 m)

Lake
Victoria

GREAT RIFT VALLEY

Seychelles

Congo
Basin

Kasai

Serengeti
Plain
L. Tanganyika

Kilimanjaro
19,340 ft (5,895 m)
Highest point in Africa

Lower Guinea

Ascension

Mitumba Mts.

GREAT RIFT VALLEY

Comoro Is.

Atlantic
Ocean

Katanga
Plateau

Lake
Malawi

Saint
Helena

Albina
Point

Zambezi

Madagascar

Mauritius

Namib Desert

Mozambique Channel

Réunion

TROPIC OF CAPRICORN

Kalahari
Desert

Drakensberg

Indian
Ocean

Orange

Thabana Ntlenyana
11,425 ft (3,482 m)

Cape of
Good Hope

Cape Agulhas

Physical

▲ Highest point
▼ Lowest point
+ Other mountain peak

0   800 Miles
0   800 Kilometers

Azimuthal Equal-Area Projection

BOUNDARIES DRAWN by colonial powers at the 1884 Berlin Conference cut across culture and language divisions. These imposed borders contribute to much of the turmoil that has plagued African countries as they have moved from the colonial era to independence.

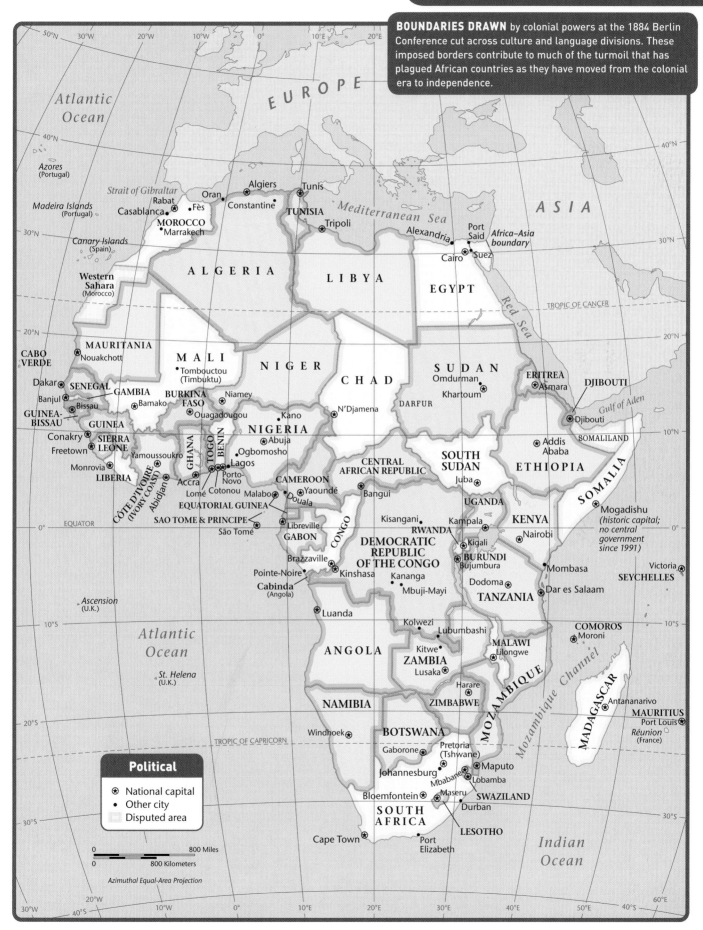

EUROPE

ASIA

Atlantic Ocean

Azores
(Portugal)

Madeira Islands
(Portugal)

Strait of Gibraltar

Canary Islands
(Spain)

Western Sahara
(Morocco)

CABO VERDE

Algiers
Tunis
Oran
Constantine
Rabat
Casablanca
Fès
Marrakech
MOROCCO

TUNISIA
Tripoli

Mediterranean Sea

Alexandria
Port Said
Cairo
Suez

Africa–Asia boundary

ALGERIA
LIBYA
EGYPT

Red Sea

TROPIC OF CANCER

MAURITANIA
Nouakchott

MALI
Tombouctou
(Timbuktu)

NIGER

CHAD

SUDAN
Omdurman
Khartoum

DARFUR

ERITREA
Asmara

DJIBOUTI
Djibouti

Gulf of Aden

Dakar
Banjul
Bissau
SENEGAL
GAMBIA
GUINEA-BISSAU
Conakry
Freetown
SIERRA LEONE
Monrovia
LIBERIA

BURKINA FASO
Niamey
Bamako
Ouagadougou

Kano
NIGERIA
Abuja
Ogbomosho
Lagos
Porto-Novo
Cotonou
Lomé
Accra
GHANA
TOGO
BENIN
Yamoussoukro
Abidjan
CÔTE D'IVOIRE
(IVORY COAST)

N'Djamena

CENTRAL AFRICAN REPUBLIC
Bangui

CAMEROON
Yaoundé
Douala
Malabo

SOUTH SUDAN
Juba

SOMALILAND

ETHIOPIA
Addis Ababa

SOMALIA

Mogadishu
(historic capital; no central government since 1991)

EQUATORIAL GUINEA
SAO TOME & PRINCIPE
São Tomé
Libreville
GABON
CONGO
Brazzaville
Pointe-Noire
Cabinda
(Angola)

EQUATOR

Kisangani
DEMOCRATIC REPUBLIC OF THE CONGO
Kinshasa
Kananga
Mbuji-Mayi

RWANDA
Kigali
BURUNDI
Bujumbura

UGANDA
Kampala

KENYA
Nairobi
Mombasa

SEYCHELLES
Victoria

Dodoma
TANZANIA
Dar es Salaam

Luanda

Kolwezi
Lubumbashi
Kitwe
ANGOLA
ZAMBIA
Lusaka

MALAWI
Lilongwe

COMOROS
Moroni

Atlantic Ocean

Ascension
(U.K.)

St. Helena
(U.K.)

NAMIBIA
Windhoek

Harare
ZIMBABWE

MOZAMBIQUE

Mozambique Channel

MADAGASCAR
Antananarivo

MAURITIUS
Port Louis
Réunion
(France)

TROPIC OF CAPRICORN

BOTSWANA
Gaborone
Pretoria
(Tshwane)
Johannesburg
Mbabane
Maputo
Lobamba
Maseru
SWAZILAND
Durban
LESOTHO

Bloemfontein
SOUTH AFRICA
Cape Town
Port Elizabeth

Indian Ocean

Political
⊛ National capital
• Other city
▢ Disputed area

0   800 Miles
0   800 Kilometers

Azimuthal Equal-Area Projection

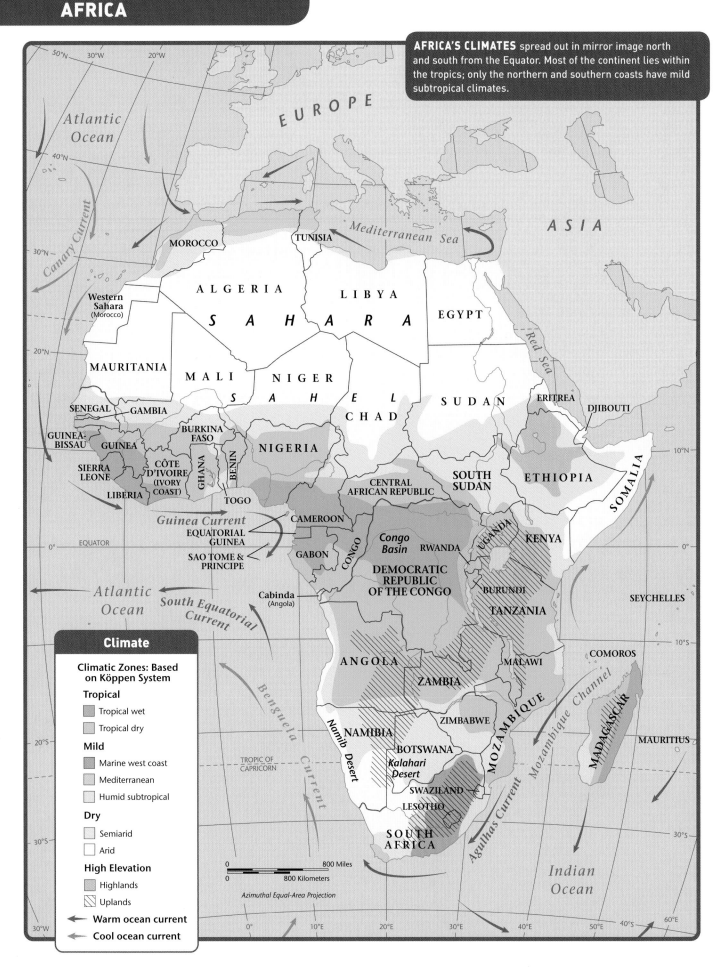

AFRICA'S CLIMATES spread out in mirror image north and south from the Equator. Most of the continent lies within the tropics; only the northern and southern coasts have mild subtropical climates.

Climate

Climatic Zones: Based on Köppen System

Tropical
- Tropical wet
- Tropical dry

Mild
- Marine west coast
- Mediterranean
- Humid subtropical

Dry
- Semiarid
- Arid

High Elevation
- Highlands
- Uplands

← Warm ocean current
← Cool ocean current

Azimuthal Equal-Area Projection

0   800 Miles
0   800 Kilometers

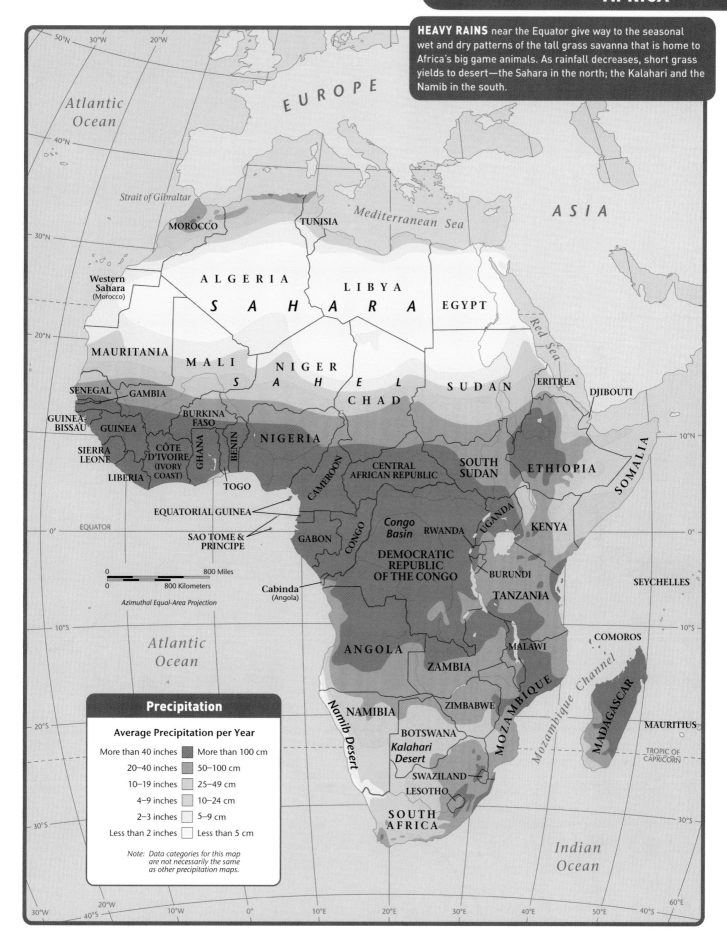

HEAVY RAINS near the Equator give way to the seasonal wet and dry patterns of the tall grass savanna that is home to Africa's big game animals. As rainfall decreases, short grass yields to desert—the Sahara in the north; the Kalahari and the Namib in the south.

Atlantic Ocean

EUROPE

Strait of Gibraltar

Mediterranean Sea

ASIA

MOROCCO

TUNISIA

Western Sahara (Morocco)

ALGERIA

LIBYA

EGYPT

SAHARA

Red Sea

MAURITANIA

MALI

NIGER

SUDAN

ERITREA

SAHEL

DJIBOUTI

SENEGAL

GAMBIA

CHAD

GUINEA-BISSAU

GUINEA

BURKINA FASO

NIGERIA

SOUTH SUDAN

ETHIOPIA

SIERRA LEONE

CÔTE D'IVOIRE (IVORY COAST)

GHANA

BENIN

CAMEROON

CENTRAL AFRICAN REPUBLIC

SOMALIA

LIBERIA

TOGO

EQUATORIAL GUINEA

GABON

CONGO

Congo Basin

RWANDA

UGANDA

KENYA

SAO TOME & PRINCIPE

EQUATOR

DEMOCRATIC REPUBLIC OF THE CONGO

BURUNDI

SEYCHELLES

Cabinda (Angola)

TANZANIA

COMOROS

Atlantic Ocean

ANGOLA

MALAWI

MADAGASCAR

ZAMBIA

MAURITIUS

Namib Desert

NAMIBIA

ZIMBABWE

MOZAMBIQUE

Mozambique Channel

TROPIC OF CAPRICORN

BOTSWANA

Kalahari Desert

SWAZILAND

LESOTHO

SOUTH AFRICA

Indian Ocean

0   800 Miles
0   800 Kilometers

Azimuthal Equal-Area Projection

Precipitation

Average Precipitation per Year

More than 40 inches	More than 100 cm
20–40 inches	50–100 cm
10–19 inches	25–49 cm
4–9 inches	10–24 cm
2–3 inches	5–9 cm
Less than 2 inches	Less than 5 cm

Note: Data categories for this map are not necessarily the same as other precipitation maps.

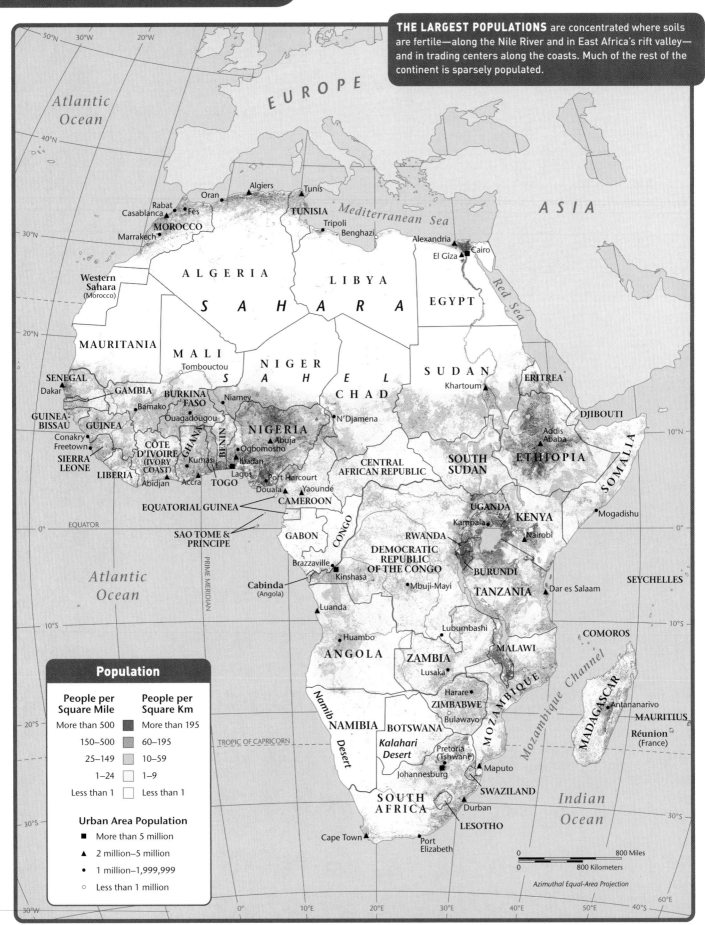

THE LARGEST POPULATIONS are concentrated where soils are fertile—along the Nile River and in East Africa's rift valley—and in trading centers along the coasts. Much of the rest of the continent is sparsely populated.

Atlantic Ocean

EUROPE

Mediterranean Sea

ASIA

Algiers Tunis
Oran
Rabat **TUNISIA**
Casablanca Fes
MOROCCO Tripoli
Marrakech Benghazi
Alexandria
El Giza Cairo

Western
Sahara
(Morocco)
A L G E R I A   L I B Y A   *Red Sea*
E G Y P T

S A H A R A

MAURITANIA
M A L I   N I G E R   S U D A N   **ERITREA**
Tombouctou S   A   H   E   L   Khartoum
SENEGAL CHAD **DJIBOUTI**
Dakar **GAMBIA** **BURKINA** Niamey
FASO N'Djamena Addis
Bamako Ababa
GUINEA- Ouagadougou **ETHIOPIA**
BISSAU **GUINEA** **NIGERIA** Abuja
Conakry Ogbomosho **CENTRAL** **SOUTH** **SOMALIA**
Freetown Kumasi Ibadan **AFRICAN REPUBLIC** **SUDAN**
SIERRA Lagos **UGANDA**
LEONE **LIBERIA** Accra Port Harcourt Mogadishu
Abidjan **TOGO** Douala Yaoundé **KENYA**
EQUATORIAL GUINEA **CAMEROON** Kampala
Nairobi
SAO TOME & **GABON** **RWANDA** **SEYCHELLES**
PRINCIPE **DEMOCRATIC**
EQUATOR **REPUBLIC** **BURUNDI**
OF THE CONGO Dar es Salaam
Atlantic Brazzaville **TANZANIA**
Ocean Kinshasa
Cabinda Mbuji-Mayi
(Angola) Lubumbashi **COMOROS**
Luanda
Huambo **MALAWI**
ANGOLA **ZAMBIA** Antananarivo
Lusaka **MADAGASCAR** **MAURITIUS**
Harare Réunion
ZIMBABWE (France)
Bulawayo
NAMIBIA **BOTSWANA**
Kalahari
Desert Pretoria
(Tshwane) Maputo
Johannesburg **SWAZILAND**
Durban
SOUTH **LESOTHO** *Indian*
AFRICA *Ocean*
Cape Town Port
Elizabeth

Namib Desert

Mozambique Channel

PRIME MERIDIAN

CONGO

MOZAMBIQUE

TROPIC OF CAPRICORN

Population

People per Square Mile	**People per Square Km**
More than 500	More than 195
150–500	60–195
25–149	10–59
1–24	1–9
Less than 1	Less than 1

Urban Area Population
■ More than 5 million
▲ 2 million–5 million
● 1 million–1,999,999
○ Less than 1 million

0   800 Miles
0   800 Kilometers

Azimuthal Equal-Area Projection

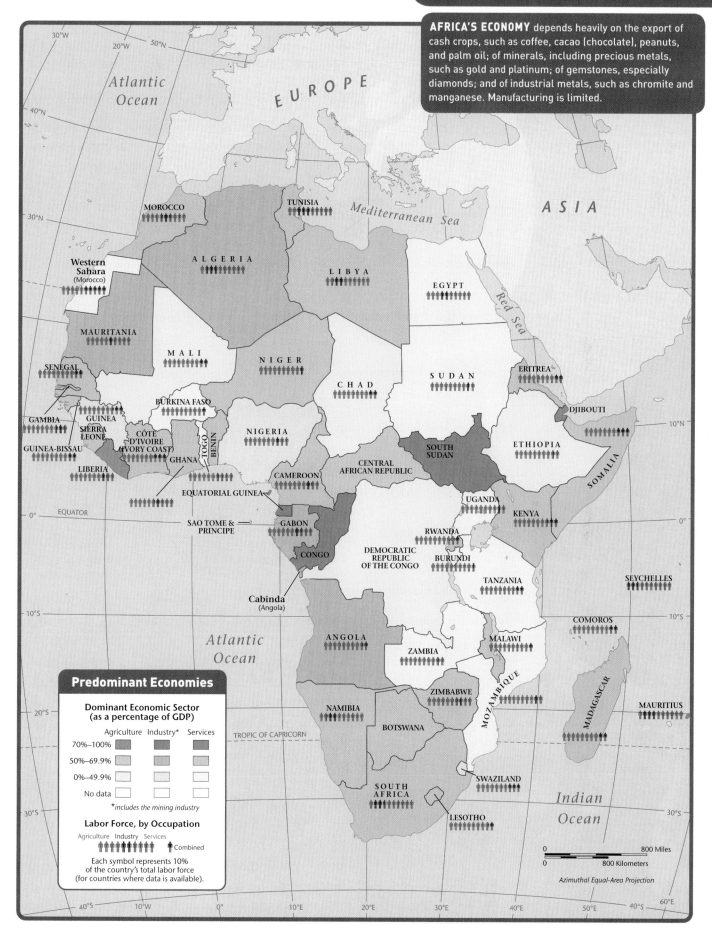

AFRICA'S ECONOMY depends heavily on the export of cash crops, such as coffee, cacao (chocolate), peanuts, and palm oil; of minerals, including precious metals, such as gold and platinum; of gemstones, especially diamonds; and of industrial metals, such as chromite and manganese. Manufacturing is limited.

Predominant Economies

**Dominant Economic Sector
(as a percentage of GDP)**

	Agriculture	Industry*	Services
70%–100%			
50%–69.9%			
0%–49.9%			
No data			

*includes the mining industry

Labor Force, by Occupation

Agriculture Industry Services   Combined

Each symbol represents 10% of the country's total labor force (for countries where data is available).

Azimuthal Equal-Area Projection

0   800 Miles
0   800 Kilometers

PROTECTED AREAS:

FACTS & FIGURES

Annual forest loss (2000–2010):
Global: 32,123,700 acres (13 million ha)
Africa: 8,401,583 acres (3.4 million ha)

Main causes: subsistence and commercial agriculture, logging, fuelwood collection

Highest annual rate of loss (2005–2010):

Togo	5.75%
Nigeria	4.00%
Uganda	2.72%
Ghana	2.19%

Threatened species (2013):

Mammals	739
Birds	744
Reptiles	355
Fish	1,906
Plants	2,474

Selected species at risk:
African elephants, black rhinoceros, eastern chimpanzees, gazelles, hippopotamus, lemurs, mountain gorillas, mountain zebras

Land protected in Africa (2010):
1,086,186 square miles (2,813,208 sq km)

Land protected in North Africa (2010): 4.0%

Land protected in Sub-Saharan Africa (2010):
11.8%

Countries with highest percent of land protected (2010):

Zambia	36.04%
Botswana	30.93%
Zimbabwe	28.01%
Tanzania	27.53%

Protected Areas

Africa is home to many different animals. Some are familiar, such as the giraffe and rhinoceros; others are rare. All are part of Earth's valuable storehouse of biodiversity, but many are at risk due to a variety of pressures. Natural changes, such as periodic drought, may put stress on both plant and animal populations, but human activity is the main threat. Africa's human population is growing on average at a rate of 2.6 percent each year. Converting land for agricultural use, hunting animals for food, and cutting trees for fuel, as well as expanding commercial logging and building roads, have led to loss of natural habitat for many of Africa's animals. Some, such as the mountain gorilla, are even at risk of extinction.

To reverse this trend of biodiversity loss, many countries have created protected areas (see map at right), which include nature reserves, wilderness areas, and national parks. Protected areas allow animals to live in a natural environment. They also provide a source of income for African countries, many of which are very poor, as tourists come on photo safaris to view these unique animals.

ENDANGERED. A silverback mountain gorilla in Rwanda watches intently. Native to the Virunga Mountains of central Africa, fewer than 700 mountain gorillas remain in the wild.

STANDING TALL. At an average height of more than 18 feet (5.7 m), giraffes are the world's tallest mammal. This giraffe stands on the grassy plain of Kenya's Masai Mara.

BIODIVERSITY THREATENED

Madagascar	869
Tanzania	724
Cameroon	636
South Africa	454
Kenya	358
Dem. Rep. of the Congo	311

2013 data

Madagascar, an island country off the southeast coast, leads all countries in Africa in number of species that are critically endangered, endangered, or vulnerable.

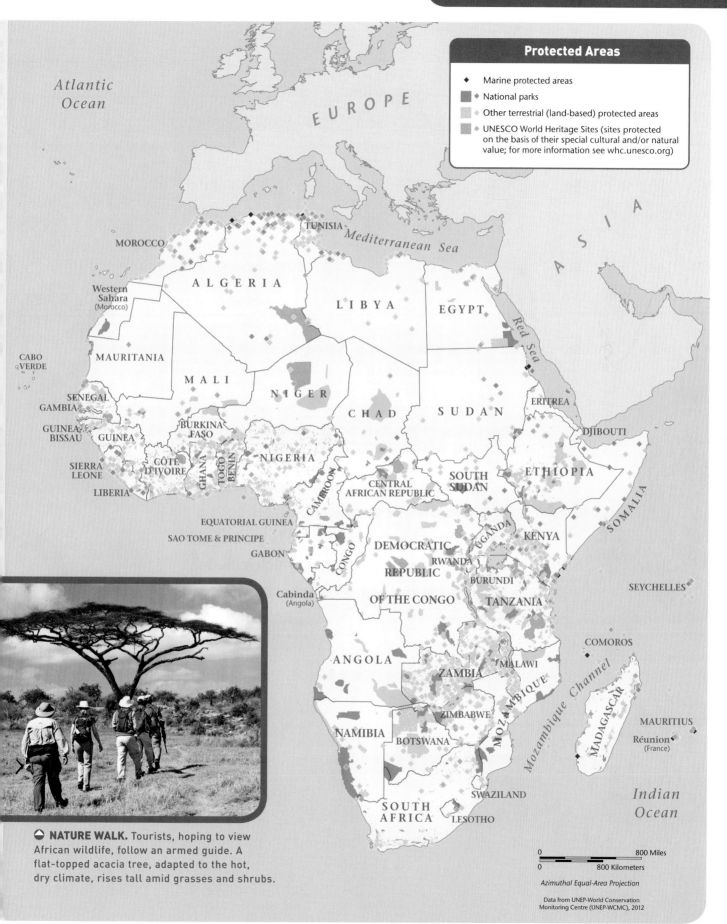

Protected Areas

- ◆ Marine protected areas
- ◆ National parks
- Other terrestrial (land-based) protected areas
- UNESCO World Heritage Sites (sites protected on the basis of their special cultural and/or natural value; for more information see whc.unesco.org)

Atlantic
Ocean

EUROPE

ASIA

Mediterranean Sea

MOROCCO

TUNISIA

Western
Sahara
(Morocco)

ALGERIA

LIBYA

EGYPT

Red Sea

CABO
VERDE

MAURITANIA

MALI

NIGER

CHAD

SUDAN

ERITREA

SENEGAL

GAMBIA

BURKINA
FASO

DJIBOUTI

GUINEA-
BISSAU

GUINEA

SIERRA
LEONE

CÔTE
D'IVOIRE

GHANA
TOGO
BENIN

NIGERIA

CENTRAL
AFRICAN REPUBLIC

SOUTH
SUDAN

ETHIOPIA

LIBERIA

CAMEROON

EQUATORIAL GUINEA

SAO TOME & PRINCIPE

GABON

CONGO

DEMOCRATIC

REPUBLIC

OF THE CONGO

UGANDA

RWANDA

BURUNDI

KENYA

SOMALIA

SEYCHELLES

Cabinda
(Angola)

TANZANIA

COMOROS

ANGOLA

MALAWI

ZAMBIA

MOZAMBIQUE

Mozambique Channel

MADAGASCAR

MAURITIUS

Réunion
(France)

ZIMBABWE

NAMIBIA

BOTSWANA

Indian
Ocean

SWAZILAND

SOUTH
AFRICA

LESOTHO

◇ **NATURE WALK.** Tourists, hoping to view African wildlife, follow an armed guide. A flat-topped acacia tree, adapted to the hot, dry climate, rises tall amid grasses and shrubs.

0   800 Miles
0   800 Kilometers

Azimuthal Equal-Area Projection

Data from UNEP-World Conservation
Monitoring Centre (UNEP-WCMC), 2012

Australia:
A View From Sp

S m
A

the g   s
New Zealand, the
Guinea, and hundreds of smaller islands
scattered across the Pacific Ocean. Although
Hawaiʻi is politically part of the United States,
geographically and culturally it is part
of Oceania.

The opera house in Sydney, Australia

Australia
& Oceania

PHYSICAL			POLITICAL		
Area and population totals are for the independent countries in the region only.	Highest point **Mount Wilhelm, Papua New Guinea** 14,793 ft (4,509 m)	Longest river **Murray-Darling, Australia** 2,310 mi (3,718 km)	Population 37,916,000	Largest country **Australia** 2,970,000 sq mi (7,692,000 sq km)	Most populous country **Australia** Pop. 23,106,000
Land area **3,278,062 sq mi (8,490,180 sq km)**	Lowest point **Lake Eyre, Australia** -52 ft (-16 m)	Largest lake **Lake Eyre, Australia** 3,430 sq mi (8,884 sq km)	Number of independent countries 14	Smallest country **Nauru** 8 sq mi (21 sq km)	Least populous country **Nauru** Pop. 11,000

THE REGION:
AUSTRALIA & OCEANIA

PHYSICAL CONTRASTS mark Oceania. Flat, arid land dominates most of Australia. Rain forest covers eastern New Guinea, and the snow-covered Southern Alps soar above New Zealand's South Island. Most of the remaining islands in this region are coral atolls or, like the Hawaiian Islands, are volcanic in origin.

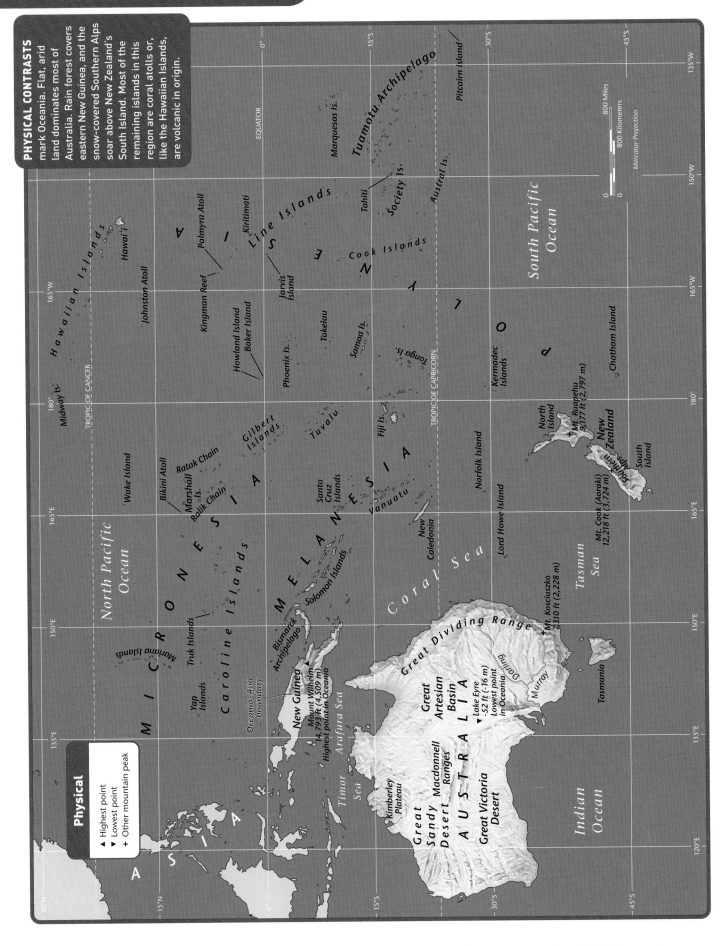

EQUATOR

800 Miles

800 Kilometers

Mercator Projection

Pitcairn Island

Tuamotu Archipelago

Marquesas Is.

Tahiti

Society Is.

Austral Is.

Line Islands

Kiritimati

Palmyra Atoll

Hawai'i

Hawaiian Islands

Johnston Atoll

Cook Islands

Kingman Reef

Jarvis Island

South Pacific Ocean

Howland Island

Baker Island

Phoenix Is.

Tokelau

Samoa Is.

Tonga Is.

Chatham Island

TROPIC OF CANCER

Midway Is.

180°

TROPIC OF CAPRICORN

Kermadec Islands

North Island

Mt. Ruapehu 9,177 ft (2,797 m)

New Zealand

Southern Alps

South Island

Gilbert Islands

Tuvalu

Fiji Is.

Norfolk Island

Mt. Cook (Aoraki) 12,218 ft (3,724 m) Lowest point in Oceania

Wake Island

Bikini Atoll

Ratak Chain

Marshall Is.

Ralik Chain

MICRONESIA

MELANESIA

Santa Cruz Islands

Vanuatu

New Caledonia

Lord Howe Island

Tasman Sea

North Pacific Ocean

Caroline Islands

Truk Islands

Mariana Islands

Yap Islands

Oceania-Asia boundary

Bismarck Archipelago

Solomon Islands

Coral Sea

Mt. Kosciuszko 7,310 ft (2,228 m)

Great Dividing Range

New Guinea

Mount Wilhelm 14,793 ft (4,509 m) Highest point in Oceania

Timor Sea

Arafura Sea

Great Artesian Basin

Lake Eyre -52 ft (-16 m) Lowest point in Oceania

Darling

Murray

Tasmania

Kimberley Plateau

Macdonnell Ranges

AUSTRALIA

Great Sandy Desert

Great Victoria Desert

Indian Ocean

A S I A

135°E

150°E

165°E

180°

165°W

150°W

135°W

30°N

15°N

0°

15°S

30°S

45°S

120°E

Physical

◄ Highest point

▶ Lowest point

+ Other mountain peak

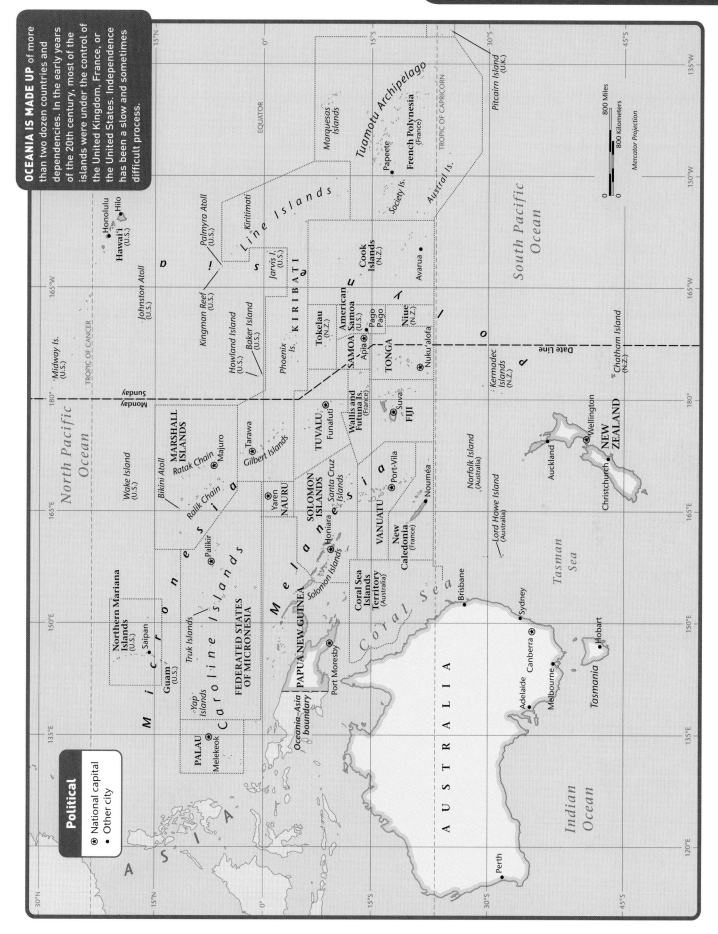

Marquesas Islands

Tuamotu Archipelago

Papeete
French Polynesia (France)

Society Is.

Austral Is.

TROPIC OF CAPRICORN

Pitcairn Island (U.K.)

South Pacific Ocean

800 Miles
800 Kilometers
Mercator Projection

EQUATOR

Honolulu
Hilo
Hawai'i (U.S.)

Johnston Atoll (U.S.)

Palmyra Atoll (U.S.)

Line Islands

Kiritimati

Kingman Reef (U.S.)

Jarvis I. (U.S.)

KIRIBATI

Cook Islands (N.Z.)

Avarua

North Pacific Ocean

Midway Is. (U.S.)

TROPIC OF CANCER

Howland Island (U.S.)

Baker Island (U.S.)

Phoenix Is.

Tokelau (N.Z.)

American Samoa (U.S.)

Niue (N.Z.)

Pago Pago

Nuku'alofa

Date Line

Chatham Island (N.Z.)

Sunday
Monday

SAMOA
Apia

TONGA

Kermadec Islands (N.Z.)

Wake Island (U.S.)

Bikini Atoll

MARSHALL ISLANDS

Ratak Chain

Majuro

Tarawa

Gilbert Islands

TUVALU
Funafuti

Wallis and Futuna Is. (France)

Suva
FIJI

NEW ZEALAND
Wellington

Ralik Chain

Micronesia

Yaren
NAURU

Palikir

SOLOMON ISLANDS

Santa Cruz Islands

Port-Vila
VANUATU

Nouméa
New Caledonia (France)

Norfolk Island (Australia)

Auckland

Christchurch

Tasman Sea

Melanesia

Honiara

Solomon Islands

Lord Howe Island (Australia)

Northern Mariana Islands (U.S.)

Saipan

Truk Islands

FEDERATED STATES OF MICRONESIA

PAPUA NEW GUINEA

Coral Sea Islands Territory (Australia)

Coral Sea

Brisbane

Sydney

Hobart

Guam (U.S.)

Yap Islands

Caroline Islands

Port Moresby

Canberra

Adelaide

Melbourne

Tasmania

PALAU
Melekeok

Oceania-Asia boundary

A S I A

Political

⊕ National capital
• Other city

A U S T R A L I A

Indian Ocean

Perth

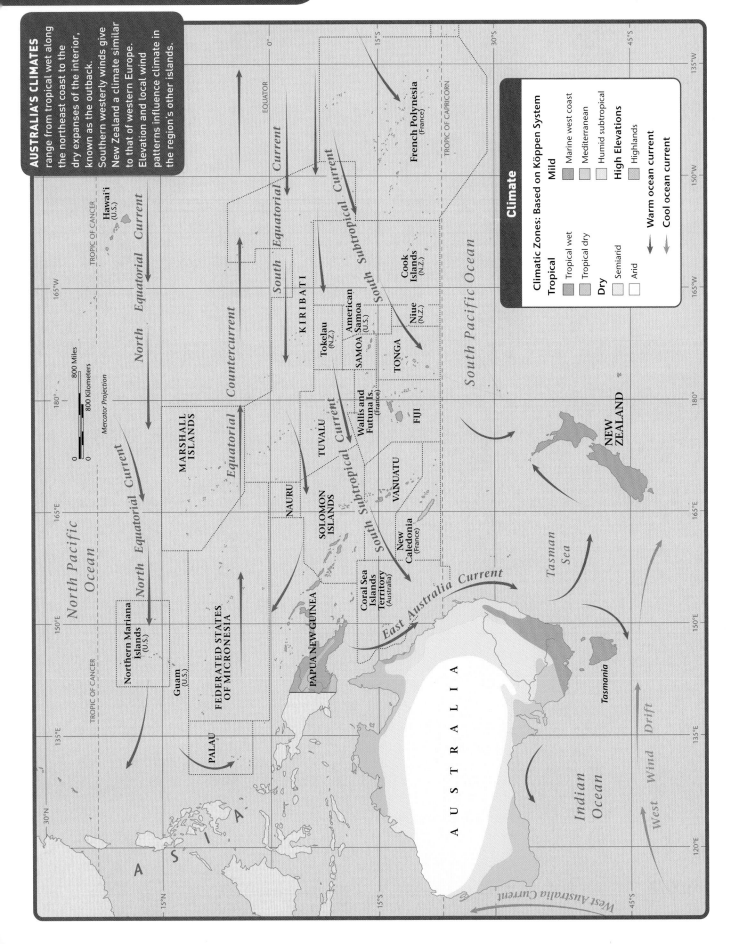

Climate

Climatic Zones: Based on Köppen System

Tropical
- Tropical wet
- Tropical dry

Dry
- Semiarid
- Arid

Mild
- Marine west coast
- Mediterranean
- Humid subtropical

High Elevations
- Highlands

→ Warm ocean current
→ Cool ocean current

800 Miles
800 Kilometers

Mercator Projection

North Pacific Ocean

North Equatorial Current

North Equatorial Current

Equatorial Countercurrent

South Equatorial Current

South Subtropical Current

Equatorial Current

South Subtropical Current

South Pacific Ocean

East Australia Current

Tasman Sea

West Wind Drift

West Wind Drift

West Australia Current

Indian Ocean

EQUATOR

TROPIC OF CANCER

TROPIC OF CAPRICORN

TROPIC OF CANCER

AUSTRALIA

Tasmania

NEW ZEALAND

PAPUA NEW GUINEA

SOLOMON ISLANDS

NAURU

MARSHALL ISLANDS

FEDERATED STATES OF MICRONESIA

PALAU

Guam (U.S.)

Northern Mariana Islands (U.S.)

Hawai'i (U.S.)

KIRIBATI

TUVALU

Tokelau (N.Z.)

SAMOA

American Samoa (U.S.)

Wallis and Futuna Is. (France)

FIJI

TONGA

Niue (N.Z.)

Cook Islands (N.Z.)

French Polynesia (France)

VANUATU

New Caledonia (France)

Coral Sea Islands Territory (Australia)

A S I A

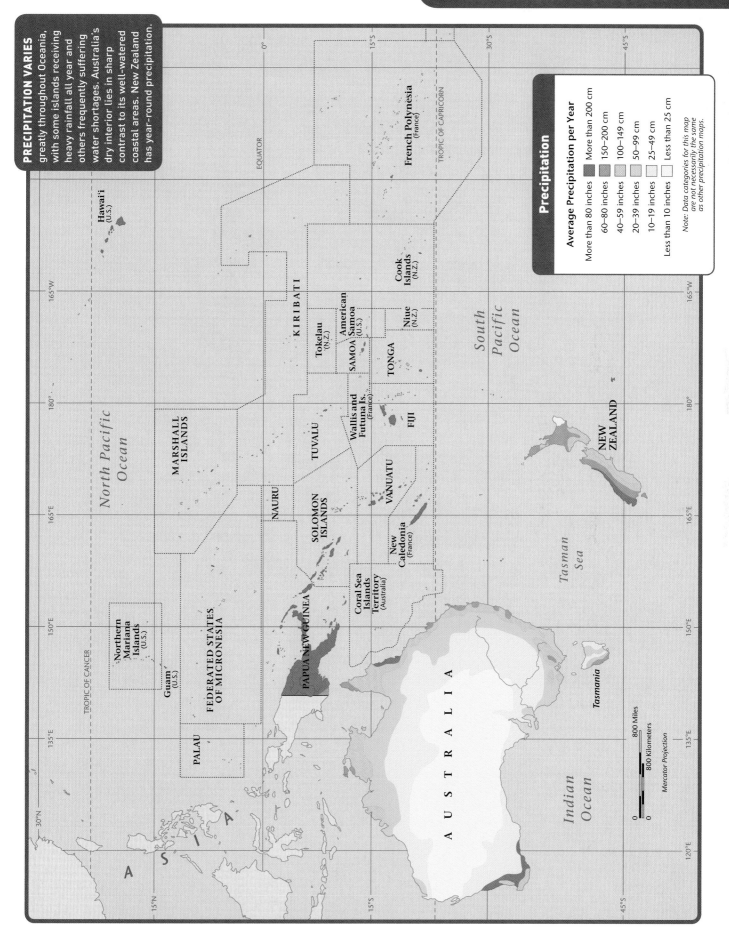

Precipitation

Average Precipitation per Year

More than 80 inches — More than 200 cm
60–80 inches — 150–200 cm
40–59 inches — 100–149 cm
20–39 inches — 50–99 cm
10–19 inches — 25–49 cm
Less than 10 inches — Less than 25 cm

Note: Data categories for this map are not necessarily the same as other precipitation maps.

Hawai'i (U.S.)

EQUATOR

French Polynesia (France)

TROPIC OF CAPRICORN

North Pacific Ocean

Cook Islands (N.Z.)

KIRIBATI

Tokelau (N.Z.)

American Samoa (U.S.)

SAMOA

Niue (N.Z.)

TONGA

South Pacific Ocean

MARSHALL ISLANDS

Wallis and Futuna Is. (France)

FIJI

TUVALU

NAURU

VANUATU

NEW ZEALAND

SOLOMON ISLANDS

New Caledonia (France)

Tasman Sea

Coral Sea Islands Territory (Australia)

Northern Mariana Islands (U.S.)

Guam (U.S.)

FEDERATED STATES OF MICRONESIA

PAPUA NEW GUINEA

TROPIC OF CANCER

Tasmania

PALAU

AUSTRALIA

Indian Ocean

ASIA

800 Miles
800 Kilometers
Mercator Projection

THE REGION:
AUSTRALIA & OCEANIA

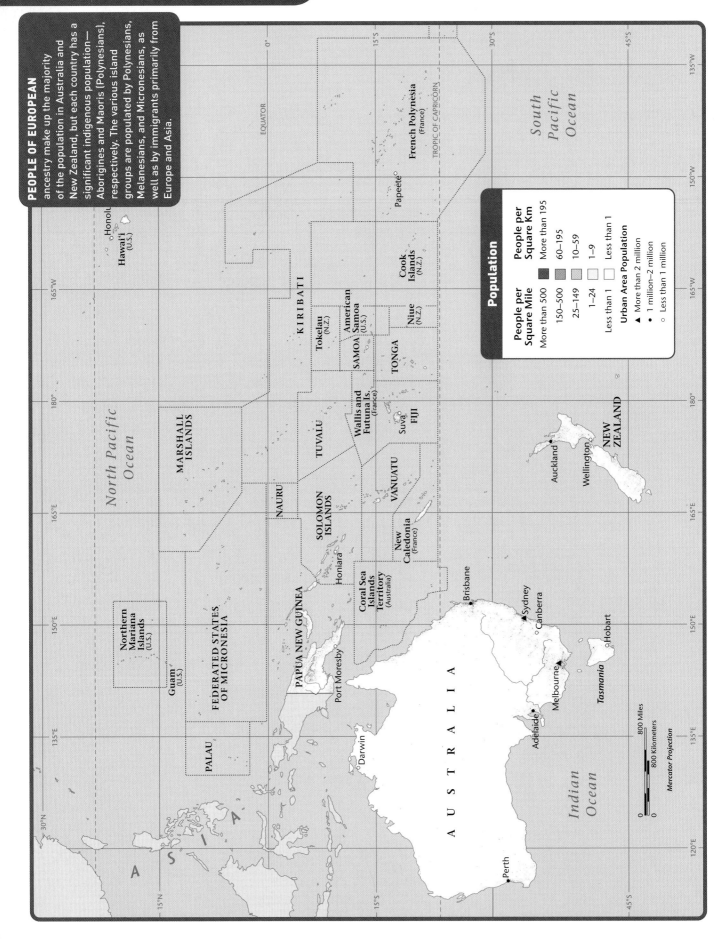

PEOPLE OF EUROPEAN ancestry make up the majority of the population in Australia and New Zealand, but each country has a significant indigenous population—Aborigines and Maoris (Polynesians), respectively. The various island groups are populated by Polynesians, Melanesians, and Micronesians, as well as by immigrants primarily from Europe and Asia.

Population

People per Square Mile	People per Square Km
More than 500	More than 195
150–500	60–195
25–149	10–59
1–24	1–9
Less than 1	Less than 1

Urban Area Population
- ▲ More than 2 million
- ● 1 million–2 million
- ○ Less than 1 million

North Pacific Ocean

South Pacific Ocean

Indian Ocean

Mercator Projection

800 Miles
800 Kilometers

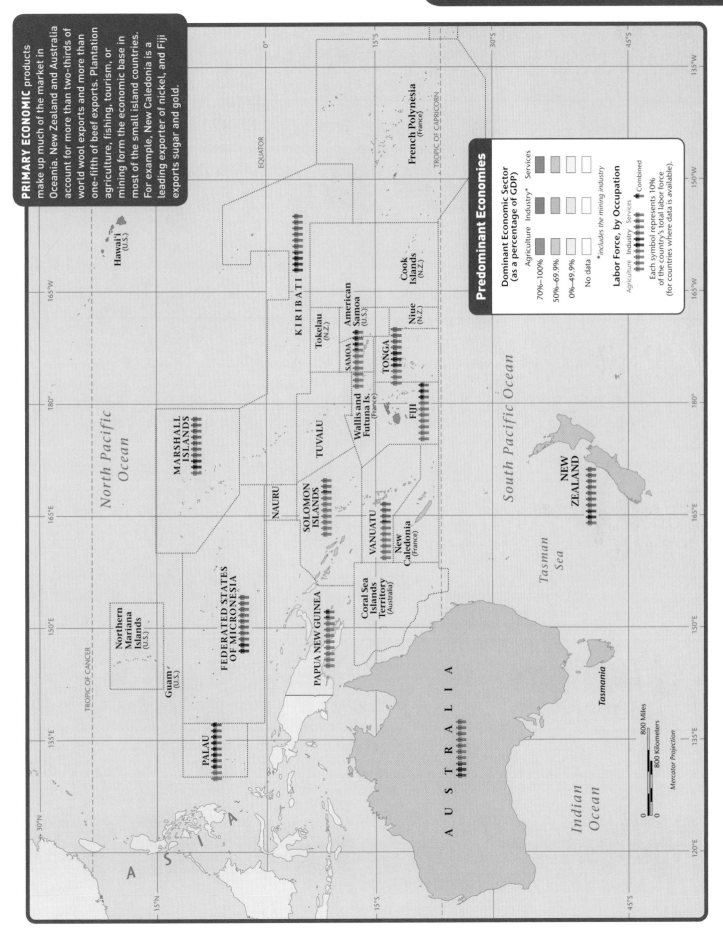

PRIMARY ECONOMIC products make up much of the market in Oceania. New Zealand and Australia account for more than two-thirds of world wool exports and more than one-fifth of beef exports. Plantation agriculture, fishing, tourism, or mining form the economic base in most of the small island countries. For example, New Caledonia is a leading exporter of nickel, and Fiji exports sugar and gold.

Predominant Economies

Dominant Economic Sector
(as a percentage of GDP)

Agriculture   Industry*   Services

70%–100%

50%–69.9%

0%–49.9%

No data

*includes the mining industry

Labor Force, by Occupation

Agriculture   Industry   Services   Combined

Each symbol represents 10%
of the country's total labor force
(for countries where data is available).

Hawai'i
(U.S.)

North Pacific Ocean

MARSHALL ISLANDS

KIRIBATI

Tokelau
(N.Z.)

SAMOA   American Samoa
(U.S.)

Wallis and Futuna Is.
(France)

TONGA

FIJI

Niue
(N.Z.)

Cook Islands
(N.Z.)

French Polynesia
(France)

TUVALU

NAURU

SOLOMON ISLANDS

VANUATU

New Caledonia
(France)

Coral Sea Islands Territory
(Australia)

South Pacific Ocean

NEW ZEALAND

Tasman Sea

Northern Mariana Islands
(U.S.)

Guam
(U.S.)

FEDERATED STATES OF MICRONESIA

PALAU

PAPUA NEW GUINEA

A   S   I   A

AUSTRALIA

Tasmania

Indian Ocean

800 Miles

800 Kilometers

Mercator Projection

EQUATOR

TROPIC OF CAPRICORN

TROPIC OF CANCER

CORAL REEFS:

SELECTED FACTS
Most coral reefs are between 5,000 and 10,000 years old, but some may have begun growing as much as 50 million years ago.

TYPES OF REEFS
FRINGING REEFS form near coastlines of islands and continents.

BARRIER REEFS form parallel to coastlines but are separated by deep lagoons.

ATOLLS form as rings of coral surrounding protected lagoons.

PATCH REEFS grow from a continental shelf to form isolated reefs.

GROWING CONDITIONS
Corals grow best in

• the **TROPICS** (30°N to 30°S) where **SUNLIGHT** is consistent year-round.

• **SHALLOW, WARM WATER,** ranging in temperature from 70° to 85°F (21° to 29°C).

• **CLEAR, CLEAN WATER** that is free of pollutants or sediments that may block sunlight or smother the coral.

• **SALTWATER** where there is a constant salt-to-water ratio.

Great Barrier Reef

Stretching like intricate necklaces along the edges of landmasses in the warm ocean waters of the tropics, coral reefs form one of nature's most complex ecosystems. Corals are tiny marine animals that thrive in shallow coastal waters of the tropics. One type of coral, called a "hard coral," produces a limestone skeleton. When the tiny animal dies, its stone-like skeleton is left behind. The accumulation of millions of these skeletons over thousands of years has produced the large reef formations found in many coastal waters of the tropics.

Most coral reefs are found between 30 degrees N and 30 degrees S latitude in waters with a temperature between 70 and 85 degrees Fahrenheit (21° and 29°C). It is estimated that Earth's coral reefs cover 110,000 square miles (284,900 sq km). Coral reefs are important because they form a habitat for marine animals such as fish, sea turtles, lobsters, and starfish. They also protect fragile coastlines from damaging ocean waves and may be a source of valuable medicines.

The world's largest coral reef, the Great Barrier Reef, lies off the northeast coast of Australia (see large map). This reef, which is made up of more than 400 different types of coral and is home to more than 1,500 species of fish, is a popular tourist destination. People visit to snorkel and dive along the reef and view the great diversity of marine life living among the corals.

⚫ **ANEMONE FISH** swim among the waving polyps of one of the reef's sea anemones. These fish are specially adapted to live safely among the venom-filled tentacles that can inject a paralyzing neurotoxin into unsuspecting prey when disturbed.

◗ **BRILLIANTLY COLORED CORALS** and the fish that live among them attract divers and snorkelers to the Great Barrier Reef every year.

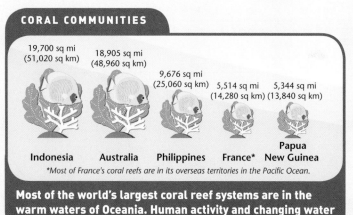

CORAL COMMUNITIES

19,700 sq mi
(51,020 sq km)

18,905 sq mi
(48,960 sq km)

9,676 sq mi
(25,060 sq km)

5,514 sq mi
(14,280 sq km)

5,344 sq mi
(13,840 sq km)

| Indonesia | Australia | Philippines | France* | Papua New Guinea |

Most of France's coral reefs are in its overseas territories in the Pacific Ocean.

Most of the world's largest coral reef systems are in the warm waters of Oceania. Human activity and changing water temperatures put some reefs at risk.

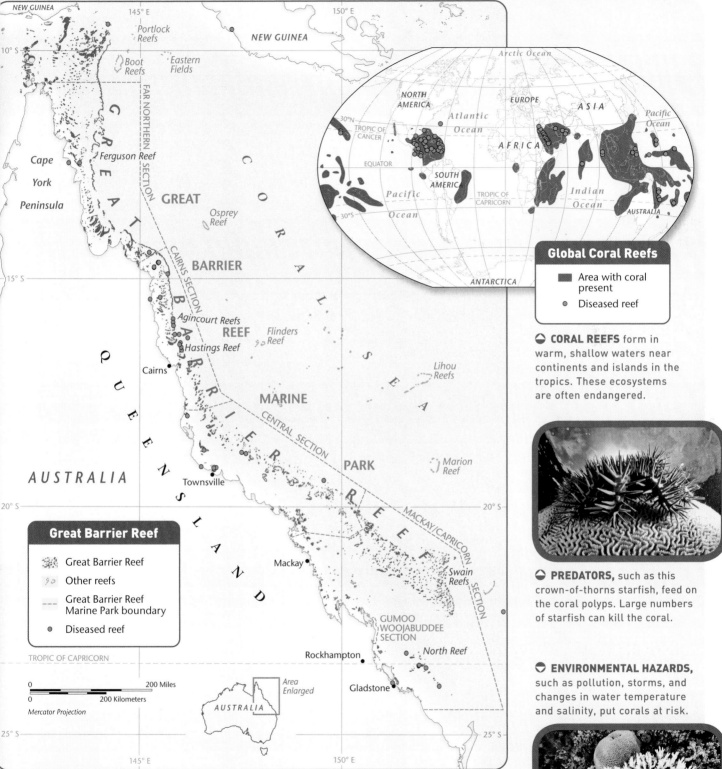

Mercator Projection

Great Barrier Reef

- Great Barrier Reef
- Other reefs
- Great Barrier Reef Marine Park boundary
- Diseased reef

0   200 Miles
0   200 Kilometers

Global Coral Reefs

- Area with coral present
- Diseased reef

CORAL REEFS form in warm, shallow waters near continents and islands in the tropics. These ecosystems are often endangered.

PREDATORS, such as this crown-of-thorns starfish, feed on the coral polyps. Large numbers of starfish can kill the coral.

ENVIRONMENTAL HAZARDS, such as pollution, storms, and changes in water temperature and salinity, put corals at risk.

THE GREAT BARRIER REEF stretches along the northeast coast of Australia for 1,429 miles (2,300 km), from the tip of the Cape York Peninsula to just north of Brisbane in the state of Queensland. The reef is actually a collection of more than 3,000 individual reef systems and is home to many different species of fish, mollusks, rays, dolphins, reptiles, and birds. There are even giant clams more than 120 years old. In addition, the reef is habitat for several endangered species, including the dugong (sea cow) and the green sea turtle. UNESCO recognized the Great Barrier Reef as a World Heritage site in 1981.

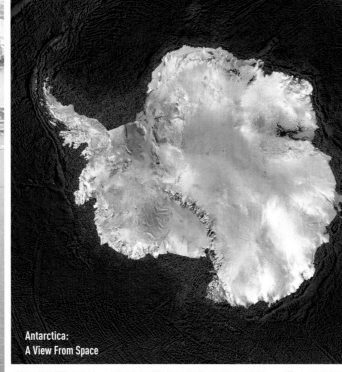

Antarctica:
A View From Space

About 180 million years ago Antarctica broke away from the ancient super-continent Gondwana. Slowly the continent drifted to its present location at the southernmost point on Earth. Antarctica has no permanent human population, but it does have many unique types of wildlife. Seals, whales, and birds such as penguins, albatrosses, petrels, and terns have adapted to the continent's bitter-cold climate and long, dark winters.

Gentoo penguins nest and raise their young in large colonies along the coastal margins of Antarctica.

PHYSICAL

Land area 5,100,000 sq mi (13,209,000 sq km)	**Lowest point** Bentley Subglacial Trench -8,383 ft (-2,555 m)	**Average precipitation on the polar plateau** Less than 2 in (5 cm) per year
Highest point Vinson Massif 16,066 ft (4,897 m)	**Coldest place** Annual average temperature Ridge A -94°F (-74°C)	

POLITICAL

Population There are no indigenous inhabitants, but there are both permanent and summer-only staffed research stations.	**Number of independent countries** 0	**Number of countries operating year-round research stations** 20
	Number of countries claiming land 7	**Number of year-round research stations** 42

Antarctica

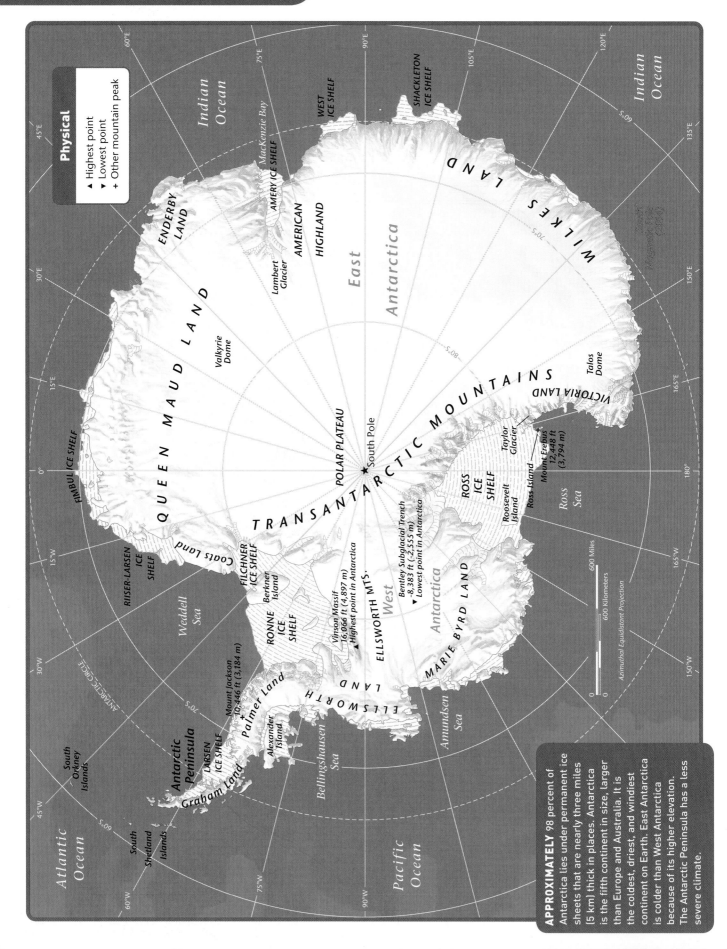

Physical
▲ Highest point
▼ Lowest point
+ Other mountain peak

Indian Ocean

Indian Ocean

WEST ICE SHELF

SHACKLETON ICE SHELF

MacKenzie Bay

AMERY ICE SHELF

ENDERBY LAND

AMERICAN HIGHLAND

WILKES LAND

Lambert Glacier

East Antarctica

QUEEN MAUD LAND

Valkyrie Dome

Talos Dome

VICTORIA LAND

Taylor Glacier

Mount Erebus
12,448 ft
(3,794 m)

Ross Island

Ross Sea

FIMBUL ICE SHELF

POLAR PLATEAU

South Pole

T R A N S A N T A R C T I C   M O U N T A I N S

ROSS ICE SHELF

Roosevelt Island

RIISER-LARSEN ICE SHELF

Coats Land

FILCHNER ICE SHELF

Berkner Island

Bentley Subglacial Trench
-8,383 ft (-2,555 m)
▼ Lowest point in Antarctica

West Antarctica

Weddell Sea

RONNE ICE SHELF

Vinson Massif
16,066 ft (4,897 m)
▲ Highest point in Antarctica

ELLSWORTH MTS.

MARIE BYRD LAND

South Orkney Islands

Mount Jackson
10,446 ft (3,184 m)

ELLSWORTH LAND

Amundsen Sea

Antarctic Peninsula

LARSEN ICE SHELF

Palmer Land

Alexander Island

Bellingshausen Sea

Graham Land

ANTARCTIC CIRCLE

South Shetland Islands

Atlantic Ocean

Pacific Ocean

600 Miles

600 Kilometers

Azimuthal Equidistant Projection

Magnetic Pole (2005)

APPROXIMATELY 98 percent of Antarctica lies under permanent ice sheets that are nearly three miles (5 km) thick in places. Antarctica is the fifth continent in size, larger than Europe and Australia. It is the coldest, driest, and windiest continent on Earth. East Antarctica is colder than West Antarctica because of its higher elevation. The Antarctic Peninsula has a less severe climate.

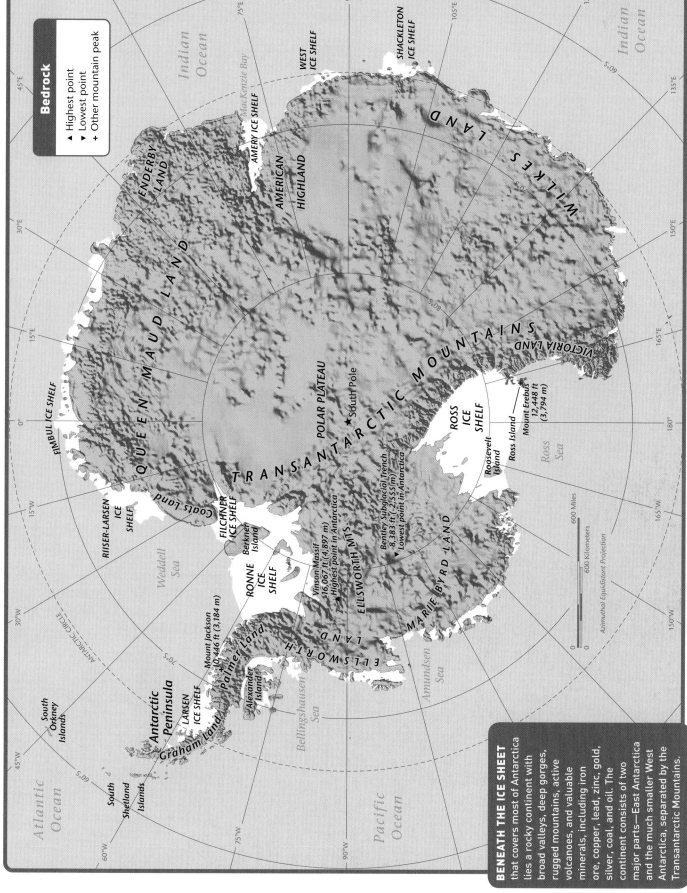

Bedrock
- ▲ Highest point
- ▼ Lowest point
- + Other mountain peak

Indian Ocean

WEST ICE SHELF

SHACKLETON ICE SHELF

Mackenzie Bay

AMERY ICE SHELF

ENDERBY LAND

AMERICAN HIGHLAND

WILKES LAND

Indian Ocean

QUEEN MAUD LAND

POLAR PLATEAU

★ South Pole

TRANSANTARCTIC MOUNTAINS

VICTORIA LAND

ROSS ICE SHELF

Mount Erebus 12,448 ft (3,794 m)

Ross Island

Roosevelt Island

Ross Sea

EMBUL ICE SHELF

RIISER-LARSEN ICE SHELF

Coats Land

FILCHNER ICE SHELF

Berkner Island

Bentley Subglacial Trench -8,383 ft (-2,555 m) ▼ Lowest point in Antarctica

MARIE BYRD LAND

Weddell Sea

RONNE ICE SHELF

Vinson Massif 16,067 ft (4,897 m) ▲ Highest point in Antarctica

ELLSWORTH MTS.

ELLSWORTH LAND

Amundsen Sea

South Orkney Islands

Mount Jackson 10,446 ft (3,184 m) +

Palmer Land

Antarctic Peninsula

LARSEN ICE SHELF

Alexander Island

Graham Land

Bellingshausen Sea

South Shetland Islands

Atlantic Ocean

Pacific Ocean

ANTARCTIC CIRCLE

600 Miles

600 Kilometers

Azimuthal Equidistant Projection

BENEATH THE ICE SHEET that covers most of Antarctica lies a rocky continent with broad valleys, deep gorges, rugged mountains, active volcanoes, and valuable minerals, including iron ore, copper, lead, zinc, gold, silver, coal, and oil. The continent consists of two major parts—East Antarctica and the much smaller West Antarctica, separated by the Transantarctic Mountains.

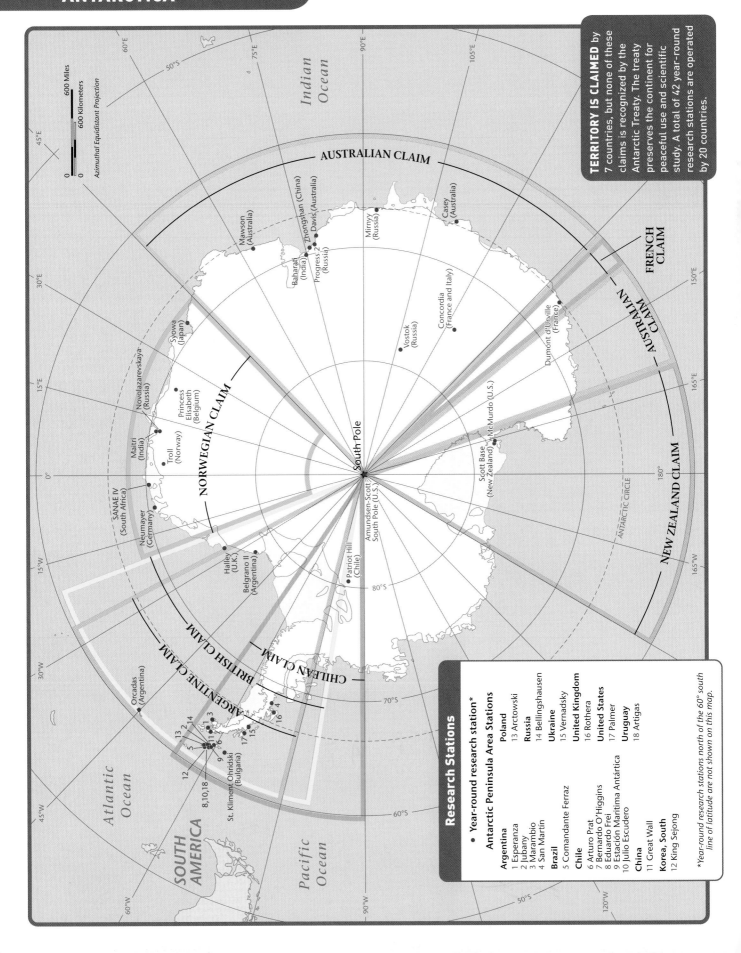

600 Miles
600 Kilometers
Azimuthal Equidistant Projection

Indian Ocean

AUSTRALIAN CLAIM

Casey (Australia)

Mirnyy (Russia)

Zhongshan (China)
Davis (Australia)
Progress 2 (Russia)
Bharati (India)

Mawson (Australia)

FRENCH CLAIM

Concordia (France and Italy)

Dumont d'Urville (France)

Vostok (Russia)

Syowa (Japan)

AUSTRALIAN CLAIM

McMurdo (U.S.)
Scott Base (New Zealand)

Novolazarevskaya (Russia)

Princess Elisabeth (Belgium)

NORWEGIAN CLAIM

Maitri (India)
Troll (Norway)

South Pole

NEW ZEALAND CLAIM

ANTARCTIC CIRCLE

SANAE IV (South Africa)

Neumayer (Germany)

Amundsen-Scott South Pole (U.S.)

Halley (U.K.)

Belgrano II (Argentina)

Patriot Hill (Chile)

CHILEAN CLAIM

Orcadas (Argentina)

ARGENTINE CLAIM

BRITISH CLAIM

St. Kliment Ohridski (Bulgaria)

SOUTH AMERICA

Atlantic Ocean

Pacific Ocean

TERRITORY IS CLAIMED by 7 countries, but none of these claims is recognized by the Antarctic Treaty. The treaty preserves the continent for peaceful use and scientific study. A total of 42 year-round research stations are operated by 20 countries.

Research Stations

• **Year-round research station***

Antarctic Peninsula Area Stations

Argentina
1 Esperanza
2 Jubany
3 Marambio
4 San Martin

Brazil
5 Comandante Ferraz

Chile
6 Arturo Prat
7 Bernardo O'Higgins
8 Eduardo Frei
9 Estación Marítima Antártica
10 Julio Escudero

China
11 Great Wall

Korea, South
12 King Sejong

Poland
13 Arctowski

Russia
14 Bellingshausen

Ukraine
15 Vernadsky

United Kingdom
16 Rothera

United States
17 Palmer

Uruguay
18 Artigas

**Year-round research stations north of the 60° south line of latitude are not shown on this map.*

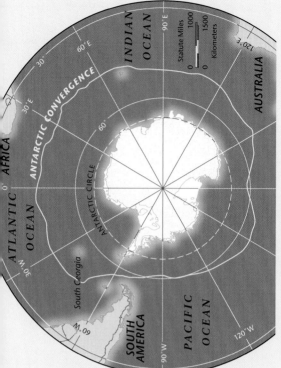

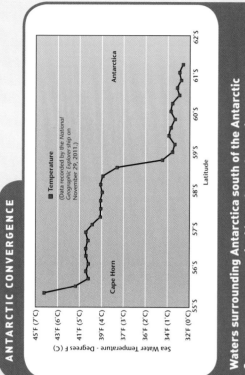

Extreme Environment

Antarctica, located at Earth's southernmost point, is one of the planet's most extreme environments. This ice-covered landmass experiences average temperatures ranging from a mild 22.5°F (-5.3°C) on the Antarctic Peninsula to a bitter -67.2°F (-55.1°C) on the high interior plateau. During the Antarctic winter, pack ice (frozen sea water) forms around the continent, making it even colder. The waters surrounding Antarctica are colder and less salty than Earth's major oceans. This results in a marine boundary called the Antarctic Convergence where the water temperature changes sharply in a short distance (see graph below, right). The mixing of waters along the convergence creates a zone extremely rich in nutrients—especially krill, which supports seals, penguins, whales, and other marine life that have adapted to the continent's extreme conditions.

⬥ **THE ANTARCTIC CONVERGENCE** (approximately 55° S–60° S) is an important climate and marine boundary where cold, slightly less saline Antarctic waters meet the southern extremes of the Atlantic, Pacific, and Indian Oceans. The waters south of the Antarctic Convergence are sometimes referred to as the Southern Ocean.

ANTARCTIC CONVERGENCE

(Data recorded by the *National Geographic Explorer* ship on November 29, 2011.)

■ Temperature

Waters surrounding Antarctica south of the Antarctic Convergence are marked by a sharp change in temperature and salinity as well as different marine life.

FROZEN CONTINENT

FACTS & FIGURES

⬥ One of the largest icebergs ever—roughly the size of the state of Connecticut—broke free from the Ross Ice Shelf in 2000.

⬥ The lowest temperature ever recorded in Antarctica—minus 128.6°F (-89.2°C)—was at Russia's Vostok station in East Antarctica.

⬥ At the beginning of the Antarctic winter, sea ice advances at a rate of 40,000 square miles (100,000 sq km) each day.

⬥ It is estimated that if all of Antarctica's ice were to melt, the global ocean level would rise more than 200 feet (60 m). The continent itself would rise more than 1,600 feet (500 m) because of lost weight—a process known as isostasy.

⬥ **THE ALBATROSS** is the largest of all sea birds. Found mainly north of the Antarctic Convergence, the albatross often stays at sea for more than five years at a time.

⬥ **ANTARCTIC KRILL,** small shrimp-like creatures that thrive in the cold Antarctic waters, are critical to the food chain around the continent.

⬥ **THE EMPEROR PENGUIN,** tallest of these flightless birds, is the only large animal that remains in Antarctica through the long, dark winter.

Flags & Stats

The following pages provide a quick glance at flags, facts, and figures for all 195 independent countries recognized by the National Geographic Society in 2013. An independent country has a national government that is accepted as the highest legal authority over its land and people.

The flags shown are national flags recognized by the United Nations. The statistical data offer a brief overview of each country. Area figures include land as well as surface areas for inland bodies of water. The languages listed are either those most commonly spoken within a country or the official language(s).

Argentina
CONTINENT: South America
AREA: 1,073,518 sq mi (2,780,400 sq km)
POPULATION: 41,267,000
CAPITAL: Buenos Aires 13,528,000
LANGUAGE: Spanish, English, Italian, German, French

Bahamas
CONTINENT: North America
AREA: 5,382 sq mi (13,939 sq km)
POPULATION: 350,000
CAPITAL: Nassau 254,000
LANGUAGE: English, Creole

Belgium
CONTINENT: Europe
AREA: 11,787 sq mi (30,528 sq km)
POPULATION: 11,164,000
CAPITAL: Brussels 1,949,000
LANGUAGE: Flemish (Dutch), French, German

Armenia
CONTINENT: Asia
AREA: 11,484 sq mi (29,743 sq km)
POPULATION: 3,048,000
CAPITAL: Yerevan 1,116,000
LANGUAGE: Armenian

Bahrain
CONTINENT: Asia
AREA: 277 sq mi (717 sq km)
POPULATION: 1,131,000
CAPITAL: Manama 262,000
LANGUAGE: Arabic, English, Persian (Farsi), Urdu

Belize
CONTINENT: North America
AREA: 8,867 sq mi (22,965 sq km)
POPULATION: 334,000
CAPITAL: Belmopan 14,000
LANGUAGE: Spanish, Creole, Maya dialects, English, Garifuna (Carib), German

Afghanistan
CONTINENT: Asia
AREA: 251,773 sq mi (652,090 sq km)
POPULATION: 30,552,000*
CAPITAL: Kabul 3,097,000
LANGUAGE: Dari (Afghan Persian), Pashto, Turkic languages

Andorra
CONTINENT: Europe
AREA: 181 sq mi (468 sq km)
POPULATION: 74,000
CAPITAL: Andorra la Vella 23,000
LANGUAGE: Catalan, French, Castilian, Portuguese

Australia
REGION: Australia/Oceania
AREA: 2,970,000 sq mi (7,692,000 sq km)
POPULATION: 23,106,000
CAPITAL: Canberra 399,000
LANGUAGE: English

Bangladesh
CONTINENT: Asia
AREA: 56,977 sq mi (147,570 sq km)
POPULATION: 156,595,000
CAPITAL: Dhaka 15,391,000
LANGUAGE: Bangla (Bengali), English

Benin
CONTINENT: Africa
AREA: 43,484 sq mi (112,622 sq km)
POPULATION: 9,645,000
CAPITAL: Porto-Novo (constitutional) 314,000; Cotonou (seat of government) 924,000
LANGUAGE: French, Fon, Yoruba

Albania
CONTINENT: Europe
AREA: 11,100 sq mi (28,748 sq km)
POPULATION: 2,774,000
CAPITAL: Tirana 419,000
LANGUAGE: Albanian, Greek, Vlach, Romani, Slavic dialects

Angola
CONTINENT: Africa
AREA: 481,354 sq mi (1,246,700 sq km)
POPULATION: 21,635,000
CAPITAL: Luanda 5,068,000
LANGUAGE: Portuguese, Bantu, other African languages

Austria
CONTINENT: Europe
AREA: 32,378 sq mi (83,858 sq km)
POPULATION: 8,511,000
CAPITAL: Vienna 1,720,000
LANGUAGE: German, Slovene, Croatian, Hungarian

Barbados
CONTINENT: North America
AREA: 166 sq mi (430 sq km)
POPULATION: 253,000
CAPITAL: Bridgetown 122,000
LANGUAGE: English

Bhutan
CONTINENT: Asia
AREA: 17,954 sq mi (46,500 sq km)
POPULATION: 733,000
CAPITAL: Thimphu 99,000
LANGUAGE: Dzongkha, Tibetan dialects, Nepali dialects

Algeria
CONTINENT: Africa
AREA: 919,595 sq mi (2,381,741 sq km)
POPULATION: 38,290,000
CAPITAL: Algiers 2,916,000
LANGUAGE: Arabic, French, Berber dialects

Antigua and Barbuda
CONTINENT: North America
AREA: 171 sq mi (442 sq km)
POPULATION: 88,000
CAPITAL: St. John's 27,000
LANGUAGE: English, local dialects

Azerbaijan
CONTINENT: Asia/Europe
AREA: 33,436 sq mi (86,600 sq km)
POPULATION: 9,418,000
CAPITAL: Baku 2,123,000
LANGUAGE: Azerbaijani (Azeri)

Belarus
CONTINENT: Europe
AREA: 80,153 sq mi (207,595 sq km)
POPULATION: 9,463,000
CAPITAL: Minsk 1,861,000
LANGUAGE: Belarusian, Russian

Bolivia
CONTINENT: South America
AREA: 424,164 sq mi (1,098,581 sq km)
POPULATION: 11,020,000
CAPITAL: La Paz (administrative) 1,715,000; Sucre (legal) 307,000
LANGUAGE: Spanish, Quechua, Aymara

*Country population figures are provided by the U.S. Population Reference Bureau (mid-2013); captial city figures are from the United Nations Population Division (metropolitan areas, 2011).

Bosnia and Herzegovina
CONTINENT: Europe
AREA: 19,741 sq mi
(51,129 sq km)
POPULATION: 3,834,000
CAPITAL: Sarajevo 389,000
LANGUAGE: Bosnian, Croatian, Serbian

Burkina Faso
CONTINENT: Africa
AREA: 105,869 sq mi
(274,200 sq km)
POPULATION: 18,015,000
CAPITAL: Ouagadougou 2,053,000
LANGUAGE: French, indigenous languages

Canada
CONTINENT: North America
AREA: 3,855,101 sq mi
(9,984,670 sq km)
POPULATION: 35,250,000
CAPITAL: Ottawa 1,208,000
LANGUAGE: English, French

Colombia
CONTINENT: South America
AREA: 440,831 sq mi
(1,141,748 sq km)
POPULATION: 48,028,000
CAPITAL: Bogotá 8,743,000
LANGUAGE: Spanish

Croatia
CONTINENT: Europe
AREA: 21,831 sq mi
(56,542 sq km)
POPULATION: 4,253,000
CAPITAL: Zagreb 686,000
LANGUAGE: Croatian

Botswana
CONTINENT: Africa
AREA: 224,607 sq mi
(581,730 sq km)
POPULATION: 1,866,000
CAPITAL: Gaborone 202,000
LANGUAGE: English, Setswana, Kalanga, Sekgalgadi

Burundi
CONTINENT: Africa
AREA: 10,747 sq mi
(27,834 sq km)
POPULATION: 10,892,000
CAPITAL: Bujumbura 605,000
LANGUAGE: Kirundi, French, Swahili

Central African Republic
CONTINENT: Africa
AREA: 240,535 sq mi
(622,984 sq km)
POPULATION: 4,676,000
CAPITAL: Bangui 740,000
LANGUAGE: French, Sangho, other indigenous languages

Comoros
CONTINENT: Africa
AREA: 719 sq mi
(1,862 sq km)
POPULATION: 792,000
CAPITAL: Moroni 54,000
LANGUAGE: Arabic, French, Shikomoro

Cuba
CONTINENT: North America
AREA: 42,803 sq mi
(110,860 sq km)
POPULATION: 11,258,000
CAPITAL: Havana 2,116,000
LANGUAGE: Spanish

Brazil
CONTINENT: South America
AREA: 3,300,169 sq mi
(8,547,403 sq km)
POPULATION: 195,527,000
CAPITAL: Brasília 3,813,000
LANGUAGE: Portuguese

Cabo Verde (Cape Verde)
CONTINENT: Africa
AREA: 1,558 sq mi
(4,036 sq km)
POPULATION: 515,000
CAPITAL: Praia 132,000
LANGUAGE: Portuguese, Crioulo

Chad
CONTINENT: Africa
AREA: 495,755 sq mi
(1,284,000 sq km)
POPULATION: 12,209,000
CAPITAL: N'Djamena 1,079,000
LANGUAGE: French, Arabic, Sara, other indigenous languages

Congo
CONTINENT: Africa
AREA: 132,047 sq mi
(342,000 sq km)
POPULATION: 4,355,000
CAPITAL: Brazzaville 1,611,000
LANGUAGE: French, Lingala, Monokutuba, other indigenous languages

Cyprus
CONTINENT: Europe
AREA: 3,572 sq mi
(9,251 sq km)
POPULATION: 1,135,000
CAPITAL: Nicosia 253,000
LANGUAGE: Greek, Turkish, English

Brunei
CONTINENT: Asia
AREA: 2,226 sq mi
(5,765 sq km)
POPULATION: 407,000
CAPITAL: Bandar Seri Begawan 16,000
LANGUAGE: Malay, English, Chinese

Cambodia
CONTINENT: Asia
AREA: 69,898 sq mi
(181,035 sq km)
POPULATION: 14,406,000
CAPITAL: Phnom Penh 1,550,000
LANGUAGE: Khmer

Chile
CONTINENT: South America
AREA: 291,930 sq mi
(756,096 sq km)
POPULATION: 17,557,000
CAPITAL: Santiago 6,034,000
LANGUAGE: Spanish

Costa Rica
CONTINENT: North America
AREA: 19,730 sq mi
(51,100 sq km)
POPULATION: 4,713,000
CAPITAL: San José 1,515,000
LANGUAGE: Spanish, English

Czech Republic (Czechia)
CONTINENT: Europe
AREA: 30,450 sq mi
(78,866 sq km)
POPULATION: 10,521,000
CAPITAL: Prague 1,276,000
LANGUAGE: Czech

Bulgaria
CONTINENT: Europe
AREA: 42,855 sq mi
(110,994 sq km)
POPULATION: 7,260,000
CAPITAL: Sofia 1,174,000
LANGUAGE: Bulgarian, Turkish, Roma

Cameroon
CONTINENT: Africa
AREA: 183,569 sq mi
(475,442 sq km)
POPULATION: 21,491,000
CAPITAL: Yaoundé 2,432,000
LANGUAGE: French, English, indigenous languages

China
CONTINENT: Asia
AREA: 3,705,405 sq mi
(9,596,960 sq km)
POPULATION: 1,357,372,000
CAPITAL: Beijing 15,594,000
LANGUAGE: Standard Chinese (Mandarin), Yue, Wu, Minbei, other dialects and minority languages

Côte d'Ivoire (Ivory Coast)
CONTINENT: Africa
AREA: 124,503 sq mi
(322,462 sq km)
POPULATION: 21,142,000
CAPITAL: Yamoussoukro (official) 966,000; Abidjan 4,288,000
LANGUAGE: French, Dioula, indigenous languages

Democratic Republic of the Congo
CONTINENT: Africa
AREA: 905,365 sq mi
(2,344,885 sq km)
POPULATION: 71,128,000
CAPITAL: Kinshasa 8,798,000
LANGUAGE: French, Lingala, Kingwana, Kikongo, Tshiluba

Denmark
CONTINENT: Europe
AREA: 16,640 sq mi (43,098 sq km)
POPULATION: 5,613,000
CAPITAL: Copenhagen 1,206,000
LANGUAGE: Danish, Faroese, Greenlandic, German, English

Egypt
CONTINENT: Africa
AREA: 386,874 sq mi (1,002,000 sq km)
POPULATION: 84,667,000
CAPITAL: Cairo 11,169,000
LANGUAGE: Arabic, English, French

Ethiopia
CONTINENT: Africa
AREA: 437,600 sq mi (1,133,380 sq km)
POPULATION: 89,209,000
CAPITAL: Addis Ababa 2,979,000
LANGUAGE: Oromo, Amharic, Tigrinya, English, Arabic, Somali

Gambia
CONTINENT: Africa
AREA: 4,361 sq mi (11,295 sq km)
POPULATION: 1,884,000
CAPITAL: Banjul 506,000
LANGUAGE: English, Mandinka, Fula, Wolof, other indigenous languages

Grenada
CONTINENT: North America
AREA: 133 sq mi (344 sq km)
POPULATION: 112,000
CAPITAL: St. George's 41,000
LANGUAGE: English, French patois

Djibouti
CONTINENT: Africa
AREA: 8,958 sq mi (23,200 sq km)
POPULATION: 939,000
CAPITAL: Djibouti 496,000
LANGUAGE: French, Arabic, Somali, Afar

El Salvador
CONTINENT: North America
AREA: 8,124 sq mi (21,041 sq km)
POPULATION: 6,307,000
CAPITAL: San Salvador 1,605,000
LANGUAGE: Spanish, Nahua

Fiji Islands
REGION: Australia/Oceania
AREA: 7,095 sq mi (18,376 sq km)
POPULATION: 860,000
CAPITAL: Suva 177,000
LANGUAGE: English, Fijian, Hindustani

Georgia
CONTINENT: Asia/Europe
AREA: 26,911 sq mi (69,700 sq km)
POPULATION: 4,541,000
CAPITAL: T'bilisi 1,121,000
LANGUAGE: Georgian, Russian, Armenian, Azeri, Abkhaz

Guatemala
CONTINENT: North America
AREA: 42,042 sq mi (108,889 sq km)
POPULATION: 15,428,000
CAPITAL: Guatemala City 1,168,000
LANGUAGE: Spanish, indigenous languages

Dominica
CONTINENT: North America
AREA: 290 sq mi (751 sq km)
POPULATION: 71,000
CAPITAL: Roseau 14,000
LANGUAGE: English, French patois

Equatorial Guinea
CONTINENT: Africa
AREA: 10,831 sq mi (28,051 sq km)
POPULATION: 761,000
CAPITAL: Malabo 137,000
LANGUAGE: Spanish, French, Fang, Bubi

Finland
CONTINENT: Europe
AREA: 130,558 sq mi (338,145 sq km)
POPULATION: 5,440,000
CAPITAL: Helsinki 1,134,000
LANGUAGE: Finnish, Swedish

Germany
CONTINENT: Europe
AREA: 137,847 sq mi (357,022 sq km)
POPULATION: 80,572,000
CAPITAL: Berlin 3,462,000
LANGUAGE: German

Guinea
CONTINENT: Africa
AREA: 94,926 sq mi (245,857 sq km)
POPULATION: 11,793,000
CAPITAL: Conakry 1,786,000
LANGUAGE: French, indigenous languages

Dominican Republic
CONTINENT: North America
AREA: 18,704 sq mi (48,442 sq km)
POPULATION: 10,260,000
CAPITAL: Santo Domingo 2,191,000
LANGUAGE: Spanish

Eritrea
CONTINENT: Africa
AREA: 46,774 sq mi (121,144 sq km)
POPULATION: 5,765,000
CAPITAL: Asmara 712,000
LANGUAGE: Afar, Arabic, Tigre, Kunama, Tigrinya, other Cushitic languages

France
CONTINENT: Europe
AREA: 210,026 sq mi (543,965 sq km)
POPULATION: 63,851,000
CAPITAL: Paris 10,620,000
LANGUAGE: French

Ghana
CONTINENT: Africa
AREA: 92,100 sq mi (238,537 sq km)
POPULATION: 26,088,000
CAPITAL: Accra 2,573,000
LANGUAGE: English, Asante, Ewe, Fante, Boron, Dagomba, Dangme, other native languages

Guinea-Bissau
CONTINENT: Africa
AREA: 13,948 sq mi (36,125 sq km)
POPULATION: 1,667,000
CAPITAL: Bissau 423,000
LANGUAGE: Portuguese, Crioulo, indigenous languages

Ecuador
CONTINENT: South America
AREA: 109,483 sq mi (283,560 sq km)
POPULATION: 15,789,000
CAPITAL: Quito 1,622,000
LANGUAGE: Spanish, Quechua, other indigenous languages

Estonia
CONTINENT: Europe
AREA: 17,462 sq mi (45,227 sq km)
POPULATION: 1,283,000
CAPITAL: Tallinn 400,000
LANGUAGE: Estonian, Russian

Gabon
CONTINENT: Africa
AREA: 103,347 sq mi (267,667 sq km)
POPULATION: 1,601,000
CAPITAL: Libreville 686,000
LANGUAGE: French, Fang, Myene, Nzebi, Bapounou/ Eschira, Bandjabi

Greece
CONTINENT: Europe
AREA: 50,949 sq mi (131,957 sq km)
POPULATION: 11,081,000
CAPITAL: Athens 3,414,000
LANGUAGE: Greek

Guyana
CONTINENT: South America
AREA: 83,000 sq mi (214,969 sq km)
POPULATION: 800,000
CAPITAL: Georgetown 127,000
LANGUAGE: English, indigenous languages, Creole, Caribbean Hindustani, Urdu

Haiti
CONTINENT: North America
AREA: 10,714 sq mi (27,750 sq km)
POPULATION: 10,421,000
CAPITAL: Port-au-Prince 2,207,000
LANGUAGE: French, Creole

Indonesia
CONTINENT: Asia
AREA: 742,308 sq mi (1,922,570 sq km)
POPULATION: 248,527,000
CAPITAL: Jakarta 9,769,000
LANGUAGE: Bahasa Indonesia, English, Dutch, Javanese, other indigenous languages

Italy
CONTINENT: Europe
AREA: 116,345 sq mi (301,333 sq km)
POPULATION: 59,831,000
CAPITAL: Rome 3,298,000
LANGUAGE: Italian, German, French, Slovene

Kenya
CONTINENT: Africa
AREA: 224,081 sq mi (580,367 sq km)
POPULATION: 44,184,000
CAPITAL: Nairobi 3,363,000
LANGUAGE: English, Kiswahili, indigenous languages

Laos
CONTINENT: Asia
AREA: 91,429 sq mi (236,800 sq km)
POPULATION: 6,736,000
CAPITAL: Vientiane 810,000
LANGUAGE: Lao, French, English, ethnic languages

Honduras
CONTINENT: North America
AREA: 43,433 sq mi (112,492 sq km)
POPULATION: 8,555,000
CAPITAL: Tegucigalpa 1,088,000
LANGUAGE: Spanish, indigenous languages

Iran
CONTINENT: Asia
AREA: 636,296 sq mi (1,648,000 sq km)
POPULATION: 76,521,000
CAPITAL: Tehran 7,304,000
LANGUAGE: Persian (Farsi), Turkic dialects, Kurdish, Luri, Gilaki, Mazandarani

Jamaica
CONTINENT: North America
AREA: 4,244 sq mi (10,991 sq km)
POPULATION: 2,712,000
CAPITAL: Kingston 571,000
LANGUAGE: English, English patois

Kiribati
REGION: Australia/Oceania
AREA: 313 sq mi (811 sq km)
POPULATION: 106,000
CAPITAL: Tarawa 44,000
LANGUAGE: I-Kiribati, English

Latvia
CONTINENT: Europe
AREA: 24,938 sq mi (64,589 sq km)
POPULATION: 2,018,000
CAPITAL: Riga 701,000
LANGUAGE: Latvian, Russian, Lithuanian

Hungary
CONTINENT: Europe
AREA: 35,919 sq mi (93,030 sq km)
POPULATION: 9,892,000
CAPITAL: Budapest 1,737,000
LANGUAGE: Hungarian

Iraq
CONTINENT: Asia
AREA: 168,754 sq mi (437,072 sq km)
POPULATION: 35,095,000
CAPITAL: Baghdad 6,036,000
LANGUAGE: Arabic, Kurdish, Assyrian, Armenian

Japan
CONTINENT: Asia
AREA: 145,902 sq mi (377,887 sq km)
POPULATION: 127,301,000
CAPITAL: Tokyo 37,217,000
LANGUAGE: Japanese

Kosovo
CONTINENT: Europe
AREA: 4,203 sq mi (10,887 sq km)
POPULATION: 1,824,000
CAPITAL: Prishtina 145,000
LANGUAGE: Albanian, Serbian, Bosnian, Turkish, Roma

Lebanon
CONTINENT: Asia
AREA: 4,036 sq mi (10,452 sq km)
POPULATION: 4,822,000
CAPITAL: Beirut 2,022,000
LANGUAGE: Arabic, French, English, Armenian

Iceland
CONTINENT: Europe
AREA: 39,769 sq mi (103,000 sq km)
POPULATION: 323,000
CAPITAL: Reykjavík 206,000
LANGUAGE: Icelandic, English, Nordic languages, German

Ireland
CONTINENT: Europe
AREA: 27,133 sq mi (70,273 sq km)
POPULATION: 4,598,000
CAPITAL: Dublin 1,121,000
LANGUAGE: Irish (Gaelic), English

Jordan
CONTINENT: Asia
AREA: 34,495 sq mi (89,342 sq km)
POPULATION: 7,309,000
CAPITAL: Amman 1,179,000
LANGUAGE: Arabic, English

Kuwait
CONTINENT: Asia
AREA: 6,880 sq mi (17,818 sq km)
POPULATION: 3,459,000
CAPITAL: Kuwait 2,406,000
LANGUAGE: Arabic, English

Lesotho
CONTINENT: Africa
AREA: 11,720 sq mi (30,355 sq km)
POPULATION: 2,242,000
CAPITAL: Maseru 239,000
LANGUAGE: Sesotho, English, Zulu, Xhosa

India
CONTINENT: Asia
AREA: 1,269,221 sq mi (3,287,270 sq km)
POPULATION: 1,276,508,000
CAPITAL: New Delhi 22,654,000 (part of Delhi metropolitan area)
LANGUAGE: Hindi, 21 other official languages, English

Israel
CONTINENT: Asia
AREA: 8,550 sq mi (22,145 sq km)
POPULATION: 8,054,000
CAPITAL: Jerusalem 791,000
LANGUAGE: Hebrew, Arabic, English

Kazakhstan
CONTINENT: Asia/Europe
AREA: 1,049,155 sq mi (2,717,300 sq km)
POPULATION: 17,031,000
CAPITAL: Astana 664,000
LANGUAGE: Kazakh (Qazaq), Russian

Kyrgyzstan
CONTINENT: Asia
AREA: 77,182 sq mi (199,900 sq km)
POPULATION: 5,665,000
CAPITAL: Bishkek 837,000
LANGUAGE: Kyrgyz, Uzbek, Russian

Liberia
CONTINENT: Africa
AREA: 43,000 sq mi (111,370 sq km)
POPULATION: 4,357,000
CAPITAL: Monrovia 750,000
LANGUAGE: English, indigenous languages

Libya
CONTINENT: Africa
AREA: 679,362 sq mi
(1,759,540 sq km)
POPULATION: 6,518,000
CAPITAL: Tripoli 1,127,000
LANGUAGE: Arabic, Italian,
English

Madagascar
CONTINENT: Africa
AREA: 226,658 sq mi
(587,041 sq km)
POPULATION: 22,550,000
CAPITAL: Antananarivo 1,987,000
LANGUAGE: French, Malagasy,
English

Malta
CONTINENT: Europe
AREA: 122 sq mi (316 sq km)
POPULATION: 448,000
CAPITAL: Valletta 198,000
LANGUAGE: Maltese, English

Micronesia
REGION: Australia/Oceania
AREA: 271 sq mi (702 sq km)
POPULATION: 107,000
CAPITAL: Palikir 7,000
LANGUAGE: English, Chuukese,
Kosrean, Pohnpeian, Yapese,
other indigenous languages

Morocco
CONTINENT: Africa
AREA: 274,461 sq mi
(710,850 sq km)
POPULATION: 32,950,000
CAPITAL: Rabat 1,843,000
LANGUAGE: Arabic, Berber
dialects, French

Liechtenstein
CONTINENT: Europe
AREA: 62 sq mi (160 sq km)
POPULATION: 37,000
CAPITAL: Vaduz 5,000
LANGUAGE: German,
Alemannic dialect

Malawi
CONTINENT: Africa
AREA: 45,747 sq mi
(118,484 sq km)
POPULATION: 16,338,000
CAPITAL: Lilongwe 772,000
LANGUAGE: English, Chichewa,
Chinyanja, Chiyao, Chitumbuka

Marshall Islands
REGION: Australia/Oceania
AREA: 70 sq mi (181 sq km)
POPULATION: 56,000
CAPITAL: Majuro 31,000
LANGUAGE: Marshallese,
English

Moldova
CONTINENT: Europe
AREA: 13,050 sq mi
(33,800 sq km)
POPULATION: 4,114,000
CAPITAL: Chisinau 677,000
LANGUAGE: Moldovan, Russian,
Gagauz

Mozambique
CONTINENT: Africa
AREA: 308,642 sq mi
(799,380 sq km)
POPULATION: 24,336,000
CAPITAL: Maputo 1,150,000
LANGUAGE: Portuguese, Emak-
huwa, Xichangana, Elomwe,
Cisena, Echuwabo

Lithuania
CONTINENT: Europe
AREA: 25,212 sq mi
(65,300 sq km)
POPULATION: 2,956,000
CAPITAL: Vilnius 546,000
LANGUAGE: Lithuanian,
Russian, Polish

Malaysia
CONTINENT: Asia
AREA: 127,355 sq mi
(329,847 sq km)
POPULATION: 29,794,000
CAPITAL: Kuala Lumpur
1,556,000
LANGUAGE: Bahasa Malaysia,
English, Chinese, Tamil, Telugu,
Malayalam, Punjabi, Thai

Mauritania
CONTINENT: Africa
AREA: 397,955 sq mi
(1,030,700 sq km)
POPULATION: 3,712,000
CAPITAL: Nouakchott 786,000
LANGUAGE: Arabic, Pulaar,
Soninke, Wolof, French,
Hassaniya

Monaco
CONTINENT: Europe
AREA: 0.8 sq mi (2.0 sq km)
POPULATION: 37,000
CAPITAL: Monaco 35,000
LANGUAGE: French, English,
Italian, Monegasque

Myanmar (Burma)
CONTINENT: Asia
AREA: 261,218 sq mi
(676,552 sq km)
POPULATION: 53,259,000
CAPITAL: Nay Pyi Taw (admin-
istrative) 1,060,000; Yangon
(Rangoon; legislative) 4,457,000
LANGUAGE: Burmese, ethnic
languages

Luxembourg
CONTINENT: Europe
AREA: 998 sq mi (2,586 sq km)
POPULATION: 543,000
CAPITAL: Luxembourg 94,000
LANGUAGE: Luxembourgish,
German, French

Maldives
CONTINENT: Asia
AREA: 115 sq mi (298 sq km)
POPULATION: 360,000
CAPITAL: Male 132,000
LANGUAGE: Maldivian Dhivehi,
English

Mauritius
CONTINENT: Africa
AREA: 788 sq mi (2,040 sq km)
POPULATION: 1,297,000
CAPITAL: Port Louis 151,000
LANGUAGE: Creole, Bhojpuri,
French

Mongolia
CONTINENT: Asia
AREA: 603,909 sq mi
(1,564,116 sq km)
POPULATION: 2,792,000
CAPITAL: Ulaanbaatar 1,184,000
LANGUAGE: Khalkha Mongol,
Turkic, Russian

Namibia
CONTINENT: Africa
AREA: 318,261 sq mi
(824,292 sq km)
POPULATION: 2,410,000
CAPITAL: Windhoek 380,000
LANGUAGE: English, Afrikaans,
German, indigenous languages

Macedonia
CONTINENT: Europe
AREA: 9,928 sq mi
(25,713 sq km)
POPULATION: 2,066,000
CAPITAL: Skopje 499,000
LANGUAGE: Macedonian,
Albanian, Turkish

Mali
CONTINENT: Africa
AREA: 478,841 sq mi
(1,240,192 sq km)
POPULATION: 15,461,000
CAPITAL: Bamako 2,037,000
LANGUAGE: French, Bambara,
other indigenous languages

Mexico
CONTINENT: North America
AREA: 758,449 sq mi
(1,964,375 sq km)
POPULATION: 117,574,000
CAPITAL: Mexico City 20,446,000
LANGUAGE: Spanish, Maya,
Nahuatl, other indigenous
languages

Montenegro
CONTINENT: Europe
AREA: 5,415 sq mi
(14,026 sq km)
POPULATION: 623,000
CAPITAL: Podgorica 156,000
LANGUAGE: Serbian, Monte-
negrin, Bosnian, Albanian,
Croatian

Nauru
REGION: Australia/Oceania
AREA: 8 sq mi (21 sq km)
POPULATION: 11,000
CAPITAL: Yaren 10,000
LANGUAGE: Nauruan, English

Nepal

CONTINENT: Asia

AREA: 56,827 sq mi (147,181 sq km)

POPULATION: 26,810,000

CAPITAL: Kathmandu 1,015,000

LANGUAGE: Nepali, Maithali, Bhojpuri, Tharu, Tamang, Newar, Magar, Awadhi

Nigeria

CONTINENT: Africa

AREA: 356,669 sq mi (923,768 sq km)

POPULATION: 173,615,000

CAPITAL: Abuja 2,153,000

LANGUAGE: English, Hausa, Yoruba, Igbo (Ibo), Fulani

Palau

REGION: Australia/Oceania

AREA: 189 sq mi (489 sq km)

POPULATION: 21,000

CAPITAL: Melekeok, 400

LANGUAGE: Palauan, Filipino, English, Chinese

Philippines

CONTINENT: Asia

AREA: 115,831 sq mi (300,000 sq km)

POPULATION: 96,209,000

CAPITAL: Manila 11,862,000

LANGUAGE: Filipino (based on Tagalog), English

Russia

CONTINENT: Europe/Asia

AREA: 6,592,850 sq mi (17,075,400 sq km)

POPULATION: 143,493,000

CAPITAL: Moscow 11,621,000

LANGUAGE: Russian, many languages

Netherlands

CONTINENT: Europe

AREA: 16,034 sq mi (41,528 sq km)

POPULATION: 16,798,000

CAPITAL: Amsterdam 1,056,000

LANGUAGE: Dutch, Frisian

North Korea

CONTINENT: Asia

AREA: 46,540 sq mi (120,538 sq km)

POPULATION: 24,720,000

CAPITAL: Pyongyang 2,843,000

LANGUAGE: Korean

Panama

CONTINENT: North America

AREA: 29,157 sq mi (75,517 sq km)

POPULATION: 3,850,000

CAPITAL: Panama City 1,426,000

LANGUAGE: Spanish, English

Poland

CONTINENT: Europe

AREA: 120,728 sq mi (312,685 sq km)

POPULATION: 38,517,000

CAPITAL: Warsaw 1,723,000

LANGUAGE: Polish

Rwanda

CONTINENT: Africa

AREA: 10,169 sq mi (26,338 sq km)

POPULATION: 11,116,000

CAPITAL: Kigali 1,004,000

LANGUAGE: Kinyarwanda, French, English, Kiswahili

New Zealand

REGION: Australia/Oceania

AREA: 104,454 sq mi (270,534 sq km)

POPULATION: 4,450,000

CAPITAL: Wellington 410,000

LANGUAGE: English, Maori

Norway

CONTINENT: Europe

AREA: 125,004 sq mi (323,758 sq km)

POPULATION: 5,084,000

CAPITAL: Oslo 915,000

LANGUAGE: Bokmal Norwegian, Nynorsk Norwegian, Sami

Papua New Guinea

REGION: Australia/Oceania

AREA: 178,703 sq mi (462,840 sq km)

POPULATION: 7,179,000

CAPITAL: Port Moresby 343,000

LANGUAGE: Melanesian pidgin, indigenous languages

Portugal

CONTINENT: Europe

AREA: 35,655 sq mi (92,345 sq km)

POPULATION: 10,460,000

CAPITAL: Lisbon 2,843,000

LANGUAGE: Portuguese, Mirandese

Samoa

REGION: Australia/Oceania

AREA: 1,093 sq mi (2,831 sq km)

POPULATION: 190,000

CAPITAL: Apia 37,000

LANGUAGE: Samoan, English

Nicaragua

CONTINENT: North America

AREA: 50,193 sq mi (130,000 sq km)

POPULATION: 6,043,000

CAPITAL: Managua 970,000

LANGUAGE: Spanish, English, Miskito, other indigenous languages

Oman

CONTINENT: Asia

AREA: 119,500 sq mi (309,500 sq km)

POPULATION: 3,983,000

CAPITAL: Muscat 743,000

LANGUAGE: Arabic, English, Baluchi, Urdu, Indian dialects

Paraguay

CONTINENT: South America

AREA: 157,048 sq mi (406,752 sq km)

POPULATION: 6,798,000

CAPITAL: Asunción 2,139,000

LANGUAGE: Spanish, Guarani

Qatar

CONTINENT: Asia

AREA: 4,448 sq mi (11,521 sq km)

POPULATION: 2,169,000

CAPITAL: Doha 567,000

LANGUAGE: Arabic, English

San Marino

CONTINENT: Europe

AREA: 24 sq mi (61 sq km)

POPULATION: 33,000

CAPITAL: San Marino 4,000

LANGUAGE: Italian

Niger

CONTINENT: Africa

AREA: 489,191 sq mi (1,267,000 sq km)

POPULATION: 16,916,000

CAPITAL: Niamey 1,297,000

LANGUAGE: French, Hausa, Djerma

Pakistan

CONTINENT: Asia

AREA: 307,374 sq mi (796,095 sq km)

POPULATION: 190,709,000

CAPITAL: Islamabad 919,000

LANGUAGE: Urdu, English, Punjabi, Sindhi, Siraiki, Pashto, Balochi, Hindko

Peru

CONTINENT: South America

AREA: 496,224 sq mi (1,285,216 sq km)

POPULATION: 30,475,000

CAPITAL: Lima 9,130,000

LANGUAGE: Spanish, Quechua, Aymara, other indigenous languages

Romania

CONTINENT: Europe

AREA: 92,043 sq mi (238,391 sq km)

POPULATION: 21,269,000

CAPITAL: Bucharest 1,937,000

LANGUAGE: Romanian, Hungarian

Sao Tome and Principe

CONTINENT: Africa

AREA: 386 sq mi (1,001 sq km)

POPULATION: 188,000

CAPITAL: São Tomé 64,000

LANGUAGE: Portuguese

Saudi Arabia
CONTINENT: Asia
AREA: 756,985 sq mi
(1,960,582 sq km)
POPULATION: 30,054,000
CAPITAL: Riyadh 5,451,000
LANGUAGE: Arabic

Singapore
CONTINENT: Asia
AREA: 255 sq mi (660 sq km)
POPULATION: 5,444,000
CAPITAL: Singapore 5,188,000
LANGUAGE: Mandarin, English,
Tamil, Malay, Hokkien, Canton-
ese, Teochew

South Africa
CONTINENT: Africa
AREA: 470,693 sq mi
(1,219,090 sq km)
POPULATION: 52,982,000
CAPITAL: Pretoria (administra-
tive) 1,501,000; Bloemfontein
(judicial) 468,000; Cape Town
(legislative) 3,562,000
LANGUAGE: IsiZulu, IsiXhosa

St. Kitts and Nevis
CONTINENT: North America
AREA: 104 sq mi (269 sq km)
POPULATION: 55,000
CAPITAL: Basseterre 12,000
LANGUAGE: English

Swaziland
CONTINENT: Africa
AREA: 6,704 sq mi
(17,363 sq km)
POPULATION: 1,238,000
CAPITAL: Mbabane (admini-
strative) 66,000; Lobamba
(legislative and royal) —
LANGUAGE: English, siSwati

Senegal
CONTINENT: Africa
AREA: 75,955 sq mi
(196,722 sq km)
POPULATION: 13,497,000
CAPITAL: Dakar 3,035,000
LANGUAGE: French, Wolof,
Pulaar, Jola, Mandinka

Slovakia
CONTINENT: Europe
AREA: 18,932 sq mi
(49,035 sq km)
POPULATION: 5,414,000
CAPITAL: Bratislava 434,000
LANGUAGE: Slovak, Hungarian

South Korea
CONTINENT: Asia
AREA: 38,321 sq mi
(99,250 sq km)
POPULATION: 50,220,000
CAPITAL: Seoul 9,736,000
LANGUAGE: Korean, English

St. Lucia
CONTINENT: North America
AREA: 238 sq mi (616 sq km)
POPULATION: 170,000
CAPITAL: Castries 21,000
LANGUAGE: English, French
patois

Sweden
CONTINENT: Europe
AREA: 173,732 sq mi
(449,964 sq km)
POPULATION: 9,592,000
CAPITAL: Stockholm 1,385,000
LANGUAGE: Swedish, Sami,
Finnish

Serbia
CONTINENT: Europe
AREA: 29,913 sq mi
(77,474 sq km)
POPULATION: 7,136,000
CAPITAL: Belgrade 1,135,000
LANGUAGE: Serbian, Hungarian,
Slovak, Romanian, Croatian,
Rusyn

Slovenia
CONTINENT: Europe
AREA: 7,827 sq mi
(20,273 sq km)
POPULATION: 2,060,000
CAPITAL: Ljubljana 273,000
LANGUAGE: Slovene,
Serbo-Croatian

South Sudan
CONTINENT: Africa
AREA: 248,795 sq mi
(644,329 sq km)
POPULATION: 9,782,000
CAPITAL: Juba 269,000
LANGUAGE: English, Arabic,
indigenous languages

St. Vincent
and the Grenadines
CONTINENT: North America
AREA: 150 sq mi (389 sq km)
POPULATION: 108,000
CAPITAL: Kingstown 31,000
LANGUAGE: English, French
patois

Switzerland
CONTINENT: Europe
AREA: 15,940 sq mi
(41,284 sq km)
POPULATION: 8,078,000
CAPITAL: Bern 353,000
LANGUAGE: German, French,
Italian, Romansch

Seychelles
CONTINENT: Africa
AREA: 176 sq mi (455 sq km)
POPULATION: 93,000
CAPITAL: Victoria 27,000
LANGUAGE: English, Creole

Solomon Islands
REGION: Australia/Oceania
AREA: 10,954 sq mi
(28,370 sq km)
POPULATION: 581,000
CAPITAL: Honiara 68,000
LANGUAGE: English, Melane-
sian pidgin, other indigenous
languages

Spain
CONTINENT: Europe
AREA: 195,363 sq mi
(505,988 sq km)
POPULATION: 46,647,000
CAPITAL: Madrid 6,574,000
LANGUAGE: Castilian Spanish,
Catalan, Galician, Basque

Sudan
CONTINENT: Africa
AREA: 718,775 sq mi
(1,861,484 sq km)
POPULATION: 34,186,000
CAPITAL: Khartoum 4,632,000
LANGUAGE: Arabic, English,
Nubian, Ta Bedawie, Fur

Syria
CONTINENT: Asia
AREA: 71,498 sq mi
(185,180 sq km)
POPULATION: 21,898,000
CAPITAL: Damascus 2,650,000
LANGUAGE: Arabic, Kurdish,
Armenian, Aramaic, Circassian

Sierra Leone
CONTINENT: Africa
AREA: 27,699 sq mi
(71,740 sq km)
POPULATION: 6,242,000
CAPITAL: Freetown 941,000
LANGUAGE: English, Mende,
Temne, Krio

Somalia
CONTINENT: Africa
AREA: 246,201 sq mi
(637,657 sq km)
POPULATION: 10,383,000
CAPITAL: Mogadishu 1,554,000
LANGUAGE: Somali, Arabic,
Italian, English

Sri Lanka
CONTINENT: Asia
AREA: 25,299 sq mi
(65,525 sq km)
POPULATION: 20,501,000
CAPITAL: Colombo (adminstra-
tive) 693,000; Sri Jayewardene-
pura Kotte (legislative) 126,000
LANGUAGE: Sinhala, Tamil

Suriname
CONTINENT: South America
AREA: 63,037 sq mi
(163,265 sq km)
POPULATION: 558,000
CAPITAL: Paramaribo 278,000
LANGUAGE: Dutch, English,
Sranang Tongo (Taki-Taki), Carib-
bean Hindustani, Javanese

Tajikistan
CONTINENT: Asia
AREA: 55,251 sq mi
(143,100 sq km)
POPULATION: 8,085,000
CAPITAL: Dushanbe 739,000
LANGUAGE: Tajik, Russian

Tanzania
CONTINENT: Africa
AREA: 364,900 sq mi
(945,087 sq km)
POPULATION: 49,122,000
CAPITAL: Dar es Salaam
2,930,000; Dodoma (legislative)
83,000
LANGUAGE: Swahili, English,
Arabic, indigenous languages

Thailand
CONTINENT: Asia
AREA: 198,115 sq mi
(513,115 sq km)
POPULATION: 66,185,000
CAPITAL: Bangkok 8,426,000
LANGUAGE: Thai, English, ethnic
and regional dialects

Timor-Leste
(East Timor)
CONTINENT: Asia
AREA: 5,640 sq mi
(14,609 sq km)
POPULATION: 1,108,000
CAPITAL: Dili 180,000
LANGUAGE: Tetum, Portuguese,
Indonesian, English

Togo
CONTINENT: Africa
AREA: 21,925 sq mi
(56,785 sq km)
POPULATION: 6,168,000
CAPITAL: Lomé 1,524,000
LANGUAGE: French, Ewe, Mina,
Kabye, Dagomba

Tonga
REGION: Australia/Oceania
AREA: 289 sq mi (748 sq km)
POPULATION: 103,000
CAPITAL: Nuku'alofa 25,000
LANGUAGE: Tongan, English

Trinidad and Tobago
CONTINENT: North America
AREA: 1,980 sq mi (5,128 sq km)
POPULATION: 1,341,000
CAPITAL: Port-of-Spain 66,000
LANGUAGE: English, Caribbean
Hindustani, French, Spanish,
Chinese

Tunisia
CONTINENT: Africa
AREA: 63,170 sq mi
(163,610 sq km)
POPULATION: 10,882,000
CAPITAL: Tunis 790,000
LANGUAGE: Arabic, French

Turkey
CONTINENT: Asia/Europe
AREA: 300,948 sq mi
(779,452 sq km)
POPULATION: 76,083,000
CAPITAL: Ankara 4,194,000
LANGUAGE: Turkish, Kurdish

Turkmenistan
CONTINENT: Asia
AREA: 188,456 sq mi
(488,100 sq km)
POPULATION: 5,240,000
CAPITAL: Ashgabat 683,000
LANGUAGE: Turkmen, Russian,
Uzbek

Tuvalu
REGION: Australia/Oceania
AREA: 10 sq mi (26 sq km)
POPULATION: 11,000
CAPITAL: Funafuti 5,000
LANGUAGE: Tuvaluan, English,
Samoan, Kiribati

Uganda
CONTINENT: Africa
AREA: 93,104 sq mi
(241,139 sq km)
POPULATION: 36,890,000
CAPITAL: Kampala 1,659,000
LANGUAGE: English, Ganda
(Luganda), other indigenous
languages, Swahili, Arabic

Ukraine
CONTINENT: Europe
AREA: 233,090 sq mi
(603,700 sq km)
POPULATION: 45,513,000
CAPITAL: Kiev 2,829,000
LANGUAGE: Ukrainian, Russian

United Arab
Emirates
CONTINENT: Asia
AREA: 30,000 sq mi
(77,700 sq km)
POPULATION: 9,346,000
CAPITAL: Abu Dhabi 942,000
LANGUAGE: Arabic, Persian
(Farsi), English, Hindi, Urdu

United Kingdom
CONTINENT: Europe
AREA: 93,788 sq mi
(242,910 sq km)
POPULATION: 64,092,000
CAPITAL: London 9,005,000
LANGUAGE: English, Welsh,
Scots, Scottish Gaelic, Irish
Gaelic, Cornish

United States
CONTINENT: North America
AREA: 3,794,083 sq mi
(9,826,630 sq km)
POPULATION: 316,158,000
CAPITAL: Washington, D.C.
4,705,000
LANGUAGE: English, Spanish

Uruguay
CONTINENT: South America
AREA: 68,037 sq mi
(176,215 sq km)
POPULATION: 3,392,000
CAPITAL: Montevideo 1,672,000
LANGUAGE: Spanish, Portunol,
Brazilero

Uzbekistan
CONTINENT: Asia
AREA: 172,742 sq mi
(447,400 sq km)
POPULATION: 30,215,000
CAPITAL: Tashkent 2,227,000
LANGUAGE: Uzbek, Russian,
Tajik, Kazakh, Karakalpak

Vanuatu
REGION: Australia/Oceania
AREA: 4,707 sq mi
(12,190 sq km)
POPULATION: 265,000
CAPITAL: Port-Vila 47,000
LANGUAGE: pidgin (known
as Bislama or Bichelama),
indigenous languages

Vatican City
CONTINENT: Europe
AREA: 0.2 sq mi (0.4 sq km)
POPULATION: 798
CAPITAL: Vatican City 798
LANGUAGE: Italian, Latin,
French

Venezuela
CONTINENT: South America
AREA: 352,144 sq mi
(912,050 sq km)
POPULATION: 29,679,000
CAPITAL: Caracas 3,242,000
LANGUAGE: Spanish, indigenous
languages

Vietnam
CONTINENT: Asia
AREA: 127,844 sq mi
(331,114 sq km)
POPULATION: 89,721,000
CAPITAL: Hanoi 2,955,000
LANGUAGE: Vietnamese,
English, French, Chinese, Khmer

Yemen
CONTINENT: Asia
AREA: 207,286 sq mi
(536,869 sq km)
POPULATION: 25,235,000
CAPITAL: Sanaa 2,419,000
LANGUAGE: Arabic

Zambia
CONTINENT: Africa
AREA: 290,586 sq mi
(752,614 sq km)
POPULATION: 14,187,000
CAPITAL: Lusaka 1,802,000
LANGUAGE: English, Bemba,
Nyanja, Tonga, Lozi, Lunda,
Kaonde, Luvale

Zimbabwe
CONTINENT: Africa
AREA: 150,872 sq mi
(390,757 sq km)
POPULATION: 13,038,000
CAPITAL: Harare 1,542,000
LANGUAGE: English, Shona,
Sindebele, other indigenous
languages

Glossary

Note: Terms defined within the main body of the atlas text are not listed below.

ANTARCTIC CONVERGENCE a climate and marine boundary (approximately 55º S–60º S) where cold, slightly less saline Antarctic waters meet the southern extremes of the Atlantic, Pacific, and Indian Oceans; waters south of the Antarctic Convergence are sometimes referred to as the Southern Ocean (p. **125**)

ARID CLIMATE type of dry climate in which annual precipitation is often less than 10 inches (25 cm); experiences great daily variations in day-night temperatures (pp. **20–21**)

ASYLUM a place where a person can go to find safety; to offer asylum means to offer protection in a safe country to people who fear being persecuted or who have been persecuted in their own country (pp. **34–35**)

BATHYMETRY measurement of depth at various places in the ocean or other body of water (p. **11**)

BIODIVERSITY biological diversity in an environment as indicated by numbers of different species of plants and animals (pp. **28, 108**)

BOREAL FOREST *see* Northern coniferous forest

BOUNDARY line established by people to separate one political or mapped area from another; physical features, such as mountains and rivers, or latitude and longitude lines sometimes act as boundaries (p. **10**)

BREADBASKET a geographic region that is a principal source of grain (p. **64**)

CANADIAN SHIELD region containing the oldest rock in North America; areas are exposed in much of eastern Canada and some bordering U.S. regions (pp. **56, 62**)

CLIMATE CHANGE any significant change in the measures of climate, such as temperature, precipitation, or wind patterns, resulting from natural variability or human activity and lasting for an extended period of time (p. **29**)

COASTAL PLAIN any comparatively level land of low elevation that borders the ocean (p. **64**)

CONTINENTAL CLIMATE midlatitude climate zone occurring on large landmasses in the Northern Hemisphere and characterized by great variations of temperature, both seasonally and between day and night; continental cool summer climates are influenced by nearby colder subarctic climates; continental warm summer climates are influenced by nearby mild or dry climates (pp. **20–21**)

COORDINATED UNIVERSAL TIME (UTC) the basis for the current worldwide system of civil (versus military) time determined by highly precise atomic clocks; also known as Universal Time; formerly known as Greenwich Mean Time (p. **13**)

CULTURE HEARTH center from which major cultural traditions spread and are adopted by people in a wide geographic area (p. **90**)

CYBERCAFÉ a café that has a collection of computers that customers can use to access the Internet (p. **52**)

DEGRADED FOREST a forested area severely damaged by overharvesting, repeated fires, overgrazing, poor management practices, or other abuse that delays or prevents forest regrowth (p. **28**)

DESERT AND DRY SHRUB vegetation region with either hot or cold temperatures that annually receives 10 inches (25 cm) or less of precipitation (pp. **24–25**)

DIFFUSE BOUNDARY an evolving boundary zone between two or more tectonic plates with edges that are not clearly defined (p. **17**)

ECOSYSTEM term for classifying Earth's natural communities according to how all things in an environment, such as a forest or a coral reef, interact with each other (pp. **10, 15, 68, 79, 118**)

FAULT break in Earth's crust along which movement up, down, or sideways occurs (pp. **16–17**)

FLOODED GRASSLAND wetland dominated by grasses and covered by water (pp. **24–25**)

FOSSIL FUEL a fuel, such as coal, petroleum, and natural gas, derived from the remains of ancient plants and animals (p. **48**)

GEOTHERMAL ENERGY heat energy generated within Earth (p. **47**)

GLACIER large, slow-moving mass of ice that forms over time from snow (p. **26**)

GLOBAL WARMING a theory about the increase of Earth's average global temperature due to a buildup of so-called greenhouse gases, such as carbon dioxide and methane, released by human activities (p. **78**)

GLOBALIZATION the purposeful spread of activities, technology, goods, and values throughout the world through the expansion of global links, such as trade, media, and the Internet (p. **50**)

GONDWANA name given to the southern part of the supercontinent Pangaea; made up of what we now call Africa, South America, Australia, Antarctica, and India (pp. **16, 120**)

GREENWICH MEAN TIME *see* Coordinated Universal Time

GROSS DOMESTIC PRODUCT (GDP) the gross national product excluding the value of net income earned abroad (p. **44**)

GROSS NATIONAL INCOME PER CAPITA a country's annual earned income divided by its population (p. **36**)

GROSS NATIONAL PRODUCT (GNP) the total value of the goods and services produced by the residents of a country during a specified period (as a year) (p. **44**)

GROUNDWATER water, primarily from rain or melted snow, that collects beneath Earth's surface, in saturated soil or in underground reservoirs, or aquifers, and that supplies springs and wells (p. **27**)

HEMISPHERE one-half of the globe; the Equator divides Earth into Northern and Southern Hemispheres; the prime meridian and the 180 degree meridian divide it into Eastern and Western Hemispheres (p. **5**)

HIGHLAND/UPLAND climate region associated with mountains or plateaus that varies depending on elevation, latitude, continental location, and exposure to sun and wind; in general, temperature decreases and precipitation increases with elevation (pp. **20–21**)

HOST COUNTRY the country where a refugee first goes to find asylum (p. **34**)

HOT SPOT in geology, an extremely hot region beneath the lithosphere that tends to stay relatively stationary while plates of Earth's outer crust move over it; environmentally, an ecological trouble spot (p. **28**)

HUMAN DEVELOPMENT INDEX (HDI) a way of measuring development that combines both social and economic factors to rank the world's countries based on health, education, and living standards (pp. **36–37**)

HUMID SUBTROPICAL CLIMATE region characterized by hot summers, mild to cool winters, and year-round precipitation that is heaviest in summer; generally located on the southeastern margins of continents (pp. **20–21**)

ICE CAP CLIMATE one of two kinds of polar climate; summer temperatures rarely rise above freezing and what little precipitation occurs is mostly in the form of snow (pp. **20–21**)

INDIGENOUS native to or occurring naturally in a specific area or environment (p. **116**)

INFILTRATION process that occurs in the water, or hydrologic, cycle when gravity causes surface water to seep down through the soil (p. **26**)

INTERNALLY DISPLACED PERSON (IDP) a person who has fled his or her home to escape armed conflict, generalized violence, human rights abuses, or natural or man-made disasters; unlike a refugee, such a person has not crossed an international border but remains in his or her own country (p. **34**)

LANDFORM physical feature shaped by uplifting, weathering, and erosion; mountains, plateaus, hills, and plains are the four major types (p. **22**)

LANGUAGE FAMILY group of languages that share a common ancestry (pp. **40–41**)

LATIN AMERICA cultural region generally considered to include Mexico, Central America, South America, and the West Indies; Portuguese and Spanish are the principal languages (p. **38**)

LIFE EXPECTANCY the average number of years a person can expect to live, based on current mortality rates and health conditions (p. **36**)

LLANOS extensive, mostly treeless grasslands in the Orinoco River basin of northern South America (p. **72**)

LOWLANDS fairly level land at a lower elevation than surrounding areas (p. **14**)

MANGROVE VEGETATION tropical trees and shrubs with dense root systems that grow in tidal mudflats and extend coastlines by trapping soil (pp. **24–25**)

MARGINAL LAND land that has little value for growing crops or for commercial or residential development (p. **28**)

MARINE WEST COAST type of mild climate common on the west coasts of continents in midlatitude regions; characterized by small variations in annual temperature range and wet, foggy winters (pp. **20–21**)

MEDIAN AGE midpoint of a population's age; half the population is older than this age; half is younger (p. **33**)

MEDITERRANEAN CLIMATE a mild climate common on the west coasts of continents, named for the dominant climate along the Mediterranean coast; characterized by mild, rainy winters and hot, dry summers (pp. **20–21**)

MEDITERRANEAN SHRUB low-growing, mostly small-leaf evergreen vegetation, such as chaparral, that thrives in Mediterranean climate regions (pp. **24–25**)

MELANESIA one of three major island groups that make up Oceania; includes the Fiji Islands, New Guinea, Vanuatu, the Solomon Islands, and New Caledonia (pp. **112–113**)

MELANESIAN indigenous to Melanesia (p. **116**)

MICROCLIMATE climate of a very limited area that varies from the overall climate of the surrounding region (p. **22**)

MICRONESIA one of three major island groups that make up Oceania; made up of some 2,000 mostly coral islands, including Guam, Kiribati, the Mariana Islands, Palau, and the Federated States of Micronesia (pp. **112–113**)

MICRONESIAN indigenous to Micronesia (p. **116**)

MONSOON seasonal change in the direction of the prevailing winds, which causes wet and dry seasons in some tropical areas (p. **94**)

MOUNTAIN GRASSLAND vegetation region characterized by clumps of long grass that grow beyond the limit of forests at high elevations (pp. **24–25**)

NONRENEWABLE RESOURCES elements of the natural environment, such as metals, minerals, and fossil fuels, that form within Earth by geological processes over millions of years and thus cannot readily be replaced (pp. **48–49**)

NORTHERN CONIFEROUS FOREST vegetation region composed primarily of cone-bearing, needle- or scale-leaf evergreen trees that grow in regions with long winters and moderate to high annual precipitation; also called boreal forest or taiga (pp. **24–25**)

OCEANIA name for the widely scattered islands of Polynesia, Micronesia, and Melanesia; often includes Australia and New Zealand (pp. **110–121**)

PAMPAS temperate grassland primarily in Argentina between the Andes and the Atlantic Ocean; one of the world's richest agricultural regions (pp. **70**, **72**)

PATAGONIA cool, windy, arid plateau region primarily in southern Argentina between the Andes and the Atlantic Ocean (p. **72**)

PER CAPITA INCOME the total national income divided by the number of people in the country (p. **37**)

PLAIN large area of relatively flat land; one of the four major kinds of landforms (p. **18**)

PLATE TECTONICS study of the interaction of slabs of Earth's crust as molten rock within Earth causes them to slowly move across the surface (pp. **16–17**)

PLATEAU large, relatively flat area that rises above the surrounding landscape; one of the four major kinds of landforms (pp. **18–19**)

POLAR CLIMATES climates that occur at very high latitudes; generally too cold to support tree growth; include tundra and ice cap (pp. **20–21**)

POLYNESIA one of three major regions in Oceania made up mostly of volcanic and coral islands, including the Hawaiian and the Society Islands, Samoa, and French Polynesia (pp. **112–113**)

POLYNESIAN indigenous to Polynesia (p. **116**)

PREDOMINANT ECONOMY main type of work that most people do to meet their wants and needs in a particular country (pp. **44–45**, **61**, **77**, **87**, **97**, **107**, **117**)

PROVINCE land governed as a political or administrative unit of a country or empire; Canadian provinces, like U.S. states, have substantial powers of self-government (p. **63**)

RAIN FOREST see Tropical moist broadleaf forest

RENEWABLE FRESH WATER water that is replenished naturally, but the supply of which can be endangered by overuse and pollution (p. **26**)

RIVER BASIN area drained by a single river and its tributaries (p. **72**)

RURAL pertaining to the countryside, where most of the economic activity centers on agriculture-related work (pp. **38–39**)

SAHEL in Africa the semiarid region of short, tropical grassland that lies between the dry Sahara and the humid savanna and that is prone to frequent droughts (p. **104**)

SALINE/SALINITY measure of all salts contained in water; average ocean salinity is 35 parts per thousand (p. **125**)

SAMPAN a flat-bottomed boat used in eastern Asia and usually propelled by two short oars (p. **98**)

SAVANNA tropical tall grassland with scattered trees (pp. **24–25**)

SELF-SUSTAINABILITY the ability of a system or community to maintain itself without benefit of external support or input (p. **39**)

SELVA Portuguese word referring to tropical rain forests, especially in the Amazon Basin (p. **78**)

SEMIARID dry climate region with great daily variation in day-night temperatures; has enough rainfall to support grasslands (pp. **20–21**)

SILT mineral particles that are larger than grains of clay but smaller than grains of sand (p. **78**)

STATELESS PEOPLE those who have no recognized country (p. **35**)

STEPPE Slavic word referring to relatively flat, mostly treeless, temperate grasslands that stretch across much of central Europe and central Asia (p. **92**)

SUBARCTIC CLIMATE region characterized by short, cool, sometimes freezing summers and long, bitter-cold winters; most precipitation falls in summer (pp. **20–21**)

SUBTROPICAL CLIMATE region between tropical and continental climates characterized by distinct seasons but with milder temperatures than continental climates (pp. **20–21**)

SUBURB a residential area on the outskirts of a town or city (p. **38**)

SUNBELT area of rapid population and economic growth south of the 37th parallel in the United States; its mild climate is attractive to retirees, and a general absence of labor unions has drawn manufacturing to the region (p. **60**)

TAIGA see Northern coniferous forest

TEMPERATE BROAD-LEAF FOREST vegetation region with distinct seasons and dependable rainfall; predominant species include oak, maple, and beech, all of which lose their leaves in the cold season (pp. **24–25**)

TEMPERATE CONIFEROUS FOREST vegetation region that has mild winters with heavy precipitation; made up of mostly evergreen, needle-leaf trees that bear seeds in cones (pp. **24–25**)

TEMPERATE GRASS-LAND vegetation region where grasses are dominant and the climate is characterized by hot summers, cold winters, and moderate rainfall (pp. **24–25**)

TERRITORY land under the jurisdiction of a country but that is not a state or a province (p. **57**)

TROPICAL CONIFEROUS FOREST vegetation region that occurs in a cooler climate than tropical rain forests; has distinct wet and dry seasons; made up of mostly evergreen trees with seed-bearing cones (pp. **24–25**)

TROPICAL DRY CLIMATE region characterized by year-round high temperatures and sufficient precipitation to support savannas (pp. **20–21**)

TROPICAL DRY FOREST vegetation region that has distinct wet and dry seasons and a cooler climate than tropical moist broad-leaf forests; has shorter trees than rain forests and many shed their leaves in the dry season (pp. **24–25**)

TROPICAL GRASSLAND AND SAVANNA vegetation region characterized by scattered individual trees; occurs in warm or hot climates with annual rainfall of 20 to 50 inches (50–130 cm) (pp. **24–25**)

TROPICAL MOIST BROADLEAF FOREST vegetation region occurring mostly in a belt between the Tropic of Cancer and the Tropic of Capricorn in areas that have at least 80 inches (200 cm) of rain annually and an average annual temperature of 80°F (27°C) (pp. **24–25**, **78–79**)

TROPICAL WET CLIMATE region characterized by year-round warm temperatures and rainfall ranging from 60 to 150 inches (150–400 cm) annually (pp. **20–21**)

TROPOSPHERE region of Earth's atmosphere closest to the surface; where weather occurs (p. **5**)

TUNDRA vegetation region at high latitudes and high elevations characterized by cold temperatures, low vegetation, and a short growing season (pp. **24–25**)

TUNDRA CLIMATE region with one or more months of temperatures slightly above freezing when the ground is free of snow (pp. **20–21**)

UNIVERSALIZING RELIGION one that attempts to appeal to all people rather than to just those in a particular region or place (p. **42**)

UPLAND CLIMATE see Highland/upland climate

URBAN pertaining to a town or city, where most of the economic activity is not based on agriculture (pp. **38–39**)

URBAN AGGLOMERATION a group of several cities and/or towns and their suburbs (p. **38**)

Web Sites

Activities and Lessons: http://education.nationalgeographic.com/education/?ar_a=1

Antarctica: http://www.coolantarctica.com

Cultural Diffusion: http://www2.geog.okstate.edu/users/lightfoot/lightfoot.html

Earth's Climates: http://www.worldclimate.com

Earth's Vegetation: http://earthobservatory.nasa.gov/Features/LandCover

Education Resource: education.nationalgeographic.com/education/standards/national-geography-standards/?ar_a=1

Environmental Hot Spots: Quiz for Students: http://www.myfootprint.org

Flags of the World: http://www.fotw.us/flags/index.html

Globalization: http://www.globalization101.org

Map Projections: http://www.colorado.edu/geography/gcraft/notes/mapproj/mapproj.bak2

National Geographic Kids Atlases Home Page: http://www.nationalgeographic.com/kids-atlases/index.html

Natural Hazards:
 Earthquakes: http://earthquake.usgs.gov
 Tsunamis: http://www.tsunami.noaa.gov
 Volcanoes: http://www.geo.mtu.edu/volcanoes

Political World: https://www.cia.gov/library/publications/the-world-factbook/index.html

Quality of Life: http://hdr.undp.org/en/content/human-development-report-2013

Reading Maps: http://education.usgs.gov/secondary.html#geography

Time Zones: http://tycho.usno.navy.mil/tzones.html

World Cities: http://esa.un.org/unup

World Conflicts: http://www.cnn.com/interactive/maps/world/fullpage.global.conflict/world.index.html

World Energy: http://www.bp.com/en/global/corporate/about-bp/energy-economics/statistical-review-of-world-energy-2013.html

World Food: http://www.cgiar.org/impact/research/index.html

World Languages: http://www.ethnologue.com/web.asp
 Interactive for Students: http://www.ipl.org/div/hello

World Population: http://www.census.gov/population/international/data/idb/informationGateway.php; http://www.prb.org/Publications/Datasheets/2013/2013-world-population-data-sheet.aspx

World Refugees: http://www.unhcr.org/cgi-bin/texis/vtx/home

World Religions: http://www.adherents.com

World Water: http://www.worldbank.org/en/topic/water

Note: All Web sites were viable as of publication date. In the event that a site has been discontinued, a reliable search engine can lead you to new sites with helpful information.

Thematic Index

Boldface indicates illustrations; *italics* indicates maps.

A

Agriculture
  crops 26, 44, 46, 78, 107
  irrigation **26,** 59, 64
  slash-and-burn 78, **78**
  subsistence 28, 44, 79, 97, 108
  world maps 44–45, 46–47
Albatrosses 120, 125, **125**
Anemone fish 118, **118**
Animistic religions 42
Antarctic Convergence 125
Arab culture 53
Arid lands 15, 58, 70, 112
Asylum-seekers: world map *34–35*
Atmosphere 5, 20, 23, 78
Atolls 112, 118

B

Banking 44, 50
Bengali (language) 41
Biodiversity 108
Boundaries, national 30, 31
Buddhism 42, 43

C

Cartograms 10, **10**
Cartographers 6, 7, 8, 9
Cellular phones 51, 52
Choropleth maps 10
Christianity 42, 43
Cities
  urban growth 28, 38
  world map *38–39*
Climate: world map *20–21*
Climate change 28, *29,* 78
Climate controls 22–23
Clothing, traditional 52, **53**
Coal 45, 48, 56, 87, 123
Communications 12, 45, 50
Container ports 98, **98, 99**

Coordinated Universal Time (UTC) 13
Coral reefs *29,* 118, **118, 119,** *119*
Corn 46, 47, **47**
Crops 26, 44, 46, 78, 107
Cultural diffusion 52–53

D

Date line 12, 13
Deforestation **28,** 78, 79, 108
Desert shrubs 24, 25
Dinosaurs: extinction 17

E

Earth
  climates 20–21
  environmental hot spots 28–29
  geologic history 16–17
  land and water features 14, 18–19
  in space 4, **4–5, 13**
  vegetation 24–25
  water 26–27
Earthquakes 16, 17, 56, 68, 69
Economies, world 44–45
Elephants **100–101,** 108
Endangered species 108, 119
Energy resources 48–49
English (language) 40, 41
Environmental hot spots 28–29
Equator 7, 8, 21, 22, 75, 104, 105
Eurasian Plate 16

F

Faults 16–17
Fiji Times (newspaper) 12
Fishing
  countries, top: graph 46
  falling fish catches *29*
  tuna 44, **44**
Flags and facts 125–133
Floods 68, **68,** 69
Food, world 46, *46–47*

Forests
  frontier forests *28–29*
  vegetation zones *24–25*
  see also Deforestation; Rain forests
Fossil fuels 48

G

Geothermal power plants *48,* **49**
German (language) 40
Giraffes 108, **108**
Glaciers 26, 29, 54, 56, 82
Global grid 8
Global warming 78
Globalization 50, *50–51*
Globes 6, **10**
Gondwana *16,* 120
Grains 46, **46,** 47, **47**
Grasslands 24, **25,** 28, 70, 100
Greenwich Mean Time 13
Gross national income 37
Groundwater 28

H

Habitat loss *29*
Hinduism 42, 43
Hot spots, environmental 28–29
Human development index *36–37*
Hurricanes 68, 69
Hydroelectric dams 27, **27**

I

Ice caps 14, 15, 19, 21, 25, 26, 58
Ice sheets 17, 122, 123
Indian Plate 16
Indigenous people 42, 116
Indo-European language family 40, 41
Internet 40, 44, 45, 50
Iron ore 45, 48, 123
Irrigation **26,** 59, 64
Islam 42, 43

J

Judaism 42

K

Kaaba (shrine), Mecca, Saudi Arabia **43**
Krill 125, **125**
Kurds 35, **35**

L

Languages, world 40, *40–41*
Latitude and longitude 6, 8, 22
Life expectancy *36*
Logging 44, **44,** 78, 108

M

Magma 16, 68
Mangroves 24, **25**
Manufacturing 44, **45,** 77, 87, 107
Maps
  projections 6–7
  reading 8–9
  time zones 12–13
  types of 10–11
Maquiladoras 50, **50**
Marine life 118, **118, 119,** 125, **125**
Mineral resources 48, *48–49*
Mountain gorillas 108, **108**
Muslims 42, 43

N

Nasca Plate 16
Natural hazards: North America 68, **68,** *69*
Nuclear reactors **49**

O

Ocean currents 22, 23, 75, 84
Ocean floor 14, *14,* 16, 17, 19
Oil producers and consumers 48
Oil-spill cleanup **29**

P

Pangaea 16
Parliament Building, Budapest, Hungary **89**
Penguins **120–121, 125**
Planets 4, **4**
Plate tectonics 16, *16–17*

Pollution 26, 28, 119
Polynesians 116
Population, world 46, *46–47*
Ports: East Asia 98, **98, 99,** *99*
Prime meridian 8, 13

Q

Quality of life 36–37

R

Rain forests 24, 58, 75, 78, **78,** *79,* 92, 100, 112
Refugees 34, **34,** *34–35,* **35**
Religions, world 42, *42–43*
Renewable resources 26, 48, *48*
Rice 46, 47, **47**
Russian (language) 40

S

Salinity 119, 125
Satellite image maps 11, **11**
Savanna 105
Seafood 46
Seasons 4–5, **4–5**
Shinto 42
Solar energy 22, 48
Solar panels **49**
Solar system 4, **4**
South American Plate 16
Starfish 118, 119, **119**
Steel production **45,** 48

T

Taj Mahal, Agra, India **90–91**
Technology 45, 50
Tectonic activity 16, 102; *see also* Earthquakes; Volcanoes
Three-toed sloths 78, **78**
Time zones 12, *12–13,* 13
Tornadoes 68, 69
Tourism, international *52–53*
Trains 12, **12**
Transnational companies 50, 51
Transportation 12, 50

Tsunamis 16
Tundra 21, 24, **24,** 32

U
United Nations
    Office of the High
    Commissioner for
    Refugees (UNHCR) 34
Urban areas 38, 38–39

V
Volcanoes 16, 17, 56, 68,
    68, 69, 102, 123

W
Water resources 26–27
Waterways: Europe 88,
    88, 89, 89
Welsh (language) 41
Wheat 46, **46**
Wildfires 68, **68,** 69
Windmills **49**
Winds, prevailing 23
World Heritage sites 88,
    109, 119
World maps
    agricultural extent
        46–47
    cities 38–39
    climate 20–21
    coral reefs 119
    dominant religions
        42–43
    energy and mineral
        resources 48–49
    globalization 50–51
    habitat loss due to
        climate change
        29
    human development
        index 36–37
    human footprint 28
    international
        tourism 52–53
    life expectancy at
        birth 36
    major language
        families 40–41
    physical systems
        14–15
    plate tectonics
        16–17
    political map 30–31
    population density
        32–33
    predominant
        economies 44–45
    refugees and
        asylum-seekers
        34–35

time zones *12–13*
vegetation zones
    24–25
water stress *26–27*

Place-Name Index

Boldface indicates
illustrations; *italics*
indicates maps.

A
Abidjan, Côte d'Ivoire
    103, 106
Abu Dhabi, United Arab
    Emirates *93*
Abuja, Nigeria *103, 106*
Acajutla, El Salvador:
    climate graph 22
Accra, Ghana *103, 106*
Aconcagua, Cerro,
    Argentina 71
Addis Ababa, Ethiopia
    103, 106
Afghanistan *93, 94, 95,
    96, 97*
Africa
    arid lands 15
    climate *104*
    indigenous people
        42
    physical map *102*
    political map *103*
    population *106,* 108
    precipitation *105*
    predominant
        economies *107*
    protected areas 108,
        109
    religions 42
    urban growth 38, 39
    view from space **100**
    wildlife 108, **108**
    see also Great Rift
        Valley
Agra, India: mausoleum
    90–91
Alaska
    natural hazards 68
    see also Fairbanks;
        McKinley, Mount
Albania *83, 84, 85, 86,
    87,* 89
Algeria
    area 100, 126
    cartogram 10, *11*
    maps *103, 104, 105,
        106, 107, 109*
Algiers, Algeria *106, 107*
Alice Springs, Australia:
    climate graph 20
Amazon rain forest,
    South America 78,
    78, 79
Amazon River and
    Basin, South
    America 70, 71, 72,

75, 77, **78,** 79
Amboseli National
    Park, Kenya:
    elephants **100–101**
American Samoa 65,
    *113, 114, 115, 116,
    117*
Amman, Jordan *93, 96*
Amsterdam,
    Netherlands *83, 86,
    89*
Andes (mountains),
    South America 14,
    18, 70, 72, 77
Andorra *83, 84, 85, 86,
    87*
Anglesey, Wales: sign
    41
Angola *103, 104, 105,
    106, 107, 109*
Ankara, Turkey *93, 96*
Antananarivo,
    Madagascar *103, 106*
Antarctica
    climate 120, 122, 125
    ice cap 14, 16, 25
    penguins **120–121,
        125**
    physical maps *122,
        123*
    political maps *31, 124*
    research stations
        27, 124
    types of wildlife 120
    view from space
        120
    see also McMurdo
Antigua and Barbuda
    57, 60, 61
Apia, Samoa *113*
Appalachian Mountains,
    U.S. 56, 64
Arabian Peninsula, Asia
    17, 92
Arctic Ocean *30*
Argentina
    agriculture 74
    Antarctic research
        stations 124
    maps *73, 74, 75, 76,
        77*
    see also Aconcagua,
        Cerro; Fitzroy,
        Mount; Laguna
        del Carbón;
        Tierra del Fuego
Armenia
    maps *93, 94, 95, 96,
        97*
    religions 43

Ashgabat,
    Turkmenistan *93*
Asia
    climate *94*
    immigrants 116
    physical map *92*
    political map *93*
    population 32, *96*
    ports 89, 98, **98,
        99,** 99
    precipitation *95*
    predominant
        economies *97*
    religions 42
    tropical forests 15
    urban growth 38, 39
    view from space **90**
    water supply 26
    see also Caucasus
        Mountains;
        Himalaya; Tibet,
        Plateau of
Asmara, Eritrea *103*
Assal, Lake, Djibouti 100
Astana, Kazakhstan *93*
Asunción, Paraguay
    73, 76
Atacama Desert, Chile
    70, 75
Athens, Greece *83, 86*
Augustine (volcano),
    Alaska 68
Australia
    area 111, 126
    arid lands 15, 112,
        115
    climate *114*
    coastal areas 115
    coral reefs 118
    indigenous
        population 116
    physical map *112*
    political map *113*
    population 111, *116,*
        126
    precipitation *115*
    predominant
        economies *117*
    total population 111
    view from space **110**
    wool and beef
        exports 117
    see also Alice
        Springs; Eyre,
        Lake; Great
        Barrier Reef;
        Murray-Darling
        River; Sydney
Austria *83, 84, 85, 86, 87,
    89; see also* Vienna
Azerbaijan
    maps *83, 84, 85, 86,
        93, 94, 95, 96, 97*
    religions 43

B

Baghdad, Iraq *93, 96*
Bahamas *57, 60, 61*
Bahrain *93, 94, 95, 96, 97*
Baikal, Lake, Russia *91*
Baku, Azerbaijan *93, 96*
Bamako, Mali *103, 106*
Bandar Seri Begawan, Brunei *93*
Bangkok, Thailand *93, 96, 99*
Bangladesh 32, *93, 94, 95, 96, 97, 99*
Bangui, Central African Republic *103*
Banjul, Gambia *103*
Barbados *57, 60, 61*
Basseterre, St. Kitts and Nevis *57*
Beijing, China *93, 96*
Beirut, Lebanon *93, 96*
Belarus *83, 84, 85, 86, 87, 89; see also* Minsk
Belém, Brazil: climate graph 20
Belgium 38, *83, 84, 85, 86, 87,* 89
Belgrade, Serbia *83, 86, 89*
Belize *57, 58, 59, 60, 61, 67*
Belmopan, Belize *57*
Benin *103, 104, 105, 106, 107, 109*
Bentley Subglacial Trench, Antarctica 121, 122, 123
Berlin, Germany *83, 86, 89*
    world time clock **12**
Bern, Switzerland *83, 86*
Bhutan *93, 94, 95, 96, 97, 99*
    farmers **44**
Bishkek, Kyrgyzstan *93*
Bissau, Guinea-Bissau *103*
Black Sea *82, 83, 88, 89, 92, 93*
Bogotá, Colombia *73, 76, 79*
Bolivia *73, 74, 75, 76, 77, 79; see also* Titicaca, Lake
Bosnia and Herzegovina *83, 85, 86, 87, 89*
Bosporus, Turkey *82, 83, 89, 92, 93*
Botswana *103, 104, 105, 106, 107, 108, 109*

Brasilia, Brazil *73, 76, 79*
Bratislava, Slovakia *83, 89*
Brazil
    Antarctic research stations 124
    area and population 71, 127
    container trade 98
    forest loss 78
    maps *73, 74, 75, 76, 77*
    rain forest 78, **78**
    see also Belém; Tucuruí
Brazzaville, Congo *103, 106*
Bridgetown, Barbados *57*
British Columbia, Canada
    earthquakes 68
    see also Columbia River
Brunei *93, 94, 95, 96, 97*
Brussels, Belgium *83, 86, 89*
Bucharest, Romania *83, 86, 89*
Budapest, Hungary *83, 86, 88,* **89,** *89*
Buenos Aires, Argentina *73, 76*
Bujumbura, Burundi *103*
Bulgaria *83, 84, 85, 86, 87, 89*
Burkina Faso *103, 104, 105, 106, 107, 109*
Burma. *see* Myanmar
Burundi *103, 104, 105, 106, 107, 109*
Busan, South Korea: shipping containers **98**

C

Cabo Verde (Cape Verde) *103, 109*
Cairo, Egypt 39, *103, 106*
California
    beach cleanup **29**
    transform fault 16
    see also Death Valley; Sacramento; San Francisco
Cambodia *93, 94, 95, 96, 97, 99*
Cameroon *103, 104, 105, 106, 107, 109*

Canada
    area 55, 62, 127
    container trade 98
    elevation *62*
    maps *56, 57, 58, 59, 60, 61, 62, 63*
    natural hazards 69
    see also British Columbia; Great Lakes; Hudson Bay; Resolute
Canadian Shield, North America 56, 62
Canberra, Australia *113, 116*
Cape Town, South Africa *93, 96*
Caracas, Venezuela *73, 76, 79*
Caspian Sea 81, *82, 83, 92, 93*
Castries, St. Lucia *57*
Caucasus Mountains, Asia-Europe 43, *82, 83, 92, 93*
Central African Republic *103, 104, 105, 106, 107, 109*
Chad *103, 104, 105, 106, 107, 109*
Chile
    agriculture 74
    Antarctic research stations 124
    maps *73, 74, 75, 76, 77*
    see also Atacama Desert; Fitzroy, Mount; Tierra del Fuego
China
    Antarctic research stations 124
    area 91, 127
    container trade 98
    maps *93, 94, 95, 96, 97, 99*
    population 47, 91, 127
    religions 43
    rice 47
    time zone 13
    see also Everest, Mount; Hong Kong; Lhasa; Shanghai; Wuhan; Yangtze River
Chinatown, New York, New York **52**
Chisinau, Moldova *86, 89*
Ciudad Juárez, Mexico: assembly plant **50**

Cologne, Germany 88, **88**
Colombia *73, 74, 75, 76, 77, 98*
Colombo, Sri Lanka *93, 99*
Columbia River, British Columbia-Washington **44**
Comoros *103, 104, 105, 106, 107, 109*
Conakry, Guinea *103, 106*
Congo *103, 104, 105, 106, 107, 109*
Congo, Democratic Republic of the
    displaced people 34
    maps *103, 104, 105, 106, 107, 109*
Congo River, Africa 14, 102
Copenhagen, Denmark *83, 86*
Costa Rica *57, 60, 61*
Côte d'Ivoire *103, 104, 105, 106, 107, 109*
Croatia *83, 85, 86, 87, 89*
Cuba *57, 60, 61*
Cyprus *83, 84, 85, 86, 87*
Czech Republic *83, 85, 86, 87, 89*

D

Dakar, Senegal *103, 106*
Damascus, Syria *93, 96*
Danube River, Europe *82, 88,* **88,** *89,* **89**
Dar es Salaam, Tanzania *103, 106*
Dardanelles, Turkey *82, 83, 89, 92, 93*
Dead Sea, Israel-Jordan 91
Death Valley, California 55
Delhi, India: population 38
Denmark *83, 84, 85, 86, 87*
Des Moines, Iowa: climate graph 21
Dhaka, Bangladesh *93, 96*
Dili, Timor-Leste *93*
Djibouti *103, 104, 105, 106, 107, 109; see also* Assal, Lake
Djibouti, Djibouti *103*
Doha, Qatar *93*
    shopping mall **53**

Dominica *57, 60, 61*
Dominican Republic
    earthquakes 68
    forested land **28**
    maps *57, 60, 61*
Dublin, Ireland *83, 86*
Dushanbe, Tajikistan *93*

E

East Asia: ports 98, **98, 99,** *99*
East Timor. *see* Timor-Leste
Ecuador *73, 74, 75, 76, 77*
Egypt *103, 104, 105, 106, 107, 109; see also* Cairo
El Salvador *57, 60, 61*
El'brus, Mount, Russia 81, *82*
England *83*
Equatorial Guinea *103, 104, 105, 106, 107, 109*
Eritrea *103, 104, 105, 106, 107, 109*
Estonia *83, 84, 85, 86, 87*
Ethiopia *103, 104, 105, 106, 107, 109*
Europe
    climate 84
    coastline 80
    physical map 82
    political map 83
    population 86
    population density 32
    precipitation 85
    predominant economies 87
    view from space **80**
    waterways 88, **88, 89,** *89*
    see also Caucasus Mountains
Everest, Mount, China-Nepal 91, 92
Eyre, Lake, Australia 111

F

Fairbanks, Alaska: climate graph 21
Fiji Islands
    date line 12, 13
    maps *112, 113, 114, 115, 116, 117*
Finland *83, 84, 85, 86, 87*
Fitzroy, Mount, Argentina-Chile **70–71**

Florence, Italy: skyline **80–81**
Florida: tornadoes 68
France 83, 84, 85, 86, 87, 89, 118
Freetown, Sierra Leone 103, 106
Funafuti, Tuvalu 113

G
Gabon 103, 104, 105, 106, 107, 109
Gambia 103, 104, 105, 106, 107, 109
Georgetown, Guyana 73, 76
Georgia (country) 43, 83, 84, 85, 86
Germany
  boundaries 30
  castle **88**
  maps 83, 84, 85, 86, 87, 89
  population 81, 128
  see also Berlin; Cologne; Ruhr
Ghana 103, 104, 105, 106, 107, 108, 109
Golden Gate Bridge, San Francisco, California **54–55**
Gran Chaco (region), South America: environmental protection 29
Great Barrier Reef, Australia 118, **118, 119,** 119
Great Lakes, Canada-U.S. 30, 54; see also Superior, Lake
Great Rift Valley, Africa 16, 17, 100, 102
Greece 83, 84, 85, 86, 87, 89
Greenland
  glaciers 56
  ice cap 25, 58
  maps 56, 57, 58, 59, 60, 61
Greenwich, United Kingdom 8
Grenada 57, 60, 61
Guatemala 57, 60, 61
Guatemala City, Guatemala 57, 60
Guinea 103, 104, 105, 106, 107, 109
Guinea-Bissau 103, 104, 105, 106, 107, 109
Guyana 73, 74, 75, 76, 77

H
Haiti
  deforestation **28**
  maps 57, 60, 61
Hanoi, Vietnam 93, 96
Harare, Zimbabwe 103, 106
Havana, Cuba 57, 60
Hawai'i 110; see also Mauna Loa
Hawaiian Islands, Hawai'i 112
Helsinki, Finland 83, 86
Himalaya, Asia 14, 16, 18
Ho Chi Minh City, Vietnam: harbor **98**
Honduras 57, 58, 59, 60, 61, 62, 67
Hong Kong, China: container cranes **99**
Honiara, Solomon Islands 113, 116
Hudson Bay, Canada 54, 56, 62, 63
Hungary 83, 84, 85, 86, 87; see also Budapest

I
Iceland
  geothermal power plant **49**
  maps 83, 84, 85, 86, 87
India
  Hinduism 42
  languages 40, 41
  maps 93, 94, 95, 96, 97, 99
  windmills **49**
  see also Agra; Delhi; Kolkata
Indonesia
  coral reefs 118
  forest loss 78
  maps 93, 94, 95, 96, 97, 99
  see also New Guinea
Iowa: tornadoes 68
Iran 93, 94, 95, 96, 97
Iraq 35, 93, 94, 95, 96, 97
Ireland 83, 84, 85, 86, 87
Iron Gates (gorge), Romania-Serbia **88**
Islamabad, Pakistan 93
Israel
  Jews 42
  maps 93, 94, 95, 96, 97
  see also Dead Sea; Jerusalem

Italy
  maps 83, 84, 85, 86, 87, 89
  population pyramid 33
  see also Florence; Rome
Ivory Coast. see Côte d'Ivoire

J
Jakarta, Indonesia 93, 96, 99
Jamaica 57, 60, 61
Japan
  container trade 98
  maps 93, 94, 95, 96, 97, 99
  see also Tokyo
Jerusalem, Israel **42,** 93
Jordan 93, 94, 95, 96, 97; see also Dead Sea
Juba, South Sudan 103

K
Kabul, Afghanistan 93, 96
Kampala, Uganda 21, 103, 106
Kansas: tornadoes 68
Kathmandu, Nepal 93
Kazakhstan 93, 94, 95, 96, 97
Kenya
  Maasai warrior **53**
  maps 103, 104, 105, 106, 107, 109
  see also Amboseli National Park; Masai Mara; Nairobi
Khartoum, Sudan 103, 106
Kiev, Ukraine 83, 86, 89
Kigali, Rwanda 103
Kilauea, Hawai'i 68
Kilimanjaro, Mount, Tanzania 100
Kingston, Jamaica 57, 60
Kingstown, St. Vincent and the Grenadines 57
Kinshasa, Democratic Republic of the Congo 103, 106
Kiribati 30, 31
Kolkata (Calcutta), India: sign **41**

Korea, North
  maps 93, 94, 95, 96, 97, 99
  religions 43
Korea, South
  Antarctic research stations 124
  container trade 98
  maps 93, 94, 95, 96, 97, 99
  religions 43
Kosovo 83, 84, 85, 86, 87, 89
Kuala Lumpur, Malaysia 93
Kurdistan (region), Asia 35
Kuwait 93, 94, 95, 96, 97
Kuwait City, Kuwait 93
Kyrgyzstan 93, 94, 95, 96, 97

L
La Paz, Bolivia 73, 76, 79
Ladoga, Lake, Russia 81, 82
Laguna del Carbón, Argentina 71
Laos 93, 94, 95, 96, 97
Latvia 83, 84, 85, 86, 87
Lebanon 93, 94, 95, 96, 97
Lesotho 30, 103, 104, 105, 106, 107, 109
Lhasa, China: climate graph 21
Liberia 103, 104, 105, 106, 107, 109
Libreville, Gabon 103
Libya 103, 104, 105, 106, 107, 109
Liechtenstein 83, 84, 85, 86, 87, 89
Lilongwe, Malawi 103
Lima, Peru 73, 76, 79
Lisbon, Portugal 83, 86
Lithuania 83, 84, 85, 86, 87, 89
Ljubljana, Slovenia 83, 89
Lomé, Togo 103
London, United Kingdom 83, 86
Los Glaciares National Park, Patagonia, Argentina **70–71**
Luanda, Angola 103, 106
Lusaka, Zambia 103, 106
Luxembourg 83, 84, 85, 86, 87, 89
Luxembourg, Luxembourg 89

M
Macedonia 83, 84, 85, 86, 87, 89
Madagascar 103, 104, 105, 106, 107, 108, 109
Madrid, Spain 83, 86
Majuro, Marshall Islands 113
Malabo, Equatorial Guinea 103
Malawi 103, 104, 105, 106, 107, 109
Malaysia 93, 94, 95, 96, 97, 99
Maldives 91, 93, 94, 95, 96, 97, 99
Male, Maldives 93
Mali 103, 104, 105, 106, 107, 109
Malmö, Sweden: climate graph 20
Malta 83, 84, 85, 86, 87
Managua, Nicaragua 57, 60
Manama, Bahrain 93
Manila, Philippines 93, 96, 99
Maputo, Mozambique 103, 106
Mariana Trench, Pacific Ocean 14
Marshall Islands 112, 113, 114, 115, 116, 117
Masai Mara, Kenya: giraffe **108**
Maseru, Lesotho 103
Mauna Loa, Hawai'i 68
Mauritania
  desert sands **28**
  maps 103, 104, 105, 106, 107, 109
Mauritius 103, 104, 105, 106, 107, 109
Mbabane, Swaziland 103
McKinley, Mount (Denali), Alaska 55
McMurdo, Antarctica: climate graph 21
Mecca, Saudi Arabia: shrine **43**
Melekeok, Palau 113
Mexico
  container trade 98
  earthquakes 68
  elevation 66
  maps 56, 57, 58, 59, 60, 61, 66, 67
  natural hazards 69
  see also Ciudad Juárez; Mexico

City; Monterrey;
Veracruz
Mexico City, Mexico
climate and
elevation 22
maps 57, 60, 67, 69
population 38
Micronesia 112, 113,
114, 115, 116, 117
Mid-Atlantic Ridge 14, 16
Minsk, Belarus 21, 83,
86
Mississippi-Missouri
River, U.S. 14, 55, 56,
64, 69
Mogadishu, Somalia
103, 106
Moldova 83, 84, 85, 86,
87, 89
Monaco 93, 94, 95, 96, 97
Mongolia 93, 94, 94, 95,
96, 97
Monrovia, Liberia 103
Montenegro 83, 84, 85,
86, 87, 89
Monterrey, Mexico:
climate graph 20
Montevideo, Uruguay
73, 76
Morocco 103, 104, 105,
106, 107, 109
Moroni, Comoros 103
Moscow, Russia
maps 83, 86
restaurant **40**
Mozambique
maps 103, 104, 105,
106, 107, 109
students **37**
Murray-Darling River,
Australia: length 111
Muscat, Oman 93
Myanmar (Burma) 93,
94, 95, 96, 97, 99

N
Nairobi, Kenya
maps 103, 106
urban slum **39**
Namibia 103, 104, 105,
106, 107, 109
Nassau, Bahamas 57
Nauru
area and population
111, 130
maps 93, 94, 95, 96,
97
Nay Pyi Taw, Myanmar
93
N'Djamena, Chad 103,
106
Nebraska: tornadoes 68

Nepal 93, 94, 95, 96, 97;
see also Everest,
Mount
Netherlands
container trade 98
maps 83, 84, 85, 86,
87, 89
petroleum company
51
population density
86
see also Rotterdam
New Delhi, India 93
New Guinea (island),
Indonesia-Papua
New Guinea: rain
forest 112
New Jersey
flooding **68**
see also Newark
New York, New York
population 38
see also Chinatown
New Zealand
climate 114
indigenous
population 116
maps 112, 113, 114,
115, 116, 117
precipitation 115
wool and beef
exports 117
see also Southern
Alps
Newark, New Jersey:
container ship 98
Niamey, Niger 103, 106
Nicaragua 57, 60, 61, 73,
74, 75, 76, 77
Nicosia, Cyprus 83
Niger 103, 104, 105, 106,
107, 109
Niger River, Africa 102,
102
Nigeria
cartogram 10, 11
forest loss 108
maps 103, 104, 105,
106, 107, 109
population 10, 100
population pyramid
33
religions 43
Nile River, Africa 100,
102, 102, 106
North America
climate 22–23, 58
natural hazards 68,
68, 69
physical map 56
political map 57
population 60
precipitation 59

predominant
economies 61
view from space **54**
see also Canadian
Shield; Rocky
Mountains
North Pole 6, 30
Norway 83, 84, 85, 86,
86, 87
Nouakchott, Mauritania
103
Nuku'alofa, Tonga 113

O
Oceania
climate 114
coral reef systems
118
physical map 112
political map 113
population 116
precipitation 115
predominant
economies 117
Oklahoma: tornadoes
68
Oman 93, 94, 95, 96, 97
Oslo, Norway 83, 86
Ottawa, Ontario, Canada
57, 60, 63, 69
Ouagadougou, Burkina
Faso 103, 106

P
Pakistan 93, 94, 95, 96,
97
Palau 112, 113, 114, 115,
116, 117
Palikir, Micronesia 113
Panama
maps 73, 74, 75, 76,
77
tropical forests 54,
58
Panama City, Panama
57, 60
Papua New Guinea
coral reefs 118
maps 112, 113, 114,
115, 116, 117
see also New
Guinea; Wilhelm,
Mount
Paraguay 73, 74, 75,
76, 77
Paramaribo, Suriname
73, 79
Paris, France 83, 86
Patagonia. see Los
Glaciares National
Park

Peru 73, 74, 75, 76, 77;
see also Titicaca,
Lake
Philippines 93, 94, 95,
96, 97, 99, 118
Phnom Penh, Cambodia
93
Podgorica, Montenegro
83, 89
Poland 83, 84, 85, 86, 87,
89, 124
Port-au-Prince, Haiti
57, 60
Port Louis, Mauritius
103
Port Moresby, Papua
New Guinea 113, 116
Port-Vila, Vanuatu 113
Portland, Oregon:
climate graph 23
Porto-Novo, Benin 103
Portugal 83, 84, 85, 86,
87
Prague, Czech Republic
83, 86, 89
Pretoria, South Africa
103, 106
Prishtina, Kosovo 83, 86
Pyongyang, North
Korea 31

Q
Qatar 93, 94, 95, 96, 97;
see also Doha
Quito, Ecuador 73, 76,
79

R
Rabat, Morocco 103, 106
Redoubt (volcano),
Alaska 68
Resolute, Nunavut,
Canada: climate
graphs 21, 22
Reykjavik, Iceland 83
Rhine-Main-Danube
Canal, Europe 88, 89
Richmond, Virginia:
climate graph 23
Riga, Latvia 83, 86
Riyadh, Saudi Arabia
93, 96
Rocky Mountains, North
America 14, 18, 62
Romania 83, 84, 85, 86,
87, 89; see also Iron
Gates
Rome, Italy 20, 93, 96,
99
Roseau, Dominica 57

Rotterdam,
Netherlands 88, 98
Ruhr (region), Germany:
industrial centers 87
Russia
Antarctic research
stations 124
container trade 98
maps 83, 84, 85, 86,
87, 89, 93, 94, 95,
96, 97
see also Baikal,
Lake; El'brus,
Mount; Ladoga,
Lake; Moscow;
Ural Mountains;
Volga River
Rwanda
maps 103, 104, 105,
106, 107, 109
mountain gorilla **108**

S
Sacramento, California:
power plant **49**
Samoa 112, 113, 114,
115, 116, 117
San Andreas Fault,
California 16
San Francisco,
California
bridge **54–55**
climate 23
San José, Costa Rica
57, 60
San Marino 83, 84, 85,
86, 87, 89
San Pedro Valley,
Arizona: irrigation
26
San Salvador, El
Salvador 57, 60
Sanaa, Yemen 93, 96
Santiago, Chile 73, 76
Santo Domingo,
Dominican Republic
57, 60
São Tomé, Sao Tome
and Principe 103
Sao Tome and Principe
103, 104, 105, 106,
107, 109
Sarajevo, Bosnia and
Herzegovina 83, 89
Saudi Arabia
climate 94
container trade 98
maps 93, 94, 95, 96, 97
see also Mecca
Scotland 83
Senegal 103, 104, 105,
106, 107, 109

Seoul, South Korea 93, 96

Serbia 83, 84, 85, 86, 87; see also Iron Gates

Seychelles 100, 103, 104, 105, 106, 107, 109

Shanghai, China 98, 99
container terminal **98**
street scene **32**

Sierra Leone 103, 104, 105, 106, 107, 109

Singapore
container trade 98
maps 93, 94, 95, 96, 97

Singapore, Singapore 99

Skopje, Macedonia 83, 89

Slovakia **45,** 83, 84, 85, 86, 87, 89

Slovenia 83, 84, 85, 86, 87, 89

Solomon Islands 112, 113, 114, 115, 116, 117

Somalia 103, 104, 105, 106, 107, 109

South Africa 103, 104, 105, 106, 107, 109

South America
climate 74
indigenous people 42
physical map 72
political map 73
population 76
precipitation 75
predominant
economies 77
religions 42
tropical forests 15, 42, 78, **78,** 79
view from space **70**
see also Amazon River and Basin; Andes; Gran Chaco

South Pole 14, 31

South Sudan
boundary (2011) 30
maps 103, 104, 105, 106, 107, 109

Southern Alps, New Zealand 112, 112

Spain 83, 84, 85, 86, 87

Sri Lanka 93, 94, 95, 96, 97, 99

St. George's, Grenada 57

St. Helens, Mount, Washington **68**

St. Kitts and Nevis 55, 57, 60, 61

St. Louis, Missouri: climate graph 22

St. Lucia 57, 60, 61

St. Vincent and the Grenadines 57, 60, 61

Stockholm, Sweden 83, 86

Sudan
maps 103, 104, 105, 106, 107, 109
new boundary (2011) 30

Superior, Lake, Canada-U.S.: area 55

Suriname 71, 73, 74, 75, 76, 77

Suva, Fiji Islands 113, 116
newspaper 12

Swaziland 103, 104, 105, 106, 107, 109

Sweden 83, 84, 85, 86, 87, 89; see also Malmö

Switzerland 83, 84, 85, 86, 87, 89

Sydney, Australia: opera house **110-111**

Syria 93, 94, 95, 96, 97

T

Taiwan 93, 94, 95, 96, 97

Tajikistan 93, 94, 95, 96, 97

Tallinn, Estonia 83, 86

Tanzania
maps 103, 104, 105, 106, 107, 109
protected areas 108
see also Kilimanjaro

Tarawa, Kiribati 113

Tashkent, Uzbekistan 93, 96

T'bilisi, Georgia 93, 96

Tegucigalpa, Honduras 57, 60

Tehran, Iran 93

Texas: tornadoes 68

Thailand 93, 94, 95, 96, 97, 99; see also Wat Chang Hom

Thimphu, Bhutan 93

Tibet, Plateau of, Asia 18, 94

Tierra del Fuego, Argentina-Chile 70, 72

Timor-Leste (East Timor) 93, 94, 95, 96, 97

Tirana, Albania 83, 89

Titicaca, Lake, Bolivia-Peru
area 71
cross section **18**

Togo 103, 104, 105, 106, 107, 108, 109

Tokyo, Japan 93, 96, 99
buildings **38**
population 38

Tonga 112, 113, 114, 115, 116, 117

Trinidad and Tobago 57, 60, 61

Tripoli, Libya 103, 106

Tucuruí, Brazil: hydroelectric dams **27**

Tunis, Tunisia 103, 106

Tunisia 103, 104, 105, 106, 107, 109

Turkey
container trade 98
Kurds 35
maps 83, 84, 85, 86, 87, 93, 94, 95, 96, 97
see also Dardanelles

Turkmenistan 93, 94, 95, 96, 97

Tuvalu 112, 113, 114, 115, 116, 117

U

Uganda
forest loss 108
maps 103, 104, 105, 106, 107, 109
refugee camp **34**
see also Kampala

Ukraine
Antarctic research stations 124
area 81, 133
maps 83, 84, 85, 86, 87, 89

Ulaanbaatar, Mongolia 93

United Arab Emirates 93, 94, 95, 96, 97

United Kingdom 83, 84, 85, 86, 87

United States
Antarctic research stations 124
climate patterns 22-23
container trade 98
cultural diffusion 52
elevation 64
maps 56, 57, 58, 59, 60, 61, 64, 65

natural hazards 69
population pyramid 33
religious groups 42
urban areas 38
water supply 26
see also Appalachian Mountains; Mississippi-Missouri River; Superior, Lake

Ural Mountains, Russia 82, 83, 90, 92, 93

Uruguay
agriculture 74
Antarctic research stations 124
maps 73, 74, 75, 76, 77

Uzbekistan 93, 94, 95, 96, 97

V

Valletta, Malta 83

Vanuatu 112, 113, 114, 115, 116, 117

Vatican City 81, 83, 84, 85, 86, 87, 89

Venezuela 73, 74, 75, 76, 77, 98

Veracruz, Mexico: climate and elevation 22

Victoria, Lake, Africa 100, 102

Victoria, Seychelles 103

Vienna, Austria 83, 86, 88

Vientiane, Laos 93

Vietnam 93, 94, 95, 96, 97, 99; see also Ho Chi Minh City

Vilnius, Lithuania 83, 86, 89

Vinson Massif, Antarctica 121, 122, 123

Virunga Mountains, Democratic Republic of the Congo-Uganda 108

Volga River, Russia 81, 82, 88

W

Wales 83; see also Anglesey

Wallowa, Oregon: climate graph 23

Warsaw, Poland 83, 86, 89

Washington
logging **44**
see also Columbia River; St. Helens, Mount

Washington, D.C. 57, 60, 65, 69

Wat Chang Hom, Thailand: statues **43**

Wellington, New Zealand 113, 116

Wichita, Kansas: climate graph 23

Wilhelm, Mount, Papua New Guinea 111

Windhoek, Namibia 103

Wuhan, China: climate graph 20

Y

Yangon, Myanmar 93, 96

Yangtze River, China 14, 91, 92, 99

Yaoundé, Cameroon 103, 106

Yaren, Nauru 113

Yemen 93, 94, 95, 96, 97

Yerevan, Armenia 93, 96

Z

Zagreb, Croatia 83, 86, 89

Zambezi River, Africa 102, 102

Zambia 103, 104, 105, 106, 107, 108, 109

Zimbabwe 103, 104, 105, 106, 107, 108, 109

Illustration Credits

FRONT COVER

(Earth), leonello calvetti/Shutterstock; (background), DTKUTOO/Shutterstock; (arch), Michal Bednarek/Shutterstock; (jaguar), Mustang_79/iStockphoto; (St. Basil's), Vladitto/Shutterstock; (Statue of Liberty), Nikada/iStockphoto; (Machu Picchu), Lori Epstein/National Geographic Creative; (koala), Joe Scherschel/National Geographic Creative

BACK COVER

(Florence, Italy), S. Borisov/Shutterstock; (Antarctic penguins), kkaplin/iStockphoto; (woman with cell phone), David Evans/National Geographic Creative

SPINE

(Earth): leonello calvetti/Shutterstock

Locator globes: Theophilius Britt Griswold

Artwork & graphs: Stuart Armstrong

FRONT OF THE BOOK

1, leonello calvetti/Shutterstock; 2 (le), Andrew Burton/Getty Images; 2 (rt), Mattias Klum/National Geographic Creative; 3 (uple), Lori Epstein/National Geographic Creative; 3 (lole), Paul Banton/iStockphoto.com; 3 (rt), kkaplin/iStockphoto; 4 (le), David Aguilar; 4–5, NASA; 10, Belinda Pretorius/Shutterstock; 12 (le), kai hecker/Shutterstock; 12 (rt), Corbis; 24 (far le), TTphoto/Shutterstock; 24 (le), Lane V. Erickson/Shutterstock; 24 (rt), Elena Elisseeva/Shutterstock; 24 (far rt), Sai Yeung Chan/Shutterstock; 25 (far le), Nic Watson/Shutterstock; 25 (le), EcoPrint/Shutterstock; 25 (rt), FloridaStock/Shutterstock; 25 (far rt), EcoPrint/Shutterstock; 26 (le), Steve Winter/National Geographic Creative; 26 (rt), Annie Griffiths Belt/National Geographic Creative; 27 (le), Hervé Collart/Sygma/Corbis; 27 (rt), Mark Thiessen, NGS; 28 (le), Steve McCurry/National Geographic Creative; 28 (rt), Scientific Visualization Studio/Goddard Space Flight Center/NASA; 29 (le), Joseph Sohm/Visions of America/Corbis; 29 (rt), © Rolex Awards/Thierry Grobet; 32, Yann Layma/The Image Bank/Getty Images; 34, Isaac Kasamani/AFP/Getty Images; 35, Patrick Barth/Getty Images; 37, Ulrich Baumgarten via Getty Images; 38, WH Chow/Shutterstock; 39 (le), Tony Karumba/AFP/Getty Images; 39 (rt), Rebecca Hale, NGS; 40, Les Stone/Sygma/Corbis; 41 (le), Jeremy Horner/Corbis; 41 (rt), Ric Ergenbright/Corbis; 42 (le), Lindsay Hebberd/Corbis; 42 (rt), Annie Griffiths Belt/Corbis; 43 (le), Adrees Latif/Reuters/Corbis; 43 (rt), Joseph Sohm/Visions of America/Corbis; 44 (le), Lynsey Addario/Corbis; 44 (ctr), Phil Schermeister/National Geographic Creative; 44 (rt), James P. Blair/National Geographic Creative; 45 (le), James L. Stanfield/National Geographic Creative; 45 (rt), Ariel Skelley/Blend Images/Getty Images; 46 (le), Mark Thiessen, NGS; 46 (rt), Merrill Dyck/Shutterstock; 47 (le), stoonn/Shutterstock; 47 (rt), Steve Raymer/National Geographic Creative; 49 (le), Sarah Leen/National Geographic Creative; 49 (ctr), Bob Krist/National Geographic Creative; 49 (rt), Ayan82/Photolibrary/Getty Images; 50, Joe Raedle/Newsmakers/Getty Images; 51, David Evans/National Geographic Creative; 52, Rich LaSalle/Stone/Getty

Images; 53 (le), Jodi Cobb/National Geographic Creative; 53 (rt), Louise Gubb/Corbis SABA

NORTH AMERICA

54–55, Noppawat/Flickr/Getty Images; 68 (uple), Woodfin Camp & Associates; 68 (uprt), Ravi Miro Fry; 68 (lo), Andrew Burton/Getty Images

SOUTH AMERICA

70–71, JLR Photography/Shutterstock; 78 (up), Mattias Klum/National Geographic Creative; 78 (lole), Bill Curtsinger/National Geographic Creative; 78 (lort), Michael Nichols/National Geographic Creative; 79, Michael Nichols/National Geographic Creative

EUROPE

80–81, S.Borisov/Shutterstock; 88 (up), Sven Hoppe/iStockphoto; 88 (lole), schmidt-z/ iStockphoto; 88 (lort), Cristian Gusa/Shutterstock; 89, Mark III Photonics/Shutterstock

ASIA

90–91, Lori Epstein/National Geographic Creative; 98 (up), China Photos/Getty Images; 98 (lole), Byun Yeong-Wook/AFP/Getty Images; 98 (lort), Hoang Dinh Nam/AFP/Getty Images; 99, VOISHMEL/AFP/Getty Images

AFRICA

100–101, DLILLC/Corbis; 108 (up), Christine Eichin/iStockphoto.com; 108 (lo), Paul Banton/iStockphoto.com; 109, Eliza Snow/iStockphoto.com

AUSTRALIA & OCEANIA

110–111, Selfiy/Shutterstock; 118 (up), Tim Laman/National Geographic Creative; 118 (lo), Reuters/Corbis; 119 (up), David Doubilet; 119 (lo), Tim Laman/National Geographic Creative

ANTARCTICA

120–121, kkaplin/iStockphoto; 125 (up), Gentoo Multimedia Limited/Shutterstock; 125 (lole), Steve Oehlenschlager/Shutterstock; 125 (lort), George F. Mobley/National Geographic Creative

Prepared by the Book Division

Hector Sierra
Senior Vice President and General Manager

Nancy Laties Feresten
Senior Vice President, Kids Publishing and Media

Jennifer Emmett
Vice President, Editorial Director, Kids Books

Eva Absher-Schantz
Design Director, Kids Publishing and Media

Jay Sumner
Director of Photography, Kids Publishing

R. Gary Colbert
Production Director

Jennifer A. Thornton
Director of Managing Editorial

Staff for This Book

Priyanka Sherman, *Project Editor*

Suzanne Patrick Fonda, *Project Manager*

Martha Sharma, *Writer, Researcher, and Chief Consultant*

David M. Seager, *Art Director*

Lori Epstein, *Senior Photo Editor*

Angela Terry, angela terry design, *Designer*

Stuart Armstrong, *Graphics Illustrator*

Ariane Szu-Tu, *Editorial Assistant*

Callie Broaddus, *Design Production Assistant*

Margaret Leist, *Photo Assistant*

Carl Mehler, *Director of Maps*

Matthew Chwastyk, *Map Production Manager*

Mapping Specialists, LTD. and XNR Productions,
Map Research and Production

Catherine Farley, *Copy Editor*

Dianne Hosmer, *Indexer*

Grace Hill, *Associate Managing Editor*

Mike O'Connor, *Production Editor*

Lewis R. Bassford, *Production Manager*

Susan Borke, *Legal and Business Affairs*

Production Services

Phillip L. Schlosser, *Senior Vice President*

Chris Brown, *Vice President, NG Book Manufacturing*

George Bounelis, *Senior Production Manager*

Nicole Elliot, *Director of Production*

Rachel Faulise and Robert Barr, *Managers*

Since 1888, the National Geographic Society has funded more than 12,000 research, exploration, and preservation projects around the world. The Society receives funds from National Geographic Partners, LLC, funded in part by your purchase. A portion of the proceeds from this book supports this vital work. To learn more, visit www.natgeo.com/info.

NATIONAL GEOGRAPHIC and Yellow Border Design are trademarks of the National Geographic Society, used under license.

For more information, please visit nationalgeographic.com, call 1-800-647-5463, or write to the following address:

NATIONAL GEOGRAPHIC PARTNERS
1145 17th Street N.W., Washington, D.C. 20036-4688 U.S.A.

Visit us online at nationalgeographic.com/books

For librarians and teachers: ngchildrensbooks.org

National Geographic supports K–12 educators with ELA Common Core Resources. Visit www.natgeoed.org/commoncore for more information.

More for kids from National Geographic: kids.nationalgeographic.com

For information about special discounts for bulk purchases, please contact National Geographic Books Special Sales: specialsales@natgeo.com

For rights or permissions inquiries, please contact National Geographic Books Subsidiary Rights: bookrights@natgeo.com

The Library of Congress has cataloged the 2001 edition as follows:

National Geographic Society (U.S.)
National Geographic student atlas of the world.
p. cm.
Includes index and glossary.
ISBN 978-1-4263-0446-0 (pbk.)
ISBN 978-1-4263-0445-3 (hc.)
ISBN 978-1-4263-0458-3 (library)
ISBN 978-1-4263-1775-0 (2014 pbk.)
ISBN 978-1-4263-1777-4 (2014 hc.)
ISBN 978-1-4263-1776-7 (2014 library)
  1. Children's atlases. 2. Earth—remote-sensing images. 3. Physical geography—Maps for children. [1.Atlases.] I. Title: Student atlas of the world. II. Title.
G1021 .N42 2001
912–dc21   00-030006

16/RRDK-RRDML/2
Printed in the United States of America

Metric Conversion Tables

CONVERSION TO METRIC MEASURES

SYMBOL	WHEN YOU KNOW	MULTIPLY BY	TO FIND	SYMBOL
LENGTH				
in	inches	2.54	centimeters	cm
ft	feet	0.30	meters	m
yd	yards	0.91	meters	m
mi	miles	1.61	kilometers	km
AREA				
in^2	square inches	6.45	square centimeters	cm^2
ft^2	square feet	0.09	square meters	m^2
yd^2	square yards	0.84	square meters	m^2
mi^2	square miles	2.59	square kilometers	km^2
—	acres	0.40	hectares	ha
MASS				
oz	ounces	28.35	grams	g
lb	pounds	0.45	kilograms	kg
—	short tons	0.91	metric tons	t
VOLUME				
in^3	cubic inches	16.39	milliliters	mL
liq oz	liquid ounces	29.57	milliliters	mL
pt	pints	0.47	liters	L
qt	quarts	0.95	liters	L
gal	gallons	3.79	liters	L
ft^3	cubic feet	0.03	cubic meters	m^3
yd^3	cubic yards	0.76	cubic meters	m^3
TEMPERATURE				
°F	degrees Fahrenheit	5/9 after subtracting 32	degrees Celsius (centigrade)	°C

CONVERSION FROM METRIC MEASURES

SYMBOL	WHEN YOU KNOW	MULTIPLY BY	TO FIND	SYMBOL
LENGTH				
cm	centimeters	0.39	inches	in
m	meters	3.28	feet	ft
m	meters	1.09	yards	yd
km	kilometers	0.62	miles	mi
AREA				
cm^2	square centimeters	0.16	square inches	in^2
m^2	square meters	10.76	square feet	ft^2
m^2	square meters	1.20	square yards	yd^2
km^2	square kilometers	0.39	square miles	mi^2
ha	hectares	2.47	acres	—
MASS				
g	grams	0.04	ounces	oz
kg	kilograms	2.20	pounds	lb
t	metric tons	1.10	short tons	—
VOLUME				
mL	milliliters	0.06	cubic inches	in^3
mL	milliliters	0.03	liquid ounces	liq oz
L	liters	2.11	pints	pt
L	liters	1.06	quarts	qt
L	liters	0.26	gallons	gal
m^3	cubic meters	35.31	cubic feet	ft^3
m^3	cubic meters	1.31	cubic yards	yd^3
TEMPERATURE				
°C	degrees Celsius (centigrade)	9/5 then add 32	degrees Fahrenheit	°F